IT HAPPENED TO ME

Series Editor: Arlene Hirschfelder

Books in the It Happened To Me series are designed for inquisitive teens digging for answers about certain illnesses, social issues, or lifestyle interests. Whether you are deep into your teen years or just entering them, these books are gold mines of up-to-date information, riveting teen views, and great visuals to help you figure out stuff. Besides special boxes highlighting singular facts, each book is enhanced with the latest reading list, websites, and an index. Perfect for browsing, there's loads of expert information by acclaimed writers to help parents, guardians, and librarians understand teen illness, tough situations, and lifestyle choices.

1. *Learning Disabilities: The Ultimate Teen Guide*, by Penny Hutchins Paquette and Cheryl Gerson Tuttle, 2003.
2. *Epilepsy: The Ultimate Teen Guide*, by Kathlyn Gay and Sean McGarrahan, 2002.
3. *Stress Relief: The Ultimate Teen Guide*, by Mark Powell, 2002.
4. *Making Sexual Decisions: The Ultimate Teen Guide*, by L. Kris Gowen, Ph.D., 2003.
5. *Asthma: The Ultimate Teen Guide*, by Penny Hutchins Paquette, 2003.
6. *Cultural Diversity: Conflicts and Challenges: The Ultimate Teen Guide*, by Kathlyn Gay, 2003.
7. *Diabetes: The Ultimate Teen Guide*, by Katherine J. Moran, 2004.
8. *When Will I Stop Hurting? Teens, Loss, and Grief: The Ultimate Teen Guide*, by Edward Myers, 2004.
9. *Volunteering: The Ultimate Teen Guide*, by Kathlyn Gay, 2004.
10. *Organ Transplant: A Survival Guide for Recipients and Their Families: The Ultimate Teen Guide*, by Tina P. Schwartz, 2005.
11. *Medications: The Ultimate Teen Guide*, by Cheryl Gerson Tuttle, 2005.

Apprenticeship

The Ultimate Teen Guide

PENNY HUTCHINS PAQUETTE

It Happened to Me, No. 13

The Scarecrow Press, Inc.
Lanham, Maryland • Toronto • Oxford
2005

SCARECROW PRESS, INC.

Published in the United States of America
by Scarecrow Press, Inc.
A wholly owned subsidiary of
The Rowman & Littlefield Publishing Group, Inc.
4501 Forbes Boulevard, Suite 200
Lanham, Maryland 20706
www.scarecrowpress.com

PO Box 317
Oxford
OX2 9RU, UK

British Library Cataloguing in Publication Information Available

Library of Congress Cataloging-in-Publication Data

Paquette, Penny Hutchins.
  Apprenticeship : the ultimate teen guide / Penny Hutchins Paquette.
    p. cm. — (It happened to me ; no. 13)
  Includes bibliographical references and index.
  ISBN 0-8108-4945-3 (hardcover : alk. paper)
  1. Apprenticeship programs—United States—Juvenile literature. 2.
Occupational training—United States—Juvenile literature. 3. Vocational
guidance—United States—Juvenile literature. I. Title. II. Series.

  HD4885.U5P28 2005
  331.25'922'0973—dc22
                                                      2005008301

∞™ The paper used in this publication meets the minimum requirements of
American National Standard for Information Sciences—Permanence of Paper
for Printed Library Materials, ANSI/NISO Z39.48-1992.
Manufactured in the United States of America.

For Cheryl and Joanie,
who helped me get started

Contents

Contents

Acknowledgments

I would like to thank John Rich, acting commissioner of the Division of Apprenticeship Training in Boston, for all of his help with this project. A special thank you also goes to all of the apprentices and apprenticeship program directors who helped bring personal voices to the many careers that can be entered through apprenticeship training.

Introduction

Apprenticeship: *The Ultimate Teen Guide* is designed to
help young adults like you explore the possibility of
apprenticeship as entry into the world of work. Apprenticeship
has many advantages for those looking for job training. Not all
apprenticeships require a college background. If you are not
planning to go to college because you think it isn't right for
you or because you prefer your instruction to be more hands-
on, apprenticeship can offer the kind of instruction you are
looking for. All apprenticeships require on-the-job training and
give you the opportunity to learn from an expert or master in
the job—someone who not only has the specific skills you are
hoping to learn, but the skills to teach as well. If you would
like to go to college, but can't afford it, there are opportunities
for you as well.

Apprentices earn while they learn. Instead of racking up
expenses for educational opportunities, you will be paid a
salary while you are training. As your knowledge and skills
improve, so will your salary. All apprenticeships pay at least
minimum wage, and many pay much more. In addition, all
apprenticeships require additional related training as well.
Depending on the program, this training may take place in a
traditional college setting, in classrooms specifically designed
by the sponsor, through online programs, in workshops, or at
conferences. Before you sigh and say, *more classwork*,
consider this. The related training is just that, related. You
won't be studying American history to learn how to lay
bricks. If you are interested in nursing, you won't be studying

the history of music. If you want to be a wardrobe designer or supervisor, you won't be working on your basic keyboarding skills. All of the classroom work will be related to what you are learning on the job. In some of these programs, you will need to pay for the related training, but in most, your employer will pay for the related instruction. To make things even sweeter, many of these courses can be applied toward college degrees. On top of that, some states require that sponsors pay you for your time in the classroom. Can you imagine? You could get paid to go to school!

Maybe you have had some experience in the workforce and know what you want to do after high school. Or, maybe you aren't quite sure and need a little more information. Either way, *Apprenticeship: The Ultimate Teen Guide* can help you decide what to do next.

The early chapters give the history of apprenticeship and an overall view of apprenticeship in general, explaining the rules and regulations. After that, each chapter presents a broad category and includes the specific jobs within that group that may appeal to you. Each job is introduced with the labor codes most often associated with that job. The O*NET/SOC code is the Standard Occupational Classification used by the Department of Labor to identify jobs. The DOT code is the Dictionary of Occupational Titles code, still used by many labor groups to classify particular jobs. The RAIS number is the Registered Apprenticeship Information System code developed by the Bureau of Apprenticeship Training and assigned to a specific apprenticeship job. With these three codes, you should be able to locate any additional information you would like about a specific job. All private and public labor sectors use one of these codes.

The book presents an overview of the work involved in each job category. The job outlook and wages section will give you an idea of the kind of salary you can expect to earn in that specific career as well as the expected growth in that area through 2012. This information comes from the Department of Labor's Bureau of Labor Statistics Occupational Employment Projections to 2012 and May 2003 National Occupational

Employment and Wage Estimates. The Bureau of Labor Statistics explains its job growth estimates in the following way.

If the percentage change is	The occupation is
Up 36% or more	Growing much faster than average
Up 21–35%	Growing faster than average
Up 10–20%	Growing about as fast as average
Up 0–9%	Growing more slowly than average, or no change
Down 1% or more	Declining

This basic information will give you an idea of what you can expect when searching for work in a particular category.

Information about apprenticeships is also presented in each job section. General descriptions of programs, including the necessary coursework involved, is presented here. Review the classroom expectations to help decide if this is the right apprenticeship for you. The related skills sections present information to help you get a head start. High school courses that can help you prepare for the jobs and the kinds of skills that are required are presented here.

Each job section ends with a resources section. Here you will find the places to go to get even more information about the jobs you are interested in.

Because each apprenticeship is different and each state has its own local contact for information, a list of state apprenticeship organizations is included in Appendix A and Appendix B. Once you have decided which jobs interest you, you can contact your local apprenticeship organization to find out about opportunities in your area.

There are more than 800 apprenticeable jobs in the United States. Although that number is quite impressive, it includes everything that can be trained for as an apprentice—not necessarily programs that are active. In addition, not all apprenticeable jobs are entry level. Some are programs designed specifically to help current employees advance in their careers. *Apprenticeship: The Ultimate Teen Guide* covers more than

200 opportunities that are currently active in the United States. As mentioned before, not all apprenticeships are available in each state. A call to your local apprenticeship organization will let you know if your state is among those offering a program in a specific job.

Either before or after reviewing the careers covered in the guide, look at the final chapter. Here is the information you will need to do some general research on your own. It includes how to find specific information for your state, including job outlooks and salaries for individual jobs in very specific areas. Also included in this section is information about alternatives to apprenticeship programs.

For those of you who are interested in doing some career exploration, *Apprenticeship: The Ultimate Teen Guide* is a great place to start.

The History of Apprenticeship

When we think of the history of apprenticeship, we most often think of young people working with master craftsmen during the middle ages, or a young person like Benjamin Franklin learning a craft in colonial America. However, on-the-job training has been a form of career education since ancient times. Young workers who could neither read nor write could learn to do a job by observation and practice.

ANCIENT APPRENTICES

Evidence of on-the-job training extends as far back as ancient Babylon, and rules for the treatment of apprentices extend that far back as well. Hammurabi, an early king of Babylon, established a code of conduct for his citizens called the Code of Hammurabi. This ancient, eight-foot-tall, black stone tablet includes rules for the treatment of apprentices: *If an artisan has undertaken to rear a child and teaches him his craft, he cannot be demanded back. If he has not taught him his craft, this adopted son may return to his father's house.*

Artisans continued to learn their craft by working directly with masters of the trade throughout ancient Egypt, Greece, and Rome.

MIDDLE AGES

By the Middle Ages, apprenticeship training was the established method of educating young people in a trade.

Image from *Johannes Gutenberg: From Lead Letter to the Computer* by Elisabeth Geck, Bad Godesberg Inter Nationes, 1968.

In the 14th and 15th centuries, one of the most lucrative trades was that of a copyist, artist/craftsmen and women who copied manuscripts. The price of these manuscripts was quite high. One copy of a written bible created by nuns in a convent was exchanged for a small farm.

Few children stayed with their families beyond their early teen years. Most were placed in other homes to learn a skill or a trade. The family's connections were the foundation for placing a son as an apprentice. During medieval times it was unusual for a child to be apprenticed with his father, even if he planned to enter the same trade. Instead, families placed their children with relatives, friends, or acquaintances. If you had lived in the Middle Ages, it is unlikely you would have chosen your trade, and there was little you could do to enter a trade that was outside your family's social situation. If your family was poor, it was highly unlikely that they would have friends in the higher-paying, well-regarded trades. In order to become a goldsmith or a stonemason, for example, your family would need to know someone in that trade.

You might learn your family's business working with a friend of the family in the same trade. More likely, however, you would be placed in a different trade. If your father had a friend who was a blacksmith, you might be apprenticed there. If your uncle was a cordwainer, you would eventually learn to design shoes.

Girls could enter trades during the Middle Ages, but they were most often taught the trade by the master's wife. Among the trades that accepted women were butchers, shoemakers, bookbinders, goldsmiths, and ironmongers as well as the more traditional women's trades, brewing, spinning, and hot-food preparation and selling. Many women learned a trade while working alongside their husbands. If a husband died, the wife was allowed to continue in the trade.

During this period, people involved in the trades formed specific guilds. These guilds were governed by master craftsmen who regulated the cost of raw materials, the quality and price of the product, wages, and working conditions. These groups were similar to modern trade unions. In England, they followed two laws, the Statute of Artificers of 1563 and the Poor Law of 1601. These laws bound an apprentice to the master and set the term of service at seven years.

Parents paid these master craftsmen to take their children on as apprentices, and in return for their work, the masters provided training, food, housing, and clothing. Skilled workers were highly regarded in the Middle Ages, and an apprentice could work his way into his own business.

COLONIAL AMERICA

The practice of training by apprenticeship came to the new world with the settlers. Craftsmen who came to America brought the master-apprentice tradition along with them. By 1716, there were written records of apprentice training here in the United States. Had you been a teenager in America during colonial times, like young people in the Middle Ages, you would have had no choice in your job training. Your parents would have made that decision for you. Many young people, like Paul Revere, learned their trade from their fathers. Others,

Benjamin Franklin working at his brother's shop, from the painting *Franklin the Printer* by Charles E. Mills. Library of Congress LC-USZ 62-48913.

THE COLONIES' MOST FAMOUS APPRENTICE

Unlike most boys during colonial times, Benjamin Franklin's father gave him some options when looking for an appropriate apprenticeship. Young Franklin wasn't happy working in his father's soap and candle shop and threatened to become a sailor. His father wanted Franklin close to home and took him to visit several master tradesmen including bricklayers, blacksmiths, cabinetmakers, roofers, brass workers, and coopers. Because the boy showed no particular interest in any of those trades, his father selected a placement for him. Twelve-year-old Benjamin Franklin was apprenticed to his older brother James and would learn to be a printer.

For a young boy who loved to read, this was a fortunate choice. His contract stipulated that he would work with his brother for nine years! In return for his work he would receive a room, food, some clothing, training as a printer, and some pay in his final year. During his apprenticeship, Franklin learned the printing trade and also honed his writing skills. James put his brother to work writing ballads that he printed and sold on the streets of Boston. By the time James was printing his own newspaper, sixteen-year-old Franklin was taking his writing skills to another level. Without his brother's knowledge, his apprentice submitted letters to the *Courant* under the name of Mrs. Silence Dogwood, proposing, among other things, that women should be educated. When James found out that his younger brother was the author of the letters, he was furious. This was one of many disputes between the brothers and in 1723, four years into his apprenticeship contract, Franklin quit. Unable to find work with any other printer, he boarded a ship and headed for a new life that would eventually find him alongside Thomas Jefferson drafting the Declaration of Independence.

like Ben Franklin, were placed with relatives. In large families, it was prudent to place boys in a variety of apprenticeships. This provided the family with the opportunity to barter for goods in several areas.

Family finances were often a factor when selecting a trade. Some artisans, like tailors and shoemakers, needed little money to get started. Unfortunately, these were often the jobs that paid the least. In some jobs, physical qualities were important. Great strength was needed to enter an apprenticeship as a blacksmith, and because few qualified, blacksmiths were well paid.

Young boys, between 10 and 17, were signed off to their teachers or masters for between four and seven years. The master was then responsible not only for the apprentice's training, but for feeding, clothing, educating (at least for the first three years), and raising the teenagers. The young person promised loyalty to the master and continued service for the period of indenture. He agreed not to gamble or visit taverns, alehouses, or theaters; not to practice any immoral behavior; and not to buy or sell anything that belonged to him or his master without the master's permission. At the end of the apprenticeship, the master was to send the now-skilled craftsman on his way with clothing, tools, and a small amount of money to get started on his own.

Parents sometimes paid a fee for the placement of their child, and the master and the parents signed contracts of indenture specifying the terms of the agreement. The term *indenture* itself came from the English practice of tearing indentions or notches in the duplicate copies of apprenticeship forms. The copy with the torn edge was kept by the apprentice or his parents.

Once parents signed contracts of indenture, they no longer had obligations to raise or train their own children. Poor or orphaned children (see sidebar next page) could be placed in apprenticeships by the courts.

Once signed over, fledgling apprentices did most of the grunt work for at least their first year. Rather than actually learning a craft, they were kept busy sweeping, cleaning, or doing any other menial job the master required. Masters were slow to teach their apprentices. An apprentice who mastered the trade

A TYPICAL APPRENTICE INDENTURE AGREEMENT

Massachusetts, 1748

This indenture witnesseth, that Joseph Lynde, Tho Wait, John Dexter, Stephen Pain, and Joseph Wilson Select-men, Overseers of the Poor of the Town of Maldon in the County of Middlesex in New-England by and with the Consent of two of his majesties Justices of the Peace for said County have placed and by these presents do place and bind out John Ramsdell a poor Child belonging to Maldon aforesaid unto Edward Wait of Maldon in the County of Middlesex yeoman, and to his Wife and Heirs, and with them after the manner of an Apprentice to dwell and Serve, from the Day of the Date of these Presents until the fifth Day of April, which will be in the Year of our Lord one Thousand Seven Hundred and Sixty Two at which time the said Apprentice if living will arrive at the age of twenty one Years, during all which said time or term the said Apprentice his said Master and Mistress well and faithfully shall Serve, their Secrets he shall keep close, their Commandments lawful and honest everywhere he shall gladly obey, he shall do no Damage to his master nor suffer it to be done by others without letting or giving Reasonable notice thereof to his Master; he shall not waste the Goods of his said Master nor lend them unlawfully to any; at Cards, Dice or any other unlawful game or Games he shall not play; Fornication he shall not commit; Matrimony he shall not contract; Tavern, Ale Houses or places of Gaming he shall not haunt or frequent; From the Service of his Master by Day nor Night he shall not absent himself; but in all things and at all times he shall carry and behave himself towards his Master and all theirs, as a good and faithful Apprentice ought to do to his utmost Ability during all the Time or term aforesaid.

And the said Master doth hereby covenant and agree for himself his Wife and heirs to teach or cause the Apprentice to be taught the Art and mystery of a Cordwainer and also to read write and cypher, and also shall and will well and truly find allow unto and provide for the Apprentice Sufficient and wholesome meat and Drink, with Washing, Lodging and apparrel, and other Necessaries meet and convenient for Such an Apprentice during all the time or term aforesaid. And at the End and Expiration thereof shall dismiss the Apprentice with two good Suits of Apparrel for all parts of his Body one for Lords-Days, the other for working Days, Suitable to his Quality. In Testimony whereof the Parties have to these Indentures interchangeably Set their Hands and Seals the thirtieth day of April, in the twenty first year of the Reign of our Sovereign Lord George, the Second King of Great Britain. Anno Domini one thousand seven hundred and forty eight.

Signed, Sealed and Delivered in presence of:

John Shute

John Wilson

Edward Wait

Source: Green Family Papers, New England Historic Genealogical Society. Transcribed from: *History of Malden, Mass, 1633–1785, Deloraine Pendre Corey, 1899.*

too early in his contract might run off, like Benjamin Franklin, and begin working on his own.

After the period of training was complete, the worker was required to produce a proof of his training. This proof was called his *masterpiece* and if judged fine by his master, the apprentice would achieve journeyman status and then qualify for a salary from his master. As a journeyman he could work at his craft wherever he pleased, but the journeyman usually remained with the master and collected a small salary. Some traveled around making or repairing goods until saving enough money to open their own shops.

Many masters treated their apprentices as members of the family. They were expected to work hard, but they were well cared for and instructed in a trade that would provide a job in the future. Most were expected to work long days at menial tasks both on the job and in the house. Eventually, the master would begin teaching the young person the finer aspects, or what master tradesmen called *the mysteries*, of the trade. Not all apprentices were so fortunate. There were cruel and abusive masters. In some colonies if the young person ran away, he could be forced to wear a chain around his neck, his time of indenture could be extended, or he could be whipped.

Not all apprentices were placed by their parents. Adventurous young men and women who wanted to come to America signed contracts or indentures and agreed to work in exchange for the cost of their journey from England. British prisoners could shorten their time in prison if they agreed to become indentured servants, and many prisoners came to America to work on southern plantations. English orphans were among those children sent to America to work, and some young people were even kidnapped off the streets of England and shipped to America, earning their kidnappers a fee. Although these workers were often referred to as apprentices, they often didn't receive the same type of training or opportunity as traditional apprentices. Eventually, laws were established to prevent this type of "apprenticeship."

FACTORY WORK BEGINS

After the American Revolution, the situation for untrained workers changed. Less expensive manufactured goods from England forced employers to look for ways to cut costs. One way was to increase the number of apprentices. As the numbers of apprentices increased, their chances of mastering the craft to the point of becoming journeymen or masters themselves was reduced. As workers lost the opportunity to become their own masters, groups of workers began to band together to protest unfair labor practices. In the mid-1780s, shoemakers, printers, and bakers all went on strike to protest low wages. By 1830, carpenters, masons, printers, and other skilled workers had organized in a quest for better pay.

By the second half of the 19th century, mass production called for a different kind of worker. No longer were the majority of workers self employed or working in a small business making hand-crafted products. The Industrial Revolution changed all that. Instead of the master craftsman looking for an assistant to learn the job, wealthy investors controlled the workspace, the tools, and the raw materials.

There were few true apprenticeship opportunities during the Industrial Revolution. It wasn't until the late 19th century that apprenticeship programs comparable to those available today became available.

Until that time, children were no longer trained in a specific craft that would lead to their own business. Instead of taking five to seven years to truly master a trade, young people were crammed into factories and taught a small piece of the process—enough to allow them to do one part in the assembly-line production of a final product. Investors and factory owners weren't interested in teaching their workers to take over the business. They were interested in making a profit. The easiest way for them to make a profit was to control costs, and the easiest way to control costs was to control wages. Factory workers could be trained quickly to do simple skills and even young children could be put to work. Poor families could no longer place their children with a master to learn a craft. If their children needed to work, and they did, they had to go into harsh environments to help their families. Very young children worked in coal mines, canneries, potteries, steel and flour mills, and textile, shoe and glass factories, and as chimney sweeps. Children were exploited wherever small hands or bodies and little pay benefited the factory owners. Even with child labor laws passed in the mid-1800s, children under the age of 13 were expected to work six-hour days and those over 13 were expected to work 12 hours! It seems unbelievable today, but young children could be expected to report to work as early as 6 a.m. and work as late as 10 p.m. in print shops.

Factory workers worked long hours in poor conditions for little pay. If they complained, they were fired. There were always more workers who could fill the gap. There was little training beyond the specific skill needed in the factory, and there was little opportunity for advancement.

Even those lucky enough to be involved in one of the few formal apprenticeship programs worked very long hours for little pay. Unlike the colonial apprentices, they were paid from the start of work. Over time, their wages increased. In 1865, the Pennsylvania Railroad paid beginning apprentices 50 cents for a 10-hour day for the first 620 days. The apprentice could earn up to 80 cents a day near the end of the apprenticeship term.

In his book *Sixty Years with Men and Machines*, Fred H. Colvin described his experience in 1883: "An apprentice in the machine shops of 1883 faced a situation not wholly unlike that of the craft guilds of the middle ages. In many cases, the boy's parents had to reimburse the shop owner for teaching him the secrets of the trade."

Colvin earned five cents an hour for a 60-hour week. His wages were increased by 50 cents a week after the first month and another 50 cents a month each six months thereafter. Businesses made no promises to educate their workers or to guarantee them a job at the end of their training.

Although there were laws passed in the late 18th and early 19th centuries to help workers, especially children, and labor unions began to fight for workers' rights and take a role in helping train workers, the first apprenticeship legislation was

THE NATIONAL APPRENTICESHIP ACT
(50 STAT. 664; 29 U.S.C. §§ 50)*
1939

§ SEC. 50. PROMOTION OF LABOR STANDARDS OF APPRENTICESHIP

The Secretary of Labor is authorized and directed to formulate and promote the furtherance of labor standards necessary to safeguard the welfare of apprentices, to extend the application of such standards by encouraging the inclusion thereof in contracts of apprenticeship, to bring together employers and labor for the formulation of programs of apprenticeship, to cooperate with State agencies engaged in the formulation and promotion of standards of apprenticeship, and to cooperate with the Secretary of Education in accordance with section 17 of title 20. For the purposes of this chapter the term "State" shall include the District of Columbia.

§ SEC. 50A. PUBLICATION OF INFORMATION; NATIONAL ADVISORY COMMITTEES

The Secretary of Labor may publish information relating to existing and proposed labor standards of apprenticeship, and may appoint national advisory committees to serve without compensation. Such committees shall include representatives of employers, representatives of labor, educators, and officers of other executive departments, with the consent of the head of any such department.

§ SEC. 50B. APPOINTMENT OF EMPLOYEES

The Secretary of Labor is authorized to appoint such employees as he may from time to time find necessary for the administration of this chapter, with regard to existing laws applicable to the appointment and compensation of employees of the United States.

This is the entire text of the National Apprenticeship Act of 1937, also known as the Fitzgerald Act.

From: DTI Associates, *A Brighter Tomorrow: Apprenticeship for the 21st Century*, Washington, D.C., U.S. Department of Labor Office of Apprenticeship Training, Employer and Labor Services (OATELS), July 2003.

Note: When legislation is first passed, it is assigned a Statute number (50 Stat. 664). These numbers are assigned chronologically as law are passed. Once the legislation is placed into the United States Code (29 U.S.C.), it is listed by subject. This section of the U.S.C. includes labor legislation. Section 50 deals with apprenticeships.

not passed until 1911. This Wisconsin law placed apprenticeship under the jurisdiction of an industrial commission and required that all apprentices spend at least five hours a week in the classroom. By the 1920s, labor organizations, educators, and government officials worked toward the establishment of a uniform apprenticeship system. When immigration was curtailed after World War I, fewer skilled workers were entering the country, and America needed a method of training apprentices for the jobs that were opening.

In 1937, the federal government was ready to promote apprenticeship and enacted the National Apprenticeship Act, sometimes called the Fitzgerald Act, named for its sponsor, Congressman William J. Fitzgerald (D-CT), to "formulate and promote the furtherance of labor standards necessary to safeguard the welfare of apprentices (see sidebar on page 10). The Federal Committee on Apprenticeship was reorganized and enlarged to include equal representation of employers and labor, plus a representative of the U.S. Office of Education. The federal government established the Apprentice-Training Service (now the Bureau of Apprenticeship and Training) as part of the Department of Labor to administer the objectives of the law. Today, the Bureau of Apprenticeship and Training (BAT) has field representatives in all 50 states. The U.S. Department of Labor Office of Apprenticeship Training, Employer and Labor Services (OATELS) publishes the overall standards for developing programs and, with cooperating states, registers the programs that have met those standards.

From its humble beginnings in American homes and craft shops, apprenticeship training has grown into more than 800 apprenticeable jobs in the United States.

Apprenticeship Today

Young people have been learning new skills from experienced workers since the beginning of civilized society. Today's apprentices still have the benefits of hands-on, on-the-job training, but many things have changed since the colonial practices that were the foundation of today's formal apprenticeship programs. If you choose to enter an apprenticeship program today, you won't rely on a master for your clothing, housing, and food. Instead of learning the basics of reading and writing in the classroom, your classroom instruction will be directly related to your career goal. And, best of all, unlike the indentured servants of the past, you will earn as you learn.

VOICES OF EXPERIENCE

Why should someone look for an apprenticeship in the trades? There are lots of reasons, says Eric Redding, the apprenticeship coordinator for the Painters and Allied Trades Council #35 in Massachusetts.

"I never wanted to go to college. My dad was in the union, so I followed. Training as an apprentice has meant the world to me. When my friends were making minimum wage, I was buying my first new car. I was 18 years old. By the time I was 24, I bought my first home, and I did not have loans to pay back."

Redding said although most young people don't think about the benefits of a union job, they are very important. He has worked in the trades for 20 years and will be able to retire while he is still in his 50s. "My pension will allow me to retire with dignity."

(continued)

Young people shouldn't think that getting an apprenticeship is a snap, however. Applicants for the apprenticeship program he coordinates must be at least 17 and have a high school diploma or a GED. After completing the initial application, they go through two days of orientation. They must pass drug tests, take an aptitude test, a physical challenge test, and complete an interview. The applicants who perform the best are accepted into the program. In 2004, his New England–area program had 231 apprentices training as painters, paper hangers, wall finishers, glaziers, and sign and display workers.

Once accepted into the program, the work is hard. Apprentices spend two nights a week going to school for related course work, in addition to working full time. The three-year program includes 6,000 hours of paid, on-the-job training. And although apprentices are not paid for the 450 hours they spend in the classroom, their education is free. His apprentices are indentured to the union, not a contractor, and they can be laid off, but as he says, "The hard worker who learns his trade is the person who is going to stay employed."

BLUE-COLLAR MENTALITY A MISTAKE

It seems a lot of people think a blue-collar job is somehow "less than," according to some of the people who work in the field. There seems to be some sort of stigma attached to working in the trades. This is unfortunate, because getting into a union apprenticeship can be as hard as getting into Stanford, Northwestern, or Harvard, says Joseph Conley, director of the apprenticeship program for the Plumbers and Gasfitters Local 12. Their selection is very competitive and they have high completion rates (99 percent) as a result.

Apprenticeship opportunities are only open once each year in this union and many others, so Conley says you need to get a head start. Each year, the members of the union's apprentice committee review work expectations and retirements to help determine how many apprentices they will take. Call the local union and ask about the opportunities and requirements. Then, be ready. When you go to apply, you will need to bring your birth certificate, a social security card, a driver's license, your high school diploma or GED certificate, a transcript of your grades, and a filing fee. Most apprenticeships require some type of aptitude testing and many require drug testing as well, says Conley. Expect to be interviewed by someone from labor and someone from management. "We are looking for people who are going to be committed to the union for 20-30-40 years with good character and good skills," says Conley. Results of tests and interview impressions are evaluated and apprentices are selected. Now the real work begins.

Once on the job, apprentices must keep a work progress report that Conley reviews each month. They work on the job during the day and then must go to school at night. Conley says he is proud of the state-of-the-art facility available to his apprentices. It has

(*continued*)

classrooms specifically designed for hands-on training in three different shops, and a welding shop that he says is "second to none." Although the minimum standard for registered apprenticeship programs is 144 hours of related instruction each year, his apprentices must complete 230 a year. "It's hard work, but it pays off," he says. Apprentices start at $12 an hour and receive full benefits packages. They get regular increases as their skills and knowledge improve, and by the time they reach journeyperson status, they make $33 an hour. "When these boys and girls finish, they can earn between $70,000 and $100,000 a year."

ORGANIZATIONAL STRUCTURE

Since the establishment of labor laws for apprentices in the 1930s, a structured program for on-the-job training has been available for those who want to take a direct approach to career development. Most formal apprenticeship programs today are registered with the U.S. Department of Labor. The Department of Labor Bureau of Apprenticeship and Training/Office of Apprenticeship Training, Employer and Labor Services (BAT/OATELS), in cooperation with State Apprenticeship Agencies or Councils (SACs), oversees the nation's apprenticeship system.

The federal agency, or BAT, oversees programs in 23 states. In 27 other states and the District of Columbia, SACs are recognized by the Department of Labor as the entity that approves and registers apprenticeship programs in those states. These SACs have adopted regulations governing apprenticeship that meet, or exceed, the minimum federal standards. A list of SACs is included in Appendix A.

Both BATs and SACs register apprenticeship programs that meet federal and state guidelines and develop requirements for businesses and industries interested in sponsoring apprenticeship programs. Once the requirements are developed, they certify that the sponsors' programs meet the requirements.

Together, these groups work to encourage the development of new programs and help protect the safety and welfare of apprentices. The oversight helps ensure that the programs provide high-quality training to registered apprentices.

THE PROGRAMS

Registered apprenticeships are certified, formal training programs that include related classroom and technical instruction designed to prepare a worker for a specific job. The Department of Labor's BAT/OATELS and SACs register programs that meet standards ensuring quality, fairness, and accessibility. Because the programs are developed by industries and businesses that depend on the specific skills they want their employees to have, the employer can be sure to have a quality workforce trained to meet the industry's need.

In order to qualify as a sponsor of a registered apprenticeship program, the sponsors must provide

- A written plan that details the terms of employment, supervision, and training
- A starting age for apprentices of at least 16 (18 in hazardous occupations)
- A full and fair opportunity to apply for apprenticeship
- An outline of the specific work processes in which an apprentice is to receive training and how much time will be spent in each area
- Organized instruction designed to provide apprentices with knowledge in technical subjects related to their trade. (A minimum of 144 hours per year is normally considered necessary.) The instruction may take place through trade or industrial courses, by correspondence courses of equivalent value, or other forms of self-study approved by the approval agency.
- Qualified training personnel and adequate supervision on the job
- A progressively increasing schedule of wages. Entry-level wages must not be less than minimum wage
- Proper supervision of on-the-job training with adequate facilities to train apprentices
- As apprentices progress, both in job performances and related instruction, they are periodically evaluated and appropriate records are maintained.

◎ **No discrimination in any phase of selection, employment, or training**

◎ **A written agreement**

In addition to these requirements, many program sponsors agree to pay for the related instruction for their apprentices. Some even pay their employees for time spent in the classroom! Sponsors may include employers, employer associations, unions, and joint labor-management organizations.

Today, there are more than 32,000 programs that represent over a quarter million employers, industries, and companies. Apprenticeship program sponsors cover the costs of the program. Sometimes funding comes through state or federal grants. The programs are registered with the Department of Labor or a federally approved state SAC.

As in the colonial days, the apprentice and the registered program sponsor sign a written agreement (indenture) called an apprenticeship agreement that covers the terms of employment. (See a sample of the apprenticeship agreement from Massachusetts on pages 18 and 19.)

It includes the length of the apprenticeship, the hours of related instruction, the wages he or she will earn, and the number of hours of on-the-job training. The sponsor promises to train the apprentice and to make every effort to keep him or her employed. The apprentice agrees to perform the work and complete the related study.

HOW IT WORKS

For young people interested in learning on the job, for those who are looking for an alternative to the traditional four-year college degree, for those who can't afford college, for those who want to be trained in a specific trade and enjoy learning in a hands-on environment, and for those who want to "earn while they learn," apprenticeship may be an excellent choice.

Requirements for specific apprenticeship programs vary. All require that applicants be at least 16, and most require applicants to be 18. Apprenticeships in construction,

The Commonwealth of Massachusetts
DEPARTMENT OF LABOR AND WORKFORCE
D E V E L O P M E N T
DIVISION OF APPRENTICE TRAINING
399 Washington Street 4th Floor, Boston, MA 02108-5223

FOR OFFICE USE ONLY
Field Rep. Number:
Sponsor Number:

APPRENTICE AGREEMENT

Pursuant to the Standards of Apprenticeship adopted by the Sponsor and registered with the Massachusetts Division of Apprentice Training, the provisions of which are hereby made part of this Agreement, and in compliance with the Massachusetts Plan for Equal Employment in Apprenticeship Training, WITNESSETH: that the Agreement is entered into by the undersigned:

_____ / _____
(Name of Apprentice)   (Address of Apprentice)

and the Program Sponsor   (Employer, JAC, JATC, Ass. of Employers or Org. of Employers.)

TRADE:_____ TERM OF APPRENTICESHIP_____ HOURS .

DATE APPRENTICESHIP BEGINS: _____ PROJECTED COMPLETION DATE: _____

CREDIT FOR PREVIOUS EXPERIENCE:_____ HOURS.

GRADUATED SCALE OF WAGES IN (PERCENTAGES TO BE PAID THE APPRENTICE. (PERCENTAGES ARE BASED ON JOURNEY PERSON WAGES)

[On projects where there is a prevailing rate set by law, the rate of pay shall comply with the wage rate or percentages stated on the wage schedules issued by the Department of Labor and Workforce Development]

PERIOD:_____

1st	5th	9th	13th
2nd	6th	10th	14th
3rd	7th	11th	15th
4th	8th	12th	16th

Minimum Journey person rate as of (Date) _____ is $_____ per hour

NUMBER OF HOURS PER DAY AND TOTAL NUMBERS OF HOURS PER WEEK TO BE WORKED BY THE APPRENTICE.

_____ hours per day _____ hours per week.   Overtime Rate:

The parties hereto agree that the terms stated on the reverse side of this form are part of this agreement

_____
(Signature of Apprentice) / (PLEASE SIGN IN BLUE INK)

_____
(Signature of Program Sponsor) / (PLEASE SIGN IN BLUE INK)

_____
Address of Program Sponsor)

_____
(Signature of Union JAC, JATC) / (PLEASE SIGN IN BLUE INK)

Approved by the Division of Apprentice Training :_____ Date:_____

manufacturing, telecommunications, information technology, service and retail industries, and health care have very different entry requirements. Some require a high school diploma or GED, some require advanced mathematics in high school, some want their apprentices to have some work-related experience,

PLEASE HAVE APPRENTICE READ AND INITIAL EVERY LINE

The Program Sponsor, the Apprentice, and her or his Parent (or Guardian) in conformity with the terms and conditions provided herein, hereby agree to the following:

========➤ The apprentice program sponsor shall ensure that the apprentice receives a minimum of 150 hours per year of related instructions in all subjects related to the trade. Such instructions may be given in a classroom or through correspondence courses or other forms of self-study, but must be approved by the Deputy Director. The sponsor will not necessarily be responsible for paying the cost of the related instruction or any books, other written materials, or supplies necessary for such instruction. If however, the apprentice is to be responsible for all or any portion of such costs it must be specified below.

COST TO BE INCURRED BY APPRENTICE: [please check item(s) that apply]

TUITION ____   BOOKS ____   TOOLS ____   NONE ____

========➤ The Program Sponsor agrees to abide by all applicable provisions of the Massachusetts Plan for Equal Employment in Apprenticeship Training.

========➤ The Apprentice agrees to be diligent and faithful in learning the stated trade or craft including mandatory attendance in 150 hrs. of related instruction classes, for each year of Apprenticeship.

========➤ The first 1000 hours of employment shall be a probationary period during which time this Agreement may be canceled by either party with notification to the other and to the Massachusetts Division of Apprentice Training.

========➤ This agreement must be approved by and filed with the Division of Apprentice Training before the apprentice starts work and copies must be returned to sponsor.

========➤ The Director of Apprentice Training may cancel the agreement subject to hearing upon application by any party.

========➤ The parties recognize that prevailing wage rates for public works projects are set by the Department of Labor and Workforce Development, Division of Occupational Safety and that the wages listed in these program standards do not supersede or replace the wage rates determined by the Department of Labor and Workforce Development.

Completion of part or all of this last section of the Apprentice Agreement is MANDATORY. The information will remain confidential and will be used for aggregate statistical data only.

TO BE COMPLETED BY APPRENTICE (Please check, circle or fill in items as appropriate)

SS#___-___-___   (Date of Birth)_____   (phone)_____

SEX	ETHNIC GROUP		VETERAN	DISABLED
1. **G** Male	1. **G** White	4. **G** Asian or Pacific Islander	1. **G** Vietnam Era Veteran	**G** YES
2. **G** Female	2. **G** Black	5. **G** Hispanic	2. **G** Other Veteran	**G** NO
	3. **G** American Ind. or Alaskan Native	6. **G** Other	3. **G** Non Veteran	

Circle highest grade of school completed 12 - GED **G**	COLLEGE 13 14 15 16 17 18

and some specialized programs require an associate's degree or other postsecondary study.

High school work counts when looking for an apprenticeship. Most sponsors want candidates who have completed classes in English, math, and science. Some may want students who have taken courses in industrial arts. Some may ask you to take aptitude tests. Some jobs require physical strength; others good interpersonal skills. As in any job search, applicants with experience have an advantage. Work or volunteer experience in related areas helps. Some companies only offer apprenticeships to those already working there. There is more information about specific requirements in the chapters that follow.

Some programs require the apprentice to complete a probationary period before signing the apprentice agreement.

All programs must offer on-the-job training supervised by a skilled worker. During your training, you will receive instruction in all areas related to the job. You will begin with simple tasks and as you learn, you will be assigned more advanced duties.

As an apprentice, you will also take classes to learn more about your job. What most apprentices say they like most about the classes they take is that the classes are directly related to their work. Students say they are motivated in the classroom because the instruction helps them on the job. Classroom instruction can come in many forms. Some apprentices attend community college classes or classes at a local vocational school several nights a week. Others go for more intense instruction for several weeks each year. Some take classes in state-of-the-art facilities built by labor organizations. Still others take classes over the Internet or through the mail. Each program is different and has different classroom components, but all programs require at least 144 hours of instruction each year. In many programs, the related study may be applied to college degree programs.

Because apprentices are employees, they are paid. Again, wages depend on the specific apprenticeship program, but all apprentices are paid at least minimum wage to start, and many are paid much more. In general, apprentices are paid 50 percent of a skilled journey worker's wage to start, and their salary increases as job skills increase. Many program sponsors offer health and retirement benefits as well.

Those interested in apprenticeship must be willing to give the time it takes for both the on-the-job and classroom training

UNUSUAL CLASSROOMS CREATE UNUSUAL WORK

When most of us think of classrooms, we think of desks, blackboards, and lectures. The classrooms of most apprenticeship programs hardly fit that model. Instead, they are often state-of-the-art training centers that provide everything an apprentice needs to learn both the theory and the hands-on work associated with a craft.

For example, apprentices in the sheet metal trade may attend schools administered by the Sheet Metal Workers' International Association (SMWIA) and the Sheet Metal Air Conditioning Contractors National Association (SMACNA). While there may be classes in math and geometry held in traditional lecture halls, the hands-on work is held in welding rooms, sheet metal shops, custom fabrication labs, and computer-assisted design (CAD) labs. These facilities provide the specific type of education that prepares apprentices for related jobs in the field. To make things even better, apprentices don't pay for this high-tech training. Instead, this program is funded by the contractors who will employ these students. In the end, the investment pays off, because they get workers trained in the specific areas.

Sheet metal workers helped build the Disney Concert Hall in Los Angeles.

Photo courtesy of the Sheet Metal and Air Conditioning Contractors' National Association (SMACNA).

Once graduated from apprenticeship programs, sheet metal workers may specialize in the air conditioning industry or in architectural sheet metal, which includes projects like the Meriden, a 20-story condominium tower in Clearwater, Florida, the Disney Concert Hall in Los Angeles, or the restoration of the Cathedral of Saint Paul in St. Paul, Minnesota.

necessary to master the skills to reach journeyman status. Apprenticeship is not a quick and easy way to get a job, but a long-term commitment to career goals. All apprenticeships require at least 2,000 hours of work experience. Some require as much as 12,000 hours! This means you will be spending between two and six years mastering your job. Some programs are competency-based and you may be given credit for past experience or for related educational background.

All of this work pays off. According to the U.S. Department of Labor, the salary for a journey-level worker competes with the salaries of college graduates. Not only do apprentices reach their salary goals, but they are likely to advance well in their chosen careers also.

A survey conducted by the Associated General Contractors of America showed that, among those that responded to the survey, 90 percent of the top officials of construction companies began their careers as apprentices. Another survey, conducted by a large manufacturer of electrical and automotive equipment, revealed that 40 percent of the 300 apprentice graduates still on the company's payroll held important supervisory or executive positions.

Apprenticeships are not only available to young people just out of school, but to ex-military, those interested in making a career change, and workers who have been laid off.

MAKING A CHOICE

Today there are close to a half million apprentices earning and learning in the United States. No matter what your interest, there is probably an apprenticeship program somewhere that can help you find the kind of work you will enjoy. There are currently over 800 apprenticeable occupations registered with the Department of Labor. Most of the apprenticeable jobs are in the construction industry—more than 7,000 apprenticeship programs. More than one-third of registered apprentices are working in this area. Another third are learning their jobs in production.

Although construction and production account for more than half of the apprenticeable occupations, there are still hundreds of other jobs that can be mastered through apprenticeship. Firefighters and police officers, stage technicians and wardrobe supervisors, funeral directors and embalmers, actors, artisans, avionics technicians, and animal

THE TOP 25 APPRENTICESHIP OCCUPATIONS
AS OF SEPTEMBER 30, 2003

Rank	Occupation	Total Number of Apprentices Enrolled	Number of Active Programs
1	Electrician	47,146	3,455
2	Carpenter	26,383	648
3	Plumber	15,611	2,280
4	Pipe Fitter (Construction)	15,174	960
5	Electrician (Maintenance)	9,842	1,135
6	Sheet Metal Worker	9,617	722
7	Electronics Mechanic	9,346	82
8	Structural Steel Worker	6,511	169
9	Roofer	5,285	191
10	Construction Craft Laborer	4,954	55
11	Bricklayer (Construction)	4,899	288
12	Painter	4,142	371
13	Operating Engineer	4,066	154
14	Maintenance Mechanic	4,050	853
15	Boilermaker	3,647	61
16	Electrician, aircraft	3,638	3
17	Machinist	3,208	2,140
18	Millwright	3,090	587
19	Tool and Die Maker	3,042	2,244
20	Telecommunications Tech	2,990	126
21	Cook (Any Industry)	2,923	167
22	Heating/AC Installer	2,677	689
23	Correction Officer	2,670	66
24	Power Plant Operator	2,601	59
25	Cook (Hotel and Restaurant)	2,533	498

Source: **Registered Apprentice Information System (RAIS)**

trainers are among the jobs that may be trained for through apprenticeship. See the complete list of all apprenticeable occupations in Appendix D. Look over the list for ideas and then begin exploring. This book covers more than 150 jobs in detail. Specific information about jobs not covered in this book can be found using the resources in the last chapter.

Your school guidance counselor can be a good source of career information. Counselors can help you sort through your areas of strength and interest and help you decide on a career path.

Trade unions can provide a wealth of information about jobs in construction and production. Your local BAT or SAC office can also provide information.

Most of these apprenticeships are in local communities. Expect to live at home. Although you will be paid about half the journeyman's wage while you are training, it probably will not be enough for independent living. If you want to get out on your own, you will need to share housing and food expenses with a roommate or two. Still, you won't be accruing expenses while you learn and you will see regular salary increases as you work your way through your apprenticeship program.

WOMEN IN APPRENTICESHIP

Apprenticeship was once considered a males-only training opportunity. Today, businesses across all occupations are seeking qualified women to help them reach their goals. According to U.S. Department of Labor Secretary Elaine L. Chao, "Apprenticeship training is a great opportunity for women to gain valuable skills that can advance their careers with better paying jobs. By expanding the skills of America's working women, we are addressing the needs of our workforce and assisting women in the development of rewarding careers. When women win, families win," she said in 2002.

In an effort to bring more women into apprenticeship programs in 2002, the Department of Labor offered $1,000,000 in grants to organizations that help employees and unions establish apprenticeship programs for women.

PROGRAM REQUIREMENTS

Registered apprenticeship programs set their own standards for qualifications for applicants, and qualifications vary greatly from program to program. As mentioned above, most programs require applicants to be 18 and have a high school diploma or GED. Some require aptitude tests, medical tests, drug tests, strength tests, or other tests to help evaluate your fitness for the job. You may be required to have a driver's license and a home or cell phone where you can be reached. Some programs require a small fee for the application process and others may require you join a union and pay union dues. Once accepted as an apprentice, you must agree to perform the on-the-job training, attend related classroom instruction, and keep a record of your work and classroom hours. These records must be submitted regularly (usually once a month). In some jobs, apprentices are expected to purchase the necessary tools for the trade.

Since there are apprenticeships available in 800 different areas, it is best to explore your area of interest and the qualifications for specific jobs. The following chapters provide job descriptions and general apprenticeship information for a wide variety of careers.

Once you have done some career exploration and know what field you are interested in, you can begin looking for apprenticeship opportunities. For information about apprenticeships, contact the nearest U.S. Department of Labor Bureau of Apprenticeship and Training office or the State Apprenticeship Council office. For a list of offices in each state, see Appendix A at the end of this book. Many apprenticeship programs are sponsored by trade unions. Contact the union engaged in the trade you want to enter.

Each state posts a list of current apprenticeship programs on the U.S. Department of Labor Employment and Training Administration site, http://bat.doleta.gov/bat.cfm. The site allows you to search by state and then by county, so you can locate the programs nearest you. Although the site is kept reasonably up to date, new programs are added continuously. This site is good for exploration, but if you want to be sure what programs are currently available and may have openings for apprentices, call your local apprenticeship agency.

Talk to people. Getting a job as an apprentice is in many ways similar to finding any other job. It is often the personal contact that opens a door. If you know people who work in a job you would like, ask them about employment opportunities and whether apprenticeships are available for that job. Sometimes a short conversation can provide essential information.

With so many different apprenticeships available, it is unlikely that individual states will offer apprenticeships in every field. Some offer a limited number of programs and others offer hundreds. If your state doesn't offer an apprenticeship in a job you are interested in, talk to your local apprenticeship organization about the likelihood of a program becoming available. If you can't find a program, explore some of the other strategies for action after high school in the final chapter of the book.

Explore the chapters that follow and good luck finding an opportunity to earn while you learn.

The Construction Industry

If you were a child who loved building with blocks, working with Tinkertoys, constructing ham radios or remote-controlled vehicles, or driving your scale-model trucks through imaginary work sites, an apprenticeship in the construction industry might be right for you. With more than six million people employed in the industry, and a

CONSTRUCTION JOBS—FAST FACTS

Workers	6,085,510
Average Annual Salary	$37,000
Expected Job Growth	Average
Expected Job Outlook	Excellent
Apprentices	170,260
Apprenticeship Averages	
3–4 Years	
144 Classroom Hours Per Year (Minimum)	
Fastest Growing Jobs	Cement Mason/Concrete Finisher, Hazardous Materials Workers, and Electricians

wide variety of jobs available, construction offers more apprenticeships than any other trade. In 2002 alone, there were 170,260 apprentices bringing home a salary while they learned about specific jobs in construction. More than one-third of all registered apprenticeships are in this category.

Anticipating shortages in skilled workers, Secretary of Labor Elaine L. Chao recently joined with a diverse group of partners from industry and organized labor to address the shortage of skilled trades workers over the next ten years. In April 2004, the group established the "Skills to Build America's Future" initiative, an outreach and education effort designed to attract both young people and transitioning workers to careers in the trades.

"Today we need the skills and talents of a new generation of skilled tradesmen and women," said Elaine Chao. "Over the next few years many jobs will be created in the skilled trades, and even more opportunities will open up as the baby boom generation retires. The skilled trades offer more than great jobs—they also play a key role in building America's future."

If you are looking for a skilled trade with great opportunities, this chapter is for you.

Construction jobs are divided into three major categories. General building contractors are responsible for the construction of residential, industrial, commercial, and other buildings. Heavy construction contractors are responsible for building sewers, roads, highways, bridges, and tunnels. Special trade contractors are specialized and include carpentry, painting, plumbing, and electrical work.

The individual worker within each category is classified as structural, finishing, mechanical, or hazardous material removal worker. Carpenters, construction equipment operators, masons, concrete finishers, and iron and metal workers fall into the structural category. Finishing workers include carpenters, drywall installers, tapers, plasterers and stucco masons, painters and paperhangers, glaziers, roofers, carpet, floor and tile installers, and finishers. Those classified as mechanical workers include pipe layers, plumbers, pipe fitters, steamfitters, electricians, sheet metal workers, and heating, air-conditioning, and refrigeration mechanics and installers. As the name implies, hazardous materials removal workers remove materials such as asbestos, lead, and radioactive and nuclear materials from buildings and the environment.

Job Outlook and Wages

Paul Abrams of Roto-Rooter Services Company thinks the trades are the place to be. He says shortages in the workforce are already a problem, and five years from now the shortages will be even greater. "At a time when white-collar jobs are vulnerable to outsourcing, the time may be right for people to take a second look at traditional trades like plumbing, which offer good income potential, good benefits, and plenty of available work. The fact is that an experienced plumber can make a great living with a six-figure income if he or she works hard. Here at Roto-Rooter, a first-year drain technician with some plumbing ability can earn $40,000 or more, depending on the locality. The more experience, the more income potential. We have plenty of guys making over $100,000 per year and many more earning between $50,000 and $70,000."

The Bureau of Labor Statistics predicts jobs in the construction industry will grow at an average rate of about 15 percent between 2002 and 2012. Remember, this is an average; growth in your area could range from 4 (Vermont) to 62 percent (Georgia). For more information about specific states, use the resources in the final chapter. Although the job growth is expected to be average, many trades are already experiencing worker shortages. As the population ages and those in the trades begin to retire, there may not be enough workers in some areas to fill all the jobs.

For those interested in working for a small company, opportunities are excellent. More than 8 out of 10 construction businesses employ fewer than 10 people, and 8 out of 10 workers in the construction industry work for one of these small companies. If you are interested in becoming self-employed or owning your own business, a construction job could provide the training necessary to start your own business—the construction industry boasts 1.6 million self-employed workers.

Wages for construction workers vary from specific occupation to specific occupation, but in general, construction work is well paid. Apprentices earn a percentage of the journeyman's wage, ranging from 40 to 60 percent to start, with regular increases as the apprentice gains experience. The average annual salary for all construction workers was $36,650 in 2003 (slightly above the national average), and special trade contractors can expect to make much more. When looking at salary information in this chapter, remember that these are annual averages across the United States. Salary levels in your area might be higher or lower. The wages listed for specific occupations below come from the Department of Labor's May, 2004 report and reflect wages for the previous year.

About 20 percent of all workers are union members or are covered by union contracts. In general, union-sponsored programs provide benefits from the start of an apprenticeship, including health and retirement packages, and pay for the classroom portion of the training. Some non-union programs do not pay for the classroom training portion of the apprenticeship, but many do. Most provide benefits. These benefits have a financial value that should also be considered when evaluating differences in wages. These are questions you will want to ask when exploring apprenticeship opportunities. Wisconsin is the only state in the country that *requires* apprentices be paid for the time they spend in the classroom as well as time spent on the job.

Unfortunately, many construction jobs are dependent on weather, and poor weather can limit work in the winter months in many states. Poor weather can also delay projects and reduce earnings. Construction work is also closely related to the economy. When things are going well, construction work booms and work is plentiful. When the economy slows, so does most of the construction industry. Again, construction activity can vary widely from region to region and from state to state. Each specific job category below shows where the highest concentrations of workers in that trade were working in 2003. The highest paying states are also included.

Apprenticeships

Apprenticeships in construction are administered by local employers, trade associations and/or trade unions, and joint labor-management organizations and are registered with a State Apprenticeship Council (SAC) or local Bureau of Apprenticeship and Training (BAT). Expect to work between three and five years for an apprenticeship in this field. In addition to on-the-job training, at least 144 hours of related classroom instruction is required; many programs require more. Some programs provide college credit for the classroom component of the apprenticeship.

Depending on the apprenticeship, this classroom component may be offered in highly specialized trade centers, local community colleges, online, in merit shop training centers, or at union training sites. Most often the classroom work is presented several nights each week, and you will be attending class after a full workday.

A few programs offer instruction one day a week. You will work on the job four days and attend school the fifth day. Some programs provide all classroom instruction in one big chunk—say full time for two months (usually during bad-weather months when construction work slows). In any case, you need to be committed to the program to succeed, and you need to attend the classes to get the necessary training for the job. The good news is that in many programs, you get this training for free, and in some programs you get college credit as well. Most people think this is a pretty good deal. You get paid while you learn on the job, you get free classroom training, and you don't have college loans to pay back at the end of the apprenticeship.

Some apprenticeship programs now use competency standards instead of time requirements, so for those with experience, programs may be completed in a shorter time. For example, in some apprenticeship programs, graduates of trade and vocational schools, or those with a military background in the field, may advance more quickly than those coming out of traditional high schools. Those with a broader background in mathematics, mechanical drawing, and woodworking, as well as trade school graduates, may also have a head start.

Those hoping to qualify for apprenticeships should pay attention to their high school course work. Communication skills are valuable in all jobs and good reading and speaking skills are always a plus. In addition to basic science courses in high school, physics courses can provide excellent preparation for some construction jobs. Vocational programs can help you get some of the hands-on experience that employers in the construction industry find desirable. Drafting and art classes can also be beneficial. You can find specific high school courses that can help with specific trades in the sections that follow.

Qualifications

Apprenticeship qualifications vary from trade to trade, from state to state, and from specific program to specific program. Some programs take applications year-round and some take applications only during specific times of the year. In order to find an apprenticeship that is right for you, you must be proactive. Apprenticeships are highly competitive and in most cases there is very little advertising for applicants. If you want this work, you will need to go out and find it. You will need to contact your local apprenticeship organization (lists by state are in Appendixes A and B), your local trade union, or contractors in your area. If you have a friends or family member in the trade, they can be excellent sources of information. Talk, talk, talk to people who work in the construction trades. Pick their brains. Ask them about their jobs. What do they like best about it? What don't they like? If they had to do it again, would they enter the same trade? Ask them what you need to do to prepare for the trade.

Most trade apprenticeship programs require a high school diploma or a GED. Entry age for most is 18, although a few take workers as young as 16. Many programs require aptitude tests and most require drug tests. Many require a driver's license. They will also want letters of recommendation when you apply. You will have a personal interview as well. You will be evaluated based on your experience, your test results, and your interview. In some cases, additional credit is given to those who take part in pre-apprenticeship programs. Those who perform the best get the apprenticeships.

Resources

For additional information on jobs in the construction industry, contact:

Associated Builders and Contractors (ABC)
Workforce Development Department
4250 N. Fairfax Dr.
Arlington, VA 22203
E-mail: gotquestions@abc.org or CraftTraining@abc.org
Internet: http://www.abc.org

Associated General Contractors of America
333 John Carlyle St., Suite 200
Alexandria, VA 22314
Phone: (703) 548-3118
Internet: http://www.agc.org

National Association of Home Builders
1201 15th St., NW
Washington, DC 20005
Phone: (800) 368-5242
Internet: http://www.nahb.org

Home Builders Institute
1201 15th St. NW, 6th Floor
Washington, DC 20005-2800
Phone: (800) 795-7955
Internet: http://www.hbi.org

AFL-CIO Building and Construction Trades
815 16th Street NW, Suite 600
Washington, D.C. 20006
Phone: (202) 377-1461
Internet: http://www.buildingtrades.org

More information about specific trades in construction follows.

Boilermakers

Boilermakers and boilermaker mechanics make, install, and repair the large vessels—boilers—that supply the steam to drive huge turbines in electric power plants and provide heat and power in buildings, factories, and ships. Some boilers are also used to store and heat chemicals or other liquids, including oil and beer.

There are more than 20,000 jobs in this trade, and 7 out of 10 boilermakers work in the construction industry. The remainder work in manufacturing or for boiler repair firms or railroads. The Department of Labor classifies several specialties in this trade (see below). However, the International Brotherhood of Boilermakers, the union that sponsors most apprenticeships in this trade, has one classification for all boilermaker apprentices.

Occupational Specialties and Job Descriptions

Boilermaker I	O*NET/SOC	47-2011.00
	DOT	805.261-014
	RAIS Apprenticeship	0040

A boilermaker I *assembles*, *analyzes* defects in, and *repairs* boilers, pressure vessels, tanks, and vats in the field, following blueprints and using hand tools and portable power tools and equipment.

Boilermaker II	O*NET/SOC	47-2011.00
	DOT	805.381-010
	RAIS Apprenticeship	0041

Boilermaker II construction workers *assemble* boilers, tanks, vats, and pressure vessels according to blueprint specifications using both power tools and hand tools.

Boilerhouse Mechanic	O*NET/SOC	47-2011.00
	DOT	805.361-010
	RAIS	0038

Boilerhouse mechanics *maintain* and *repair* steam boilers.

The tasks of boilermakers may include all or some of the following:

- Lay out plate, sheet steel, or other heavy metal
- Mark bending and cutting lines
- Attach rigging or signal the crane operator to lift parts into position
- Align structures or plate sections to assemble boiler frame tanks, or vats
- Hammer, cut, or grind edges of sections to help fit the edges together
- Bolt or weld sections together
- Weld parts to provide leakproof joints
- Install connections
- Assist in testing assembled boilers
- Clean (or direct the cleaning of) boilers and auxiliary equipment

⑨ **Inspect and repair boiler fittings, including safety valves, regulators, automatic control mechanisms, water columns, and auxiliary machines**

Job Outlook and Wages

Boilermaking is a physically demanding job, and many workers retire early. Although there is little growth expected in this trade, many openings will be created to replace those workers who leave. Relatively small numbers of people seek entry into this job, so right now there are shortages of applicants for apprenticeship programs.

In 2003, the highest-paid boilermakers earned up to $30 an hour. The average annual salary for boilermakers was $43,510, with the top workers averaging more than $60,000 a year. Although boilermakers sometimes work in industry, those working in construction were the highest paid. In 2003, the top-paying states for this occupation were Michigan, New Jersey, Minnesota, Washington, and Hawaii. Texas led the way in the highest concentration of workers in any state followed by Tennessee, Louisiana, Mississippi, and Montana.

Apprenticeships

Boilermaker apprenticeships run between three and four years and require a minimum of 144 hours of training each year. Most construction boilermakers belong to the International Brotherhood of Boilermakers. In addition to classroom training, union boilermakers must complete a self-study program provided by the union. Some locals have their own training centers for many of the classroom sessions. In other areas, classroom training is provided by a state or regional institution. Many locals send their apprentices to the International Brotherhood of Boilermakers' National Training School in Kansas City, Kansas. Boilermaker apprentices spend the majority of the year learning on the job and then spend up to three weeks at a time covering classroom requirements. Among the classroom training courses offered by the Boilermakers National Joint Apprenticeship Program are safety programs, drug and alcohol awareness, tools training, multi-level classes in rigging, welding, burning (both theory and hands on), drafting, blueprint reading, boiler/scrubber technology, layout, drafting, field construction mathematics, and fiberglass shop. Applicants with welding experience are given preference.

Related Skills

Technology education in blueprint reading, drafting, and welding will help you prepare for the job. Manual dexterity and strength are very important on this job. In addition, boilermakers often have to work at extreme heights (up to 1,000 feet above ground) and/or inside enclosed areas in all kinds of weather, including extreme heat and extreme cold. People interested in this job should feel comfortable in those environments. In addition, boilermakers often have to travel distances from job to job as projects are completed.

Resources

For more information about apprenticeships in your area, contact your local apprenticeship organization. For more information about boilermakers, contact:

International Brotherhood of Boilermakers, Iron Ship
    Builders, Blacksmiths, Forgers and Helpers
753 State Avenue, Suite 570
Kansas City KS 66102
Phone: (913) 371-2640
Internet: http://www.boilermakers.org

For more information about apprenticeships, visit Boilermakers National Joint Apprenticeship Program, http://www.bnap.com. Click on the map to find contact information for your area.

Masonry Trades

Like the wisest of the three little pigs, brickmasons and blockmasons (often called bricklayers) and stonemasons use durable materials to build and repair walls, partitions, arches, sewers, fireplaces, chimneys, walkways, and other structures. Some specialized workers install firebrick linings in industrial furnaces, while most bricklayers and stonemasons work in the construction industry.

Occupational Specialties and Job Descriptions

Bricklayer, construction	*O*NET/SOC*	*47-2021*
	DOT	863.131-018
	RAIS	0052

When we think of bricklayers, we often visualize workers repairing chimneys or installing walkways of brick. Actually bricklayers use a variety of materials, including brick, structural tile, concrete cinder blocks, glass, gypsum, and terra-cotta blocks. They may work on small projects like a chimney or a walkway, but they also work on the structural wall panels used in high-rise buildings. No matter what the project, their work includes binding together the building materials to create a strong and attractive product. The workers use plumb bobs and levels to determine the vertical and horizontal alignment of the building materials. They use mortar (a mix of cement, sand, and water) to bind the materials together, placing the mortar on the building material using a trowel.

When building structures, they may begin with the complex corner, building a pyramidlike structure, called a corner lead. This requires a great deal of time and precision and a highly skilled mason. Once the corner leads are constructed, less experienced bricklayers can fill in the walls between the corners.

More often, bricklayers use a less time-consuming method—corner poles. They position the poles and then stretch a line between them that acts as a guide for each row, or course, of brick or other material. They then spread the mortar, place the brick, and tap it into place. Of course, the material must be cut to fit around windows and doors, and bricklayers may use a chisel or a saw for this part of the project. Once the building material is in place, the mortar joints are finished, leaving a sealed, uniform, and attractive appearance.

Many bricklayers work on repair and reconstruction jobs as well, replacing damaged materials and mortar. They may reinforce damaged walls or repair cracks that form as buildings settle.

Stonemason	O*NET/SOC	47-2022
	DOT	861.381-038
	RAIS	0540

Stonemasons and brickmasons do similar work, but stonemasons use natural and artificial stones including marble, granite, limestone, cast concrete, and other masonry materials. The worker sets the stone to build structures including piers, walls, and abutments or may lay walks or curbstones. Before the project begins, the stonemason must shape the material using a chisel, hammer, or other tool. Although the stonemason may use the same binding material and a trowel in the work and sometimes places the materials by hand, this craftsman may need heavy equipment like a crane or forklift to move the building material in place. In some projects, the stones may be numbered before installation to ensure proper placement. Once the building material is set, the stonemason uses muriatic acid and a brush to clean the finished surface.

The work of stonemasons can be seen on homes, churches, hotels, and commercial buildings.

Cement Mason and	O*NET/SOC	47-2051.00
Concrete Finishers	DOT	844.364-010
	RAIS	0075

Cement masons and concrete finishers work with concrete to create floors, walks, sidewalks, roads, stairways, or curbs. They work on highway projects, bridges, shopping malls, schools, hospitals, and other large buildings.

To begin a project, they must first build the forms to hold the concrete and then direct the laborers who pour the material and spread it. Masons then spread and level the mix to ensure a level surface. Once leveled, they must smooth the surface using what they call a bull float to level the ridges, fill any voids, and bring a mixture of fine cement paste to the surface.

DO YOU KNOW THE DIFFERENCE BETWEEN CONCRETE AND CEMENT?

According to the Portland Cement Association, the terms are often used interchangeably, but cement is actually one of the ingredients in concrete. Concrete is a mix of aggregates (sand, gravel, or crushed stone) and paste (water and portland cement).

Portland cement is not a brand name, but the generic name used for the type of cement used in concrete.

Cement comprises from 10 to 15 percent of the concrete mix. Through a process called hydration, the cement and water harden and bind the aggregates into a rocklike mass, and the material continues to harden over time.

For more information about cement and concrete, visit the Portland Cement Association's website, http://cement.org. You can also take a virtual tour of the cement-making process at http://www.cement.org/basics/images/flashtour.html.

A masonry apprentice practices her skills. Photo provided by the International Masonry Institute.

To finish the concrete, workers use an edger between the forms and the concrete, creating slightly rounded edges. Then, the finishers create grooves in the material to help prevent cracking. They retrowel the surface to create a smooth finish. To create nonskid surfaces, they brush the concrete with a broom or add small gravel chips to the surface. If the surface is to remain exposed, they further smooth the material by cutting away high spots and loose concrete. They fill any gaps with portland cement paste (see sidebar), and further smooth the surface with a carborundum stone. For the final step, the worker coats the exposed area with a rich cement mixture and then rubs it to a smooth finish.

Terrazzo Workers	*O*NET/SOC*	*47-2053*
and Finishers	*DOT*	*861.664-014 (finisher)*
	RAIS	*0972*

DOT   861.381-046 *(worker)*
RAIS   0548

A small, but important, part of the trowel trades is the work of terrazzo workers. These craft specialists apply a mix of cement, sand, pigment, or marble chips to floors, stairways, and cabinet fixtures to fashion durable and decorative surfaces. This is a layering process. After building a three to four-inch foundation for concrete, a one-inch layer of sandy concrete is added. Before the material hardens, workers embed metal divider strips into the concrete, setting apart areas where the color will change or where a joint will be placed. Patterns can be pictorial or geometric. For the final step, they place a fine marble-chip mixture into each of the panels. While the mix is still wet, terrazzo workers toss additional color chips into the mix and then smooth it with a lightweight roller. Finishers then grind and polish the surface and fill any depressions with grout, creating a smooth finish. They clean, polish, and seal the surface.

Job Outlook and Wages

In 2003, there were more than 310,000 workers in these masonry trades. The majority were in the bricklaying and cement mason field. They work primarily for building, trade, and special contractors and most work in major metropolitan areas. If you think you might like to own your own business someday, this may be a desirable field for you. One in four workers in this trade owns his or her own business.

The outlook for masons is expected to be excellent. The Bureau of Labor expects general employment in this trade to grow about as fast at average through 2012, and employment of cement masons and concrete finishers is expected to grow even faster—up 25 percent! Terrazzo workers represent a small population in this trade, with only about 6,140 specifically trained workers nationally. During periods of building activity, these workers are highly sought after. Job growth is expected to be about average—15 percent.

Many openings in the masonry trades will become available as workers retire or move to other occupations. In addition to an expected growth in building, more and more older masonry buildings will need repair and the attention of experienced masons.

In 2003, the average salary for bricklayers was $42,350; stonemasons earned an average of $36,111; cement masons averaged $33,760; and terrazzo workers averaged $30,460. The most experienced and best-paid workers in this trade averaged over $60,000 a year. In 2003, the highest paying states for stonemasons were New York, Hawaii, Vermont, Nevada, and California. The highest concentrations of workers were found in Arizona, Colorado, Mississippi, Vermont, and Rhode Island.

Cement masons earned the highest salaries in Alaska, Hawaii, Illinois, New Jersey, and Massachusetts, and the highest concentration of workers were found in Arizona, Utah, Nevada, South Dakota, and Montana.

Terrazzo workers received the best wages in Missouri, New York, Indiana, Massachusetts, and Illinois. By far the highest concentration of workers is in California, followed by Illinois, Alabama, Wisconsin, and Pennsylvania.

Apprenticeships

Many masons pick up their skills informally on the job, but contractors agree that the most thorough training comes through registered apprenticeships. Apprenticeships in this trade are usually sponsored by local contractors, trade associations, or local union-management committees. Most apprenticeships require two to four years of on-the-job training and up to 160 hours of classroom skills training each year. Depending on the program and specialty, the course work might be completed in intensive programs lasting several weeks or may be completed in weekend classes or night programs. Course work may include programs such as safety courses, bricklaying technique, multilevel methods classes, trade arithmetic, blueprint reading, construction materials, estimating for bricklayers, building codes, economic relations, and physical and chemical properties of cement.

Masonry apprentices and architectural interns show off their joint project at IMI's annual Masonry Camp. Photo provided by the International Masonry Institute.

MASONRY CAMP BREAKS DOWN BARRIERS BETWEEN DESIGN SPECIALISTS AND MASONRY CRAFTS WORKERS

Although working as an apprentice in the masonry trade is hard work, both on the job and in the classroom, each June, union apprentices have the opportunity to spend a week at summer camp in Swan Island, Maine. This is not a camp of pine trees, canoe rides, and camp songs, but Masonry Camp, sponsored by the International Masonry Institute (IMI). Here, apprentice bricklayers, plasterers, stonemasons, terrazzo workers, and tile setters are brought together with architecture students and interns to learn about the trowel trades through hands-on instruction. Together they design and build a special project, breaking down the barriers between design and function.

IMI is a joint labor-management cooperative trust of the International Union of Bricklayers and Allied Craftworkers and contractors that focuses on quality craft training programs in all the masonry trades.

Related Skills

If you want to join the masonry trade, it is best if you feel comfortable in high places. Although some masonry work, like brick walkways, is firmly planted on the ground, much of this work takes place on scaffolding well above the ground. You will need good eyesight and good manual dexterity, coordination, and balance. It is extremely helpful to have good information ordering skills—being able to arrange tasks in an appropriate sequence—and good visualization skills. You should also be willing to work outdoors, exposed to poor weather conditions.

High school courses that can help prepare you for a job in the masonry trade include blueprint reading, drafting, industrial arts courses, math (including algebra and business math), and mechanical drawing.

Resources

You can get information about masonry trades apprenticeships at your local apprenticeship organization, local craft union, or at the following organizations:

Associated General Contractors of America
333 John Carlyle St., Suite 200
Alexandria, VA 22314
Phone: (703) 548-3118
Internet: http://www.agc.org

Brick Industry Association
11490 Commerce Park Dr.
Reston, VA 22091-1525
Phone: (703) 620-0010
Internet: http://www.brickinfo.org

Home Builders Institute
1201 15th St. NW, 6th Floor
Washington, DC 20005
Phone: (800) 795-7955
Internet: http://www.hbi.org

International Union of Bricklayers and Allied Craftworkers
1776 Eye St. NW
Washington, DC 20006-3700
Phone: (202) 783-3788
Internet: http://www.bacweb.org

Associated Builders and Contractors (ABC)
Workforce Development Department
4250 N. Fairfax Dr., 9th Floor
Arlington, VA 22203-1607
Phone: (703) 812-2000
E-mail: gotquestions@abc.org or CraftTraining@abc.org
Internet: http://www.abc.org

National Terrazzo and Mosaic Association
201 North Maple Ave., Suite 208
Purcellville, VA 20132
Phone: (800) 323-9736
E-mail: info@ntma.com
Internet: http://www.ntma.com

International Masonry Institute
Apprenticeship and Training
The James Brice House
42 East St.
Annapolis, MD 21401
Internet: http://www.imiweb.org

National Concrete Masons Association
13750 Sunrise Valley Dr.
Herndon, VA 20171-3499
Phone: (703) 713-1900
Internet: http://www.ncma.org

The Operative Plasterers' and Cement Masons' International
    Association of the United States and Canada
Director of Training, Safety and Health
14405 Laurel Place, Suite 300
Laurel, MD 20707
Phone: (301) 470-4200
Internet: http://www.opcmia.org/

Construction Carpenters

Carpenters are trades workers who traditionally work with
wood. Today, however, they may also work with metal, plastics,
fiberglass, styrofoam, and composites of several different
materials to construct and repair not only buildings, but bridges,
tunnels, and highways as well. They build homes and they build
skyscrapers. Some do the work we are all familiar with, but
others work in specialized areas of the trade including interior
systems installers, floor layers, and pile drivers. Some also
specialize in work in the manufacturing industry. Carpenters do
studding, framing, and joist work. They build the rafters
necessary to construct all types of buildings and install the siding
on the exteriors as well. In addition to working on the general
framing of a building, they work on the inside as well, installing
cabinetry, hardwood floors, drywall, and the wooden strips
called laths that are necessary for plaster walls. Some specialize
in brattice work, the support systems for underground

The First Labor Day Parade—Union Square, New York City.
Library of Congress—LC-USZ 62-83164

DID YOU KNOW?
A CARPENTER HELPED ESTABLISH LABOR DAY

For more than 100 years we have been celebrating Labor Day in the United States. The origins of this special day go back as far as the late 1800s when Peter J. McGuire, a New York City carpenter and founder of the United Brotherhood of Carpenters and Joiners, and Matthew Maguire, a machinist from New Jersey, suggested we celebrate the role of labor in America. The first Labor Day parade was held in New York City on Tuesday, September 5, 1882. In June of 1894, Labor Day became a national holiday, which is still celebrated on the first Monday in September.

passageways that control the proper circulation of air in the work place. Carpentry is the largest of the building trades with 1.2 million people working in the trade today. There are many apprenticeship opportunities within the carpentry trade.

Occupational Specialties and Job Descriptions

Residential Carpenters	O*NET/SOC	47-2031.01
	DOT	860.381-022
	RAIS	0067

As the title implies, residential carpenters are the primary craft workers on homes, apartments, and condominiums. They not only create the framework of these homes, they build the partitions that divide the rooms, and they may also install the floors and cabinetry. They are knowledgeable about every phase of home building.

Interior Systems	*O*NET/SOC*	*47-2031.01*
	DOT	*869.381-583*
	RAIS	*0653*

Interior systems carpenters cut, fit, and assemble materials for the insides of buildings. They are not involved in the exterior framing or finishing, but they may do some of the same tasks as a general carpenter. According to the New York City District Council of Carpenters, this is a specialized and expanding field of work. Workers in this trade install prefabricated materials and equipment in residential and commercial buildings. Among the tasks performed by interior systems carpenters are the installation of

- **Acoustical ceilings**
- **Raised floors for computers**
- **Office furniture systems**
- **Wall partitions**
- **Forms for concrete flooring**
- **Doors and windows**
- **Flooring**
- **Drywall**
- **Floor tiles**

These specialists may work from blueprints or instructions from supervisors. They must be able to work with a variety of hand and power tools including saws, planes, sanders, hammers, chisels, drills, and drivers. Attention to detail is essential because workers measure, mark, and arrange materials for installation. A few inches off here or there and the installation will not work. Good reading skills are also essential as much of the material to be installed comes with written instructions and specifications.

Maintenance Carpenters	O*NET/SOC	47-2031-01
	DOT	860.281-010
	RAIS	0068

Maintenance carpenters need to be skilled in a variety of areas to help keep residential and commercial buildings in good repair, and they need to know how to use the specific tools required for each repair. They may perform both rough and finish carpentry projects including the following:

- Build and repair cabinetry and other wooden articles (bookcases, shelving, partitions, moldings, trim work, etc.)
- Frame new construction
- Remodel small structures
- Remodel building interiors
- Build forms for concrete foundations, catch basins, etc.
- Install, repair, and adjust door closures, locks, and hardware
- Hang windows and doors
- Replace floor and ceiling materials
- Repair furniture
- Paint and stain building surfaces
- Apply wall and floor covering materials
- Install tile work
- Make routine electrical and mechanical repairs of building equipment

Lathers	O*NET/SOC	47-2031.01
	DOT	842.361-010
	RAIS	0272

Drywall Applicators	O*NET/SOC	47-2081.02
	DOT	842.684-014
	RAIS	0145

Lathers install lath, a thin strip of wood or metal, on walls and ceilings. This material provides the support system for plaster, stucco, fireproofing, or acoustical materials that are applied later.

As part of their jobs, lathers

- Erect a light metal framework (furring) to which laths are fastened
- Drill holes in the floor and ceiling and drive the ends of the wood or metal studs into the halls, providing an anchor for furring or rockboard lath
- Wire horizontal strips to the furring to stiffen the framework
- Cut lath to fit openings and projections
- Wire, nail, clip, or staple lath to framework, ceiling joists, and flat concrete supports
- Bend metal lath to fit corners
- Wire plasterers' channels to the overhead framework that provides support for a plaster or acoustical ceiling tile.

Drywall applicators work as either installers or finishers. Installers measure, cut, fit, and fasten drywall panels to the inside framework of buildings. They also install the metal or vinyl beaded edge around the corners. Drywall finishers:

- Use hand and power tools, such as sanding poles, hand scrapers, stilts, mixers, spray guns
- Erect, move, and dismantle scaffolding
- Prepare panels for painting by taping and finishing joints and other imperfections
- Spread and smooth cementing material over tape, using a trowel or floating machine to blend joint with wall surface
- Sand rough spots after cement has dried
- Fill cracks and holes in walls and ceiling with sealing compound

Rough Carpenters	*O*NET/SOC*	*47-2031.02*
	DOT	*860.381-042*
	RAIS	*0069*

Rough carpenters build the frames of homes, commercial buildings, and other structures, including bridges and highways. They also build concrete forms, scaffolds, and support systems. They may install subflooring and construct the plywood surround that hides many building projects from view. Rough carpenters:

- Use bolts, nails, or screws to construct the framework of a structure
- Use power drills to bore holes into wood, masonry, or concrete walls
- Cut boards, timbers, or plywood to the required size
- Erect forms, frameworks, scaffolds, hoists, roof supports, or chutes
- Install rough door and window frames, subflooring, and temporary supports
- Build chutes for pouring concrete (a mold carpenter specializes in this job as well)

Pile Driver Carpenters	O*NET/SOC	47-2031.02
	DOT	860.381-581
	RAIS	1009

Pile drivers are often the first workers on site when a construction project begins. They cut, fit, assemble, and drive heavy timber, steel, concrete, and other materials used to construct bridges, highways, roadways, subways, ports and docks, dams and power plants, deep foundation commercial or industrial structures, and other ground or underwater projects. They use large machines, mounted on skids, barges, or cranes, that hammer piles (long, heavy beams of wood or steel) into the ground. As part of their jobs they:

- Drive metal sheet piling to hold back dirt during excavation
- Drive the wood, concrete, and/or metal piling portions of a foundation system
- Drive wood and concrete pilings to hold up docks, wharfs, and bridges
- May work on offshore oil rigs
- May work in underwater construction
- Install heavy timbers and may weld or cut large metal beams

Pile drivers use heavy equipment to drive heavy timber, metal, or concrete to support structures. Photo by Penny Hutchins Paquette.

Training for pile drivers includes specialized carpentry skills as they work with very large and heavy materials. They build and drive pilings into soil or rock. Because pile driving is so specialized, apprentices will need to take specialized course work such as classes in welding, specialized tools, land and water pile driving, wharf and marine structures, heavy timber framing, formwork, and shoring for pile drivers.

Most pile drivers learn their trade through formal apprenticeship programs or other on-the-job training programs.

Job Outlook and Wages

The outlook for carpentry jobs is excellent. The most recent Bureau of Labor Statistics data indicate that there will be increases in construction activity through 2012. A demand for new housing coupled with an increase in demand for commercial and industrial plants will keep carpenters busy. Baby boomers are just reaching their peak earning years and can now afford to spend more on housing. Growing numbers will be purchasing larger homes (some new construction) or renovating existing homes. At the same time, children of the baby boomers (what the Bureau of Labor Statistics calls the *echo boomers*) are now looking for starter homes, condominiums, or apartments. This will make for an increase in the development of smaller homes and manufactured housing.

Although there may be some reductions in carpenters in the construction area because of an increased use of prefabricated materials, the overall outlook is strong.

In 2003, the average annual salary for carpenters was $34,250, with the highest paid averaging more than $58,000 a year. Carpenters working in specialized areas made more. For example, those working on nonresidential projects earned $40,660. The top-paying states for carpenters were Hawaii, where the average annual income was close to $50,000 a year, followed by Alaska, New Jersey, Illinois, and Massachusetts. Arizona has the highest concentration of workers in the field, followed by Nevada, Montana, Alaska, and Vermont.

Apprenticeships

Apprenticeships for carpenters are often sponsored by joint training committees made up of local unions such as the United Brotherhood of Carpenters and Joiners or local trade groups such as the Associated General Contractors of America or the National Association of Home Builders and management. Carpentry apprenticeship is generally a four-year, 8,000-hour on-the-job training program with a minimum of 144 hours of related technical training each year. Many trade organizations, both union and non-union, require more related training.

Related Skills

You can prepare for an apprenticeship by taking related courses in high school. General math, algebra, and business math can help with the measurement calculations often needed on the job. In addition to the basic academic programs you will need for graduation, technical courses such as woodworking, cabinetmaking, blueprint reading, and drafting provide skills that are directly transferred to the job. Because many carpenters eventually run their own businesses, business courses and accounting courses can be a plus.

Those interested in carpentry apprenticeships should have good math skills and good mechanical skills. Strength is required for much of this type of work and physical coordination, manual dexterity, and flexibility is essential. Carpenters need to have steady hands and good eyesight, especially in their near vision. Carpenters need good visualization skills—the ability to picture a finished project before construction begins. Since carpenters work as part of a construction team, communication skills are very important in this job.

Resources

For more information about carpentry apprenticeships, contact your local apprenticeship organization and:

Associated Builders and Contractors (ABC)
4250 N. Fairfax Dr., 9th Floor
Arlington, VA 22203-1607
Phone: (703) 812-2000
E-mail: gotquestions@abc.org or CraftTraining@abc.org
Internet: http://www.abc.org

Associated General Contractors of America
333 John Carlyle St., Suite 200
Alexandria, VA 22314
Phone: (703) 548-3118
Internet: http://www.agc.org

National Association of Home Builders
1201 15th St., NW
Washington, DC 20005
Phone: (800) 368-5242
Internet: http://www.nahb.org

United Brotherhood of Carpenters and Joiners of America
50 F St., NW
Washington, DC 20001
Internet: http://www.carpenters.org
Click on the "Local Contacts" tab for local information

International Union of Painters and Allied Trades
(for drywall apprenticeships)
The Joint Apprenticeship Training Fund
1750 New York Ave., NW
Washington, DC 20006
Phone: (800) 276-7289
Internet: http://www.jatf.org

Construction Craft Laborers (CCL)

Occupational Specialties

CCLs are responsible for much of the physically demanding work at construction projects, tunnel and shaft excavations, hazardous waste remediation jobs, and demolition sites. Today's construction laborers may do a variety of jobs, or they may specialize in commercial construction, highway construction, underground utilities, or environmental construction. Each of these fields requires specialized training.

Construction	*O*NET/SOC*	*47-2061*
Craft Laborers	*DOT*	*869.463-580*
	RIAS	*0061*

Construction craft laborers have long been the strong backs of the construction industry. Most of us think of them as relatively unskilled laborers digging a trench or unloading a truck. Today, however, construction craft workers are responsible for a wide variety of jobs, many of which require very specialized training. Construction workers today use complex equipment and machinery to get the job done and work best when they are trained to use, manage, and understand their new tools. New technologies in this field allow the remote camera inspection of pipelines and repairs that don't require digging. According to the Department of Labor, formal apprenticeships provide a thorough preparation for these jobs.

In 1994, the Bureau of Apprenticeship Training recognized the multilevel training that construction craft laborers need to be proficient in their jobs and first recognized construction craft laborer as an apprenticeable trade. The Department of Labor distinguishes this job from the helpers or assistants who work with skilled workers in the trades.

Highway Construction   *Codes the same as CCL, above*

Those who specialize in highway construction are responsible for clearing and preparing the highway work zones. Workers may need to know how to operate a wide range of equipment including pavement breakers, jackhammers, earth tampers, concrete mixers, boring machines, torches, mechanical hoists, laser beam equipment, and surveying and measuring equipment. They break up the old road surface and haul away the old materials and then help level and grade the surface for the new road. These workers then assist in the final stages of completing the new road. They are the ones who place those barricades, cones, and markers we see on the highways, and they are the ones who help control the traffic in the construction area. These workers may also install sewer, water, and storm drain pipes.

Hazardous Waste	*O*NET/SOC*	*47-0499.99*
Materials Technician	*DOT*	*168.364-640*
	RAIS	*0591*

Concern for the environment has created a specialty that addresses health and welfare of our communities. These workers receive special training and licenses in environmental cleanup qualifying them to remove lead paint and asbestos, clean up hazardous waste sites, handle mold contamination, and decommission nuclear power plants. Before any work can take place, these laborers need to learn and fully understand the federal and local laws involving hazardous materials. At hazardous waste sites, hazardous materials removal workers prepare the site and then safely pack, and remove the lead, asbestos, mold, radioactive waste, underground storage tanks, or other hazardous material. As they do their job, they need to operate and maintain the air monitoring and other sampling devices used on the site. These specialists need the skills to identify, handle, pack, and transport the hazardous waste, and then they need to decontaminate the equipment and buildings on the site. Once the cleanup is complete, they are responsible for restoring the site, including landscaping if necessary.

Workers on hazardous waste sites wear protective clothing and devices to help protect their respiratory systems and eyes. Obviously, workers in this field need special training and require special licenses or certifications.

| *Underground utilities* | *Codes the same as CCL, above* |
| *construction laborers* | |

This job is a blast, literally. In addition to other tasks, workers in this specialty help with the explosives that blast tunnels for underground utilities. Underground workers may install water, gas, sewer, storm drainage networks, or telecommunications cables, and may be responsible for other tunneling projects. They may take care of a wide variety of tasks from excavating dirt to operating the laser guidance equipment to place pipes. They operate air, electric, and pneumatic drills, and may use mining equipment including drills, rock bolts, timbers, hoists, and cages. They need special safety training including air quality monitoring, ventilation systems, underground electrical safety, and explosives.

Job Outlook and Wages

Because this work is strenuous and can be hazardous, many workers are reluctant to enter the field and many choose to leave. If you consider this kind of work a challenge, this is good news. A continuing emphasis on environmental remediation will create specialty jobs in that area. In general, job growth will continue at an average rate, but growing concern for the environment will mean a much faster-than-average growth in jobs for those who specialize in hazardous materials removal. Job growth for construction laborers in general is expected to be about 14 percent through 2012; for hazardous materials workers, the increase is expected to be a whopping 43 percent. For those who are willing to relocate as jobs open, opportunities are especially good.

Salary ranges in this field have been among the most extreme. In 2003, the lowest-paid workers in these jobs earned in the $15,000 range, with the national average for workers at $28,380. Those who specialized in hazardous materials removal averaged more, $32,710. At the high end of the salary range, workers in Leominster, Massachusetts, averaged more than $50,000.

The top-paying states for this trade in 2003 were Alaska, Massachusetts, New Jersey, New York, and Illinois. Texas was far ahead in the highest concentration of workers, followed at some distance by Nevada, New Mexico, Wyoming, and Alaska.

Apprenticeships

Construction craft laborer apprenticeships are under the guidelines established by the Laborer's International Union/

Associated General Contractors of American Education and Training Fund. Apprentices spend 4,000 hours of supervised on-the-job training over a two-to-three year period and up to 440 hours of related skills training during the apprenticeship. Basic course work includes blueprint reading, use of tools and equipment, and safety and health procedures. Course work is then geared to the trade specialty—building construction, highway construction, or environmental remediation. Depending on the specialty, course work might include flagging and traffic control, hazardous waste operations and emergency response (Hazwoper) training, specialty equipment training, pipe fusion, pipe laying, scaffold erecting, torch cutting, welding, drilling and blasting, tunnel mining, mold remediation, asbestos and lead paint abatement, and trenchless technology.

Apprentices usually start at 60 to 75 percent of the journeyman's wage and salaries increase with experience.

Related Skills

High school courses in blueprint reading, mathematics, computer skills, science, physics, and chemistry can help you prepare for a CCL job. Good reading skills are essential as workers need to comprehend warning signs and labels and understand plans, specifications, and other written instructions. Strength, manual dexterity, and strength are all important in the CCL trade.

Those who choose to specialize in hazardous materials jobs will need to pass physical tests that measure the ability to wear protective gear like respirators.

Resources

In addition to contacting your local apprenticeship organization, the following organizations can provide information about the work and training of construction labors, including hazardous waste removal workers:

Laborers' International Union of North America
905 16th St. NW
Washington, DC 20006
Internet: http://www.liuna.org

Laborers-AGC Education and Training Fund
37 Deerfield Road
P.O. Box 37
Pomfred Center, CT 06259
Internet: http://www.laborerslearn.org

National Center for Construction Education and Research
P.O. Box 141101
Gainesville, FL 32614-1104
Internet: http://nccer.org

Construction Equipment Operators

Ever stand in amazement at a construction site as those huge
trucks move about digging, pushing, lifting, or demolishing?
Ever wanted to get behind the wheel and take control of one of
those huge machines? If so, a job as a construction equipment
operator might be for you.

Occupational Specialties and Job Descriptions

Paving, Surfacing, and	*O*NET/SOC*	*47-2071*
Tamping Equipment	*DOT*	*853.683-01*
Operators	*RAIS*	*0872*

Those huge machines that smooth and surface roads,
parking lots, and runways are operated by paving, surfacing,
and tamping equipment operators. These heavy equipment
operators specialize in roadwork and must be sure that the
equipment distributes the paving material, whether asphalt or
concrete, evenly. There were 57,980 workers in this specialty in
2003.

Operating Engineers	*O*NET/SOC*	*47-2073.02*
	DOT	*859.683-010*
	RAIS	*0365*

Operating engineers are qualified to operate a variety of
large construction vehicles, including motor graders,
bulldozers, scrapers, compressors, pumps, derricks, shovels,
tractors, or front-end loaders. They may also be qualified to

A backhoe with a grapple attachment pulls apart decking concrete at Haymarket Square in Boston during the Big Dig project. Photo provided by the Massachusetts Turnpike Authority.

THE BIG DIG

Heavy equipment operators are now working on "the largest, most complex, and technologically challenging project ever attempted in the United States." In 2004, Boston's "Big Dig" project was nearing completion. As part of the massive project, workers replaced a six-lane elevated highway with an eight-to-ten-lane underground expressway and dug a new tunnel beneath South Boston and Boston Harbor. As the underground parts of the project were completed, the crumbling elevated road was demolished.

The project spans 7.8 miles of highway, 161 lane miles in all, and will use 3.8 million cubic tons of concrete, the equivalent of 2,350 acres, one foot thick!

Among the pieces of equipment used on this project are concrete pumping machines, highly specialized cranes, bulldozers, trench cutters, excavators, mining excavators, mining loaders, hydraulic alpine miners, front-end excavators, launching gantries, compressed-air and vacuum excavation machines, and demolition hammers. Operating engineers operate this equipment and keep it running.

If you would like to see operating engineers in action, visit the Big Dig website, http://www.masspike.com/bigdig/index.html.

maintain and repair the equipment. There were 343,640 operating engineers working on construction sites in 2003. The majority of these heavy equipment operators work in the construction industry. Others work in mining and manufacturing as well. Operating engineers:

- ◎ Drive, maneuver, or navigate vehicles or equipment
- ◎ Watch gauges, dials, or other indicators to ensure the equipment is operating properly
- ◎ Determine what is causing an operating problem and what needs to be done to fix it
- ◎ Perform routine maintenance and determine when and what is needed
- ◎ Repair machines or systems

Job Outlook and Wages

Jobs for construction equipment operators are expected to grow about as fast as average between 2002 and 2012—about 11 percent. During that time, the Department of Labor estimates that there will be 144,000 job openings for those who want to get behind the wheels of those big trucks. Growth will be the result of increases in population and business, creating a need for new houses, industrial facilities, schools, hospitals, offices, and other structures. Highway, bridge, and street construction are expected to grow as well.

The average salary for equipment operators in road construction (paving, surfacing, tamping) was $32,980 in 2003. Those at the top end of wages averaged $55,540. The states with the highest concentration of workers included Arkansas, Mississippi, Montana, South Dakota, and Wyoming. Top wages were paid in Illinois, Nevada, New Jersey, California, and New York.

Salaries for operating engineers in 2003 averaged $38,260, with top wage earners averaging over $60,000. The highest concentration of workers was in Kentucky, West Virginia, Wyoming, Alaska, and Montana. Workers earned the highest wages in Illinois, Alaska, California, Massachusetts, and Hawaii.

Apprenticeships

Three-year apprenticeships are offered by joint labor-management committees of the International Union of Operating Engineers and the Associated General Contractors of America. Apprentices in this apprenticeship program have a distinct advantage over other beginning-level workers who learn on the job. This apprenticeship program trains workers to operate a wider variety of machines, providing greater job opportunities after the program is complete.

You can learn to operate those huge machines in a three- to four-year (6,000-hour) apprenticeship program that also requires 144 hours a year of related classroom instruction. Some apprentices get related training doing community projects, such as building a neighborhood baseball diamond. Salary ranges for starting apprentices vary from about 40 to 60 percent of a journey-level worker, with regular increases as the apprentice becomes more experienced.

In addition to classes in union history and safety, apprentices learn the operation of construction equipment and study trade math, grades and planes, multilevel courses in electricity, welding, equipment maintenance and repair, and licensing preparation for a variety of construction vehicles.

Related Skills

Obviously, in order to operate this type of equipment, you must have a driver's license. High school vocational courses in electricity and automobile, diesel, or farm machinery mechanics are helpful. Those who have experience operating farm tractors and harvesters will also be at an advantage. Science courses and mechanical drawing courses provide useful background as well.

Equipment operators need excellent eye-hand-foot coordination to operate all the levers, pedals, switches, and valves that are part of this type of equipment.

Some workers in this field specialize in maintenance and repair. Those workers need good mechanical skills and must be able to lift heavy objects.

If you have problems with noise, with being shaken around, or don't like getting dirty, this is probably not the job area for you.

Resources

For more information about apprenticeships as a construction equipment operator, contact your local operating engineers union (see link below) or your local apprenticeship agency. For further information, contact:

Associated General Contractors of America
333 John Carlyle St., Suite 200
Alexandria, VA 22314
Phone: (703) 548-3118
Internet: http://www.agc.org (click "locate a chapter" on the left side of the page to find an AGC in your area)

International Union of Operating Engineers
1125 17th St., NW
Washington, DC 20036
Phone: (202) 429-9100
Internet: http://www.iuoe.org (Use the "find a local union near you" link)

Electricians

Electricians	O*NET/SOC	47-2111
	DOT	824.261-010
	RAIS	0159

Working at your computer? Talking on the phone? Switching on the light to read? You couldn't do any of that without the help of electricians. Today, more than 400,000 electricians work in the construction industry, helping all of us with out electrical needs.

In the past, electricians specialized in installation or maintenance. Today, most do both. Electricians install, test, and maintain electrical systems. They may install electrical systems in the smallest homes or the largest industrial buildings. They begin by reviewing the blueprints that show where circuits, outlets, and other equipment will be placed. In factories and offices, they must install conduit (pipe or tubing) within the partitions, wall, or other concealed areas. They fasten the metal or plastic boxes that will hold the electrical switches and outlets to the walls. They then pull the wires or cables through the conduit to complete the circuits. On smaller jobs, like residential construction, plastic-covered wire is used instead of conduit.

Once all the wires are placed, electricians connect them to circuit breakers, transformers, or other components. They may twists the ends of wires together and connect them with plastic caps or they may solder metal onto the ends to fuse them. When all is connected, they test to be sure that all circuits are operating properly. All electricians must follow the National Electric Code and all state and local building codes when they install electrical systems.

More and more electricians are now installing low-voltage wiring systems as well. This work provides the voice, data, and video wiring necessary for telephones, computers, intercoms, fire alarms, and security systems. They install coaxial and fiber optic cables for computers and other telecommunications equipment.

Maintenance electricians keep everything in good working order, helping prevent problems. When problems do occur, they are in charge of repairs.

Job Outlook and Wages

The average salary for electricians in 2003 was $44,090, with wages averaging up to $66,000 a year for experienced workers in some areas of the country. Job opportunities for electricians are expected to be good, with jobs growing a little faster than average—up about 23.4 percent through 2012. As the population and the economy grow, there will be work installing and maintaining electrical systems in homes, factories, offices, and other buildings. Although fewer workers leave this occupation for other jobs than workers in other trades, the number of retirements is expected to rise as more electricians reach retirement age. As with most jobs in the construction industry, opportunities can vary widely from area to area. In 2003, New Jersey, New York, Minnesota, Oregon, and Washington were among the top-paying states for electricians. The highest concentrations of workers were in Wyoming, Alaska, Delaware, Louisiana, and Alabama.

Apprenticeships

Most electricians begin learning the trade in apprenticeship programs lasting from three to five years, with residential electricians having the shorter apprenticeships. Local chapters of the International Brotherhood of Electrical Workers and local chapters of the National Electrical Contractors Association form joint training committees that sponsor apprenticeships. Apprenticeships may also be sponsored by local chapters of the Associated Builders and Contractors with the Independent Electrical Contractors Association. Management committees of individual electrical contracting companies may sponsor apprentices as well.

Classroom training for electricians runs between 144 and 200 hours each year. Among the courses offered for electrical apprentices are workplace safety, labor history, tools of the trade, A/C and D/C electrical theory and math, conduit bending, National Electrical Code, blueprint reading, transformers, semiconductor devices and circuits, transformers, fiber optics, fire alarm systems, structured cabling systems, high-voltage testing, and related mathematics and algebra.

Apprentices generally start at between 40 and 50 percent of the rate paid to a fully trained electrician, with regular increases during the apprenticeship.

Related Skills

While still in high school, you can help prepare for an apprenticeship by studying mathematics, including algebra, blueprint reading, electricity, electronics, mechanical drawing, and science.

Because wires are often color coded, electricians must have good color discrimination skills. Good near-vision eyesight is also essential. To work with the wiring and conduit, good manual dexterity is important. Memorization skills are also important because electrical work must follow specific codes.

Resources

For information about apprenticeships in your area, you can contact your local apprenticeship organization. For more information about apprenticeship programs, contact:

Associated Builders and Contractors (ABC)
Workforce Development Department
4250 N. Fairfax Dr., 9th Floor
Arlington, VA 22203-1607
Phone: (703) 812-2000
E-mail: gotquestions@abc.org or CraftTraining@abc.org
Internet: http://www.abc.org

Independent Electrical Contractors
4401 Ford Ave., Suite 1100
Alexandria, VA 22302
E-mail: bbaird@ieci.org
Internet: http://www.ieci.org

International Brotherhood of Electrical Workers
900 7th St., NW
Washington, DC 20001
Internet: http://www.ibew.org
Click on the "Training" section and click on Apprenticeship

National Association of Home Builders
1201 15th St., NW, 6th Floor
Washington, DC 20005
Internet: http://www.hbi.org
Click on the HBI Programs link, then "Craft Skills" for
    apprenticeship information

National Electrical Contractors Association
3 Metro Center, Suite 1100
Bethesda, MD 20814
Internet: http://www.necanet.org

National Joint Apprenticeship Committee
301 Prince George's Blvd.
Upper Marlboro, MD 20774
Internet: http://www.njatc.org
Click on Apprentice Training link

Elevator Constructors and Repairers

Elevator	*O*NET/SOC*	*47-4021.00*
Constructors	*DOT*	*825.361-010 (const.)*
and Repairers		*825.281.030 (repair)*
	RAIS	*0173 (const.)*
		0174 (repair)

We couldn't make our way through a department store, the airport, a high-rise, a hospital, or any other multilevel building without them. Elevator constructors and repairers, also called elevator installers and repairers, assemble, install, and replace elevators, escalators, dumbwaiters, moving walkways, and similar equipment in new and old buildings. They also maintain, repair, and modernize the equipment once it is in place.

These workers are very knowledgeable in electronics, electricity, and hydraulics, all of which are necessary to run the equipment. Many of today's elevators have microprocessors that analyze traffic conditions and dispatch the elevators in response to traffic, so elevator workers must have a working knowledge of computer technology as well.

These workers begin by studying blueprints detailing the project and determine what materials and equipment will be necessary to complete the job. They install the equipment by bolting or welding the steel guide rails to the shaft. They install the electrical wires and controls within conduit secured within the shaft. Then they install the electrical components and other devices on each floor and at the main control panel. They install the safety and control devices, the cables, drives, rails, motors, and elevator cars and then inspect the work to be sure it is all safe and done to specifications. Once the job is complete, specialty workers called adjusters fine-tune all the equipment and make sure everything is operating properly. Repairers maintain the equipment, oiling and greasing moving parts, replacing worn parts, and making necessary adjustments. Service crews handle major repairs like replacing motors, pumps, or control panels or replacing cables, doors, or bearings.

Job Outlook and Wages

Job growth in this area is expected to be about as fast as average—up 17.1 percent through 2012. Growth in nonresidential construction will keep elevator installers working and the need to maintain and upgrade existing equipment will provide work for repairers.

On the downside, this is a small career field, with only 21,470 workers nationwide, and workers in this industry are less likely to change jobs than workers in other fields. Many of these jobs are unionized and require a great deal of training. The commitment to training combined with good wages and benefits keeps most workers from leaving the field.

The average annual salary for elevator installers and repairers was $55,860 in 2003. Most workers worked for building equipment contractors where the average annual salary was $57,080. Hawaii was the top-paying state, with workers averaging $76,670 a year. Massachusetts, California, Connecticut, and Illinois followed with salary ranges between $60,000 and $68,000. The highest concentrations of workers were in New York, Minnesota, Maryland, Louisiana, and Hawaii.

Apprenticeships

Most apprenticeships in this field are sponsored by the International Union of Elevator Constructors and local employers. These programs require 8,000 hours of on-the-job training in all areas from installation to repair. An additional minimum of 144 hours of related training is also required each year. Related training may include elevator history and safety, blueprint reading, rigging and hoisting equipment, guide rail, pit equipment, general maintenance practices, traction and hydraulic elevator maintenance, maintenance of escalators and moving walks, electrical wiring and equipment, hydraulic theory, basic electronics, contracts, test equipment, shaft alignment, and A/C and D/C motors.

There is usually a six-month probationary period for elevator installer and repairer apprentices and the program usually takes about four years to complete. Workers then take standard exams to be certified as certified electrical technicians (CET) or as a certified accessibility and private residence lift technician (CAT). Most states require workers in this field to pass a licensing exam.

Related Skills

Those with a solid background in electronics will have the best opportunities in this field. High school courses in electricity, mechanics, mathematics, and physics will be beneficial. Workers in this field are expected to have "problem sensitivity"—the ability to tell when something is wrong or is likely to go wrong. They also need good manual dexterity and good near vision.

Resources

For information about apprenticeships in your area, contact your local apprenticeship organization. For more information about the union and to locate a local near you:

International Union of Elevator Constructors
7154 Columbia Gateway Dr.
Columbia, MD 21046
Internet: http://www.iuec.org

For more information about the CAT and CET programs, contact:

National Association of Elevator Contractors
1298 Wellbrook Circle, Suite A
Conyers, GA 30012
Internet: http://www.naec.org

Finishing Trades

Finishing trades include all of the jobs required to put the final touches on a construction project—wall finishing, painting, wallpapering, floor covering, glasswork, and signs (for commercial projects). Each of the trades can be learned through apprenticeship programs. For a quick look at a video that provides information about all of the finishing trades, visit the joint labor-management apprenticeship training fund site of the International Union of Painters and Allied Trades (IUPAT), http://www.jatf.org/edu_appren.html.

Occupational Specialties and Job Descriptions

Drywall Finishers (see interior systems carpenters, under carpenters)

Glaziers	*O*NET/SOC*	*47-2121*
	DOT	*865.381-010*
	RAIS	*0221*

Ever wonder how all that glass gets set in one of those gigantic high-rise buildings? Can you imagine installing glass panels on the 100th floor? Glaziers do just that. They select, cut, install, replace, and remove all types of glass, including the glass in skyscrapers. In addition, they also work on residential projects replacing home windows and installing mirrors, shower doors, and bathtub enclosures. They may also cut and fit glass for tabletops and display cases.

Today, glaziers don't just work with glass. They also work with plastics, granite, marble, and other materials that may be used for glass substitutes. In addition to working directly with the glass, they also take care of the steel or aluminum sashes or frames that hold the windows or doors, and may attach hinges and locks as well.

In securing the glass, the material is sometimes precut and mounted into frames at the factory and is ready to be placed in position. Once the glass is in place, it must be secured. Glaziers use mastic, putty, or other types of cement to secure the glass, or they may use metal clips, rubber gaskets, or metal or wood moldings.

For some projects, glaziers must cut the glass on site using special equipment to secure the material before cutting it with a specially designed metal wheel. Once the glass is scored, the

glazier breaks away the smaller pieces, leaving the finished
piece ready for the project.

Glaziers also work on automobiles, replacing windows.

Job Outlook and Wages

Growth in the glazier trade is expected to be about average—
up just over 17 percent between 2002 and 2012, but the Bureau
of Labor Statistics projects that job opportunities will be
excellent. There were only 50,000 glaziers in 2002, and as
residential and nonresidential projects grow, so will the demand
for well-trained glass experts. Energy-efficient glass products
will be in demand as many homeowners and businesses opt for
high-efficiency products. In addition, the requirement for higher
levels of security will create an increased demand for safety
glass products in government and commercial buildings. New
positions will open as retiring workers leave the trade.

Because most glazing contractors are located in large
metropolitan areas, that is where many glaziers are employed.
The top-paying metropolitan areas for glaziers were Chicago,
Illinois; Newark, New Jersey; Trenton, New Jersey; Lowell,
Massachusetts; and Boston, Massachusetts. The metropolitan
areas with the highest numbers of glaziers were Great Falls,
Montana; Cedar Rapids, Iowa; Fort Walton Beach, Florida;
Myrtle Beach, South Carolina; and Duluth-Superior, Minnesota.

Apprenticeships

Both union and non-union apprenticeship programs are
available for glaziers. The National Glass Association and local
union-management committees or local contractors'
associations provide training programs for apprentice glaziers.
As might be expected, apprenticeships are more readily
available in large metropolitan areas. Apprentices can specialize
in installation and repair or fabrication.

Apprenticeships are generally three to five years, with an
additional 144 hours a year of related classroom work. The
IUPAT offers separate apprenticeships in installation and
fabrication. In the classroom, glaziers might study blueprint
reading; power tool safety and application; ladder, scaffold and

manlifting devices; the cutting and handling of glass and mirror; the cutting and fastening of aluminum and other metals; and the proper use of sealants. Those in union apprenticeship programs may also take courses in union history.

Related Skills

Glaziers need high levels of strength, coordination, arm-hand steadiness, and finger dexterity. Because many glaziers work on scaffolds high above the ground, they must be comfortable at heights and have good balance. A good background in mathematics is very helpful. In addition, high school students might take courses in blueprint reading, mechanical drawing, and general construction to help prepare for an apprenticeship.

Resources

For information about apprenticeships in your area, contact your local apprenticeship organization, the National Glass Association, or the local office of one of the following organizations:

Finishing Contractors Association
FCA National
Association Office
8150 Leesburg Pike, Suite 1210
Vienna, VA 22182
Phone: (703) 448-9001
Internet: http://www.finishingcontractors.org

International Union of Painters and Allied Trades
1750 New York Ave. NW
Washington, DC 20006
Internet: http://www.iupat.org

National Glass Association
Education and Training Department
8200 Greensboro Dr., Suite 302
McLean, VA 22101-3881
Internet: http://www.glass.org

Flooring

Floor installers held about 164,000 jobs in 2003, and 43 percent had their own businesses. If you are looking to learn a trade that will allow you to be your own boss, this might be the field for you.

Carpet Installers	O*NET/SOC	47-2041
	DOT	864.381-010
	RAIS	0071

Carpet installers start by ensuring that they have a smooth surface for installation. Part of the complexity of the trade is in planning the layout of the material. Seams must be placed in areas with low traffic and in places where they will least affect appearance. They install tack strips around the corners of the room and then install a carpet pad or underlay. They roll out, measure, mark, and cut the carpet and then stretch it to fit snugly, attaching it to the edging strip.

Floor Layers	O*NET/SOC	47-2042
	DOT	864.410-010
	RAIS	0199

Workers who specialize in flooring may also work with materials including rubber, vinyl, linoleum, cork, or other materials that can be installed in blocks or sheets. This type of flooring may be installed in residential environments, but may also have specialized properties, including sound-deadening and/or shock absorbing qualities that may be required in some commercial environments. After applying a wooden underlay, floor layers install the material using adhesive cement.

Tile and Marble Setters	O*NET/SOC	47-2044
	DOT	861.381-054
	RAIS	0573

Closely linked to other masonry trades, tile and marble setters finish floors with hard surfaces. They may also install the tile and marble to walls, ceilings, and roof decks. Tiles may be set with mortar or with a sticky paste called mastic. When using mortar, the work is like that of other masonry workers.

They begin with a scratch coat of cement mortar, raking the surface. They then apply another layer of cement, smoothing the surface, apply mortar to the tile or marble, and then apply it to the floor or wall. When using mastic, they must begin with a drywall, concrete, plaster, or wood surface. They spread the mastic paste or cement adhesive and then place the tile.

When the setting materials are dry, craftsmen grout the surface to fill the joints, remove the excess, and clean with a damp sponge.

Job Outlook and Wages

Jobs for carpeting specialists will grow about as fast as average—up 16.8 percent, with 53,000 job openings through 2012. In 2003, wages averaged $35,360 nationally, with workers in some states averaging more than $56,000. Top earnings for carpet installers were paid in Rhode Island, Illinois, Montana, Massachusetts, and New Jersey. The highest concentrations of workers were in Nevada, California, Delaware, Alaska, and Oregon.

Jobs for floor layers are expected to grow at an average rate—up about 13 percent from 2002–2012. In 2003, the average wage for floor layers was $35,760. The average wage for floor layers was the highest in Nebraska, $51,370, followed by Alaska, Maryland, Nevada, and Connecticut. The highest concentrations of workers were in Oregon, Nevada, Pennsylvania, Wisconsin, and California.

Tiles setters averaged about $35,600 nationally in 2003, up to $59,950 in Massachusetts. Washington, Hawaii, Connecticut, and Michigan were also among the high-paying states for this trade. Nevada, Arizona, Utah, Florida, and New Mexico had the highest concentration of workers.

Apprenticeships

Most flooring workers learn informally on the job, but formal apprenticeships are available to teach all phases of the flooring trade. Most are union sponsored and last three to four years, with a minimum of 144 hours a year of classroom training. Tile and marble setters can also train through masonry apprenticeship programs.

Related Skills

Good floor installers have to be in good physical condition and have good manual dexterity and flexibility. The job requires bending, kneeling, and stretching to place the flooring materials. Because this is decorative work, a good sense of design and color is also a plus. Good preparatory classes for an apprenticeship in this trade would include general and business math and mechanical drawing.

Resources

For information about apprenticeships in flooring, contact your local apprenticeship office and:

United Brotherhood of Carpenters and Joiners of America
50 F St., NW
Washington, DC 20001
Internet: http://www.carpenters.org
Follow the "Apprenticeship" links
For tile work, see the resources section of the masonry trades.

Painters and Paperhangers

Painters	*SOC/O*NET*	*47-2141*
	DOT	*840.381-010*
	RAIS	*0379*
Paperhangers	*O*NET/SOC*	*47-2142*
	DOT	*841.381-010*
	RAIS	*0390*

More than a quarter of a million workers were employed as painters in 2003, although many of them worked part time. Painters paint, stain, or varnish interior and exterior surfaces, providing an attractive and durable surface. When working on renovations, painters must also prepare the surfaces to be painted to ensure the paint will adhere and create a smooth and even finish. This may include washing walls, filling cracks and holes, sanding rough spots, and removing any dust.

Although we all know about the painters who work on residential properties using scaffolds and ladders to reach the highest areas, painters also work on tall buildings where they may work on scaffolds suspended by ropes, called "swing scaffolds." Flat surfaces can be painted this way, but what about conical surfaces, like church steeples or those towers in the Green Bay Packer's Lambeau Field stadium? In that case, the painter swings from a bosun's chair, a swinging seat often used when painting boats.

Like painters, paperhangers must have a thorough understanding of wall preparation before applying wall coverings made of paper, vinyl, or fabric to walls or ceilings. They may need to patch holes or cracks before starting. Walls are then covered with sizing to seal the surface and make the wall coverings adhere. When working on redecorating projects, paperhangers may need to remove old wallpaper with solvents or steam. Paperhangers must take care

WHY DO YOU NEED APPRENTICESHIP TRAINING TO PAINT?

Why should someone enter an apprenticeship in painting, rather than just pick up a brush and start a business? Because at the end of an apprenticeship you will know what you are doing, says Eric Redding, coordinator of apprenticeship training for the Painters and Allied Trades Council #35 in Roslindale, Massachusetts.

Redding says those people who just take brushes in hand present problems for all trained painters. "They give all painters a bad name." They think if you can slap on a coat of paint, you are a painter. Not so, he says. He often hears from consumers who have had that type of work done, and they are dismayed when the paint starts peeling off after a year or two.

Trained apprentices know about the chemical makeup of the materials they use. They understand the importance of preparation before the painting even begins. They understand the paint surfaces they are working with and which materials are right for which job. They receive 6,000 hours of on-the-job training, not only in painting, but in paperhanging and wall finishing as well. Then they spend an additional 450 hours in the classroom. Trained painters adhere to the standards of the Society for Protective Coatings and understand the complexities of painting on a variety of surfaces. "Unlike that kid on his summer vacation, trained painters know what they are doing," says the apprentice coordinator.

Painters, like all craft workers, sometimes face periods of unemployment. Those who are well-trained have the best chances of staying employed. Union-trained workers can work on a variety of projects, from small office jobs to the heights of Boston's new Leonard Zakim Bridge, with towers 266 feet above the roadway, says Redding.

to ensure edges are butted tightly, that bubbles and wrinkles are smoothed out, and that patterns match.

Job Outlook and Wages

The expected growth in painting and paperhanging jobs is about average through 2012—up about 11 percent from 2002 to 2012.

Because this field is an easy-entry field, many unskilled workers work in this field. Unfortunately, they provide competition for the highly trained worker who received his or her training through an apprenticeship program. More than half of the painters worked for building finishing contractors.

The average wage for painters in 2003 was $31,960. Those earning the highest salaries averaged more than $50,000. The states with the highest concentration of workers included Louisiana, Hawaii, Maine, Nevada, and Maryland. The highest-paid workers were in Alaska, Hawaii, Illinois, New Jersey, and Minnesota.

The outlook is not as good for paperhangers. There were only 8,900 full-time paperhangers in 2003. With fewer jobs, there are naturally fewer openings, and growth in the paperhanging business is not expected to grow as quickly as painting. The Department of Labor expects job growth in paperhanging to grow more slowly than average, just under 6 percent between 2002 and 2012.

The average wage for a paperhanger in 2003 was $34,220, with the highest wage earners averaging about $54,000 a year. The top-paying states for paperhangers were Minnesota, California, Missouri, Massachusetts, and New Jersey. The highest concentrations of workers were in Delaware, Arizona, North Dakota, Maine, and Pennsylvania.

Apprenticeships

Apprenticeships for painters run about three years with a minimum of 144 hours of classroom study each year. Some programs cross-train workers in wallpapering and wall finishing as well. Classroom work may include safety practices, blueprint reading, wood finishing, paint mixing and matching, paint technique, ladders and scaffolds, color theory, related math, surface preparation, application techniques, solvents, spray painting, and wall coverings. Apprenticeships for paperhangers are generally about two years, and longer if cross-trained with painting.

Related Skills

If you are interested in a painting or paperhanging as a career, you need good visual skills, including good visual color discrimination skills (the ability to detect variations in color, including shades and brightness, and to match color), the necessary muscle strength for repetitive motions, good manual dexterity, wrist-finger speed, and arm-hand steadiness.

General industrial arts courses, art classes, interior decorating, basic math, blueprint reading, and chemistry are all good preparatory courses for this job.

Resources

Contact your local apprenticeship organization or the groups listed below for more information about work in the finishing trades.

Associated Builders and Contractors (ABC)
Workforce Development Department
4250 N. Fairfax Dr., 9th Floor
Arlington, VA 22203
E-mail: gotquestions@abc.org or CraftTraining@abc.org
Internet: http://www.abc.org

International Union of Painters and Allied Trades
   (covers workers in all finishing trades)
1750 New York Ave., NW
Washington, DC 20006
Internet: http://www.iupat.org

Painting and Decorating Contractors of America
3913 Old Lee Highway
Fairfax, VA 22030
Internet: http://www.pdca.org

Sign, Display, and	*O*NET/SOC*	*47-4099.99*
Screen Process	*DOT*	*869.684-054*
	RAIS	*0517*

Another subspecialty of the painting and allied trades is the sign, display, and screen-process apprenticeship. Because this job is part of an "all other" classification in the Department of Labor's construction worker category, there is no specific breakdown of information for this particular job. There are, however, apprenticeships available for those who want to learn to design, construct, paint, or erect the display signs used for buildings and trade show exhibits. For information about this program, contact the International Union of Painters and Allied Trades. See address above.

Plasterers

Plasterers	*O*NET/SOC*	*47-2161*
	DOT	*842.361-018*
	RAIS	*0423*

Plasterers, stucco masons, and exterior insulation and finish systems (EIFS) installers put highly durable finishes on interior and exterior walls. These workers can work on a wide range of projects from small private homes to huge projects including shopping malls and cathedrals. Their work may be sleek and clean or might include the very intricate detailing found inside a church or theater. Their work may include both new construction projects and highly sophisticated restoration jobs that require masters of the trade.

Occupational Specialties and Job Descriptions

Plasterers The work of plasterers goes back to ancient times when frescoes were painted on plaster surfaces. Today, plasterers work on interior walls and ceilings, layering coats of plaster to create a smooth or decorative finished surface. Plaster may be spread over wooden or metal strips called lath, or it may be spread over solid surfaces, such as concrete block. It takes several coats of plaster to complete the job, and each coat is made of a different composition. The first coat, or scratch coat, is applied over the lath and is then roughed up with a special tool to create ridges that help hold the next coat. Next, they apply a "brown" coat made of gypsum plaster that provides a base for the finish coat. The finish coat is white and is made of a lime, plaster of paris, and water. Skilled plasterers may add intricate and complex design details to the finish. This type of specialist may also create custom mold designs and then pour or spray special plaster into the mold. After it dries, the decorative material is removed and becomes an intricate design element.

In some cases, plasterers work with a single thin coat smoothed onto other surfaces, such as interior masonry surfaces, gypsum baseboard, or drywalls.

Stucco Masons   Stucco masons work on exterior surfaces, laying a coat of stucco (portland cement, lime, and sand) over cement, concrete, masonry, or lath surfaces. Again, several layers of stucco must be applied before the project is complete. In the final stage, stucco masons can add marble or gravel chips to the finish coat for a decorative finish.

EIFS Installers   Exterior insulation and finish systems (EIFS) plasterers use a special adhesive to secure foam insulation boards to the exterior walls. Then they add a water-resistant base coat and reinforce it with fiberglass mesh for added strength. The EIFS workers then trowel on a polymer-based finish coat.

Job Outlook and Wages

New jobs for plasterers are expected to grow by about 14 percent—about as fast as average—between 2002 and 2012. Although consumers had turned away from plaster finishes in the past, today more consumers are looking for the hand-finished, Old World–quality of fine plaster and stucco work. In addition, the newer polymer finishes are less expensive than traditional stucco finishes and are becoming more popular in some areas of the country. Thin coat, or veneer, applications, are becoming more and more popular because they are easier to apply and provide a durable finish with good soundproofing qualities.

Plaster, stucco, and EIFS work is very regional and one method may be used more often in some areas than others. In 2003, the highest concentrations of workers in this trade were found in California, Arizona, Nevada, Utah, and New Mexico—all areas where stucco architecture is popular. The top-paying states in this field were New York, Illinois, Washington, Hawaii, and Massachusetts. Most workers were employed by building finishing contractors and building foundation and exterior contractors.

The average salary for this type of work was $35,720 in 2003. The highest-paid workers averaged more than $67,000 a year.

Apprenticeships

Contractors and unions or trade organizations jointly sponsor apprenticeship programs. Apprentice programs in plastering usually run three and a half to four years and require a minimum of 144 hours of classroom training. Classroom work could include job-related courses such as history of plastering, portland cement/stucco, gypsum systems (including veneers), ornamental and shop work, fireproofing, EIFS, knowledge of various lathing and substrates, specialty finishes, safety, applied mathematics, blueprint reading, tool and equipment use, and maintenance.

Related Skills

Because this work is hand applied, you will need to have good manual and finger dexterity. The job requires strength because your arms will be reaching above your head as you apply plaster and stucco. You need good coordination skills to climb up and down ladders and walk along scaffolds.

You should also feel comfortable wearing protective clothing and equipment because plaster and stucco work can be very dusty and dirty.

Masonry courses at vocational high schools can help prepare young people for this kind of work. Courses in drafting, shop, and mathematics, including algebra, are also beneficial.

Resources

For information about apprenticeships in this trade, contact your local apprenticeship organization or local unions in the field. Information about this field can be found at many of the same resources as found in the brickmasons and stonemasons section of this chapter including:

Association of Wall and Ceiling Industries International
803 West Broad Street
Falls Church, VA 22047
Phone: (703) 534-8300
Internet: http://www.awci.org

The Operative Plasterers' and Cement Masons' International
    Association of the United States and Canada
Director of Training, Safety and Health
14405 Laurel Place, Suite 300
Laurel, Maryland 20707
Phone: (301) 470-4200
Internet: http://www.opcmia.org/

International Masonry Institute
The James Brice House
42 East Street
Annapolis, MD 21401
Internet: http://www.imiweb.org

International Union of Bricklayers and Allied Craftworkers
1776 Eye St. NW
Washington, DC 20006-3700
Phone: (202) 783-3788
Internet: http://www.bacweb.org

Plumbers, Pipe Fitters, Steamfitters, and Sprinklerfitters

For young people interested in working in the construction industry, plumbing may offer some of the best opportunities. According to the Department of Labor job opportunities are excellent in this field because not enough people seek training.

When most of us think about plumbers, we think of that person who has arrived at our home to help deal with a plumbing emergency. Maybe the toilet is clogged, or the water heater has leaked all over the floor, or a ceiling has fallen in because of a leaky pipe. But there is more to the plumbing industry than that.

The plumbing industry is divided into four specialized trades: plumbers, pipe fitters, steamfitters, and sprinklerfitters. Together these jobs make up one of the largest and highest-paid construction occupations. More than half a million workers hold jobs in the plumbing field.

Photo provided by Roto-Rooter Services.

CREATIVE BRAIN CLEARS A DRAIN

Clogged drains have been a problem for years, but Samuel Blanc helped find a solution to the problem. Blanc was inspired when a clogged drain in his son's house in Des Moines, Iowa, took hours to clear, and he set about looking for a solution to the problem. In 1933, he took a 1/6-horsepower engine from a Maytag washing machine, some roller skate wheels, some special blades, and some 3/8-inch cable and made the prototype for the first Roto-Rooter. The rest is history.

Occupational Specialties and Job Descriptions

Plumber	O*NET/SOC	47-2152.02
	DOT	862.381-030
	RAIS	0431

Plumbers do the jobs we are most familiar with. They repair and install the systems that keep our houses, schools, and businesses functioning. Plumbers repair the water, waste disposal, drainage, and gas systems in homes and commercial and industrial buildings. They also install the plumbing fixtures we take for granted every day—bathtubs, showers, sinks, toilets, dishwashers, and water heaters.

Although all workers in the plumbing industry work with pipe, the specifics of the particular job require additional skills as well. All plumbers need to be able to read blueprints. Pipes for a new home can't be laid willy-nilly. They must follow precise plans in order to avoid interfering with other systems within the building (electrical wiring, for example). Jobs need to be planned to avoid wasting materials and to keep individual projects within budget guidelines. In addition to working with pipe, plumbers also need to be able to provide the support systems needed to hold the pipe. Sometimes, for example, it is necessary to install steel supports from the ceiling joists to hold pipe in place. When doing repairs, it is sometimes necessary to cut holes in walls, floors, ceilings in order to reach and repair damaged pipes.

In order to install a plumbing system, plumbers need to use saws, pipe cutters, and pipe-bending machines to cut and bend lengths of pipe. Then, they must connect the pieces to keep the whole system running, without leaks. Depending on the type of pipe used for the project, they may connect individual pieces with adhesives (for plastic pipe) or solder (for copper pipe). Once all the piping is complete, the plumber will install and connect the fixtures and appliances. Then they connect all of the equipment to the outside water and sewer lines. The final step includes checking the system to be sure everything is working properly.

Pipe Fitters	O*NET/SOC	47-2152.01
	DOT	862.281-022
	RAIS	0414

Pipe fitters install and repair the piping systems used in manufacturing, the generation of electricity, and in heating and cooling buildings. They also install the controls that regulate these systems. Some pipe fitters do all types of work, but most specialize in one of the following areas.

Occupational Specialties

Steamfitters   Steamfitters install pipe systems that move liquids or gases under high pressure. They are responsible for designing, fabricating, assembling, laying out, installing, and maintaining complex piping systems. Steamfitters install piping and tubing made of carbon steel, copper, plastic, glass, or other metals using a variety of processes. These processes include brazing, welding, screwing, gluing, bending, and mechanical joining. Steamfitters install valves, controls, pumps, vessels, and hangers, as well as refrigeration equipment, air-conditioning equipment, compressors, coils, and boilers.

Sprinklerfitters   Sprinklerfitters are pipe-fitting specialists who install automatic fire sprinkler systems in residential and commercial buildings. Sprinklerfitters help protect lives and property. Sprinklerfitters must understand fire protection systems, including the layout and installation of underground fire mains. A sprinklerfitter works from blueprints or drawings to lay out the job, installing individual fire sprinklers throughout the ceiling of a building. Then they measure, mark, cut, and thread pipe and connect it to the sprinklers and to the water supply. After connecting the integrated system, they test for leaks.

A sprinklerfitter must understand fire and building codes. In addition to installing sprinkler systems, they may also install other fire protection equipment including standpipes, carbon dioxide systems, halon (fire-suppressant chemical) systems, foam systems, and dry-chemical systems.

Job Outlook and Wages

Job growth in this trade is expected be about average, but the demand for workers in this trade is expected to be higher than the number of workers entering the field. In addition to an

83

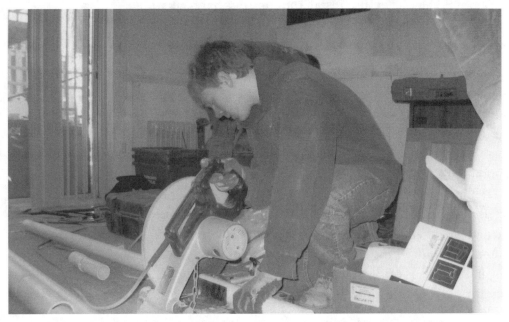
Brendan Cheever cuts pipe as part of his on-site cooperative education program.

PRE-APPRENTICESHIP PROGRAM ALLOWS HIGH SCHOOL STUDENT TO LEARN TRADE

Brendan knew even before entering high school that he wasn't interested in going to college. He enjoyed working with his hands and decided a vocational school was the best place for him to learn a trade. Fortunately, Brendan found a school that participates in a pre-apprenticeship program that allows him to learn the plumbing trade even before graduating from high school. Brendan's school allows students to do what they call a cooperative educational program in the third semester of their junior year, if their grades are "up to snuff." Brendan spends one week in the classroom and one week at his apprenticeship job in the field. While in the classroom, he learns about the basic codes, and studies English, math, and history. He does the shop portion of his day out in the field where he learns to use the equipment associated with the trade.

For Brendan, this program will give him a head start when he graduates from high school. Massachusetts requires a three-year apprenticeship program to qualify for a license. Brendan will have eighteen months toward his official apprenticeship by the time he graduates from high school.

(continued)

Master plumber Bob Hackett says he enjoys having the opportunity to teach young people like Brendan.

"When he first starts, the apprentice is the helper. I explain how things work, what we are doing, and what each job entails. Essentially his job is to help me do my job faster. Eventually, I expect him to be able to think ahead and plan what we need to do, so he is capable of doing the job himself."

Hackett says this type of program helps him find and train workers for his business.

"We feel we are training our future employees to do the type and quality of work that we want. We try to help them develop good habits. We hope young people who work for us as apprentices will choose to stay on when their apprenticeship is complete. We have no guarantees, however."

Hackett says he prefers to take apprentices from a vocational/technical school. "They are more prepared and have more experience.

"There is an enormous need for apprentices today. We have a big void in qualified people. We have a big need for people to come into this field."

Hackett says interest in computer technology took some young people away from the trades, and that unfortunately there is still a stigma attached to working with your hands. "There is a misperception out there that young people who make a career in the trades are some how regarded as less than. That's a mistake," he says. "Young people trained in a trade can find work and are well paid."

Master plumber Bob Hackett supervises Brendan's work.

increase in building renovations, the installation of sprinkler systems is steadily increasing.

In the past, many companies with extensive pipe systems had workers on staff to take care of maintenance issues. Increasingly, companies are outsourcing that work to plumbing contractors. This means a reduction of jobs within private companies, but an increase in the numbers of service contracts with independent plumbing companies. This, then, produces an increase in jobs with plumbing and pipe-fitting contractors.

As with most jobs in the construction industry, plumbers can experience times of unemployment as the work on specific projects ends. Workers in the pipes trades were among the highest paid in the construction industry. The average annual wage for workers in this field was $43,450 in 2003. The most highly trained workers earned up to $70,000. Sprinklerfitters were among the highest paid in the plumbing industry. The states with the highest salaries for workers in this trade included Illinois, Alaska, New York, Oregon, and Washington. States employing the largest number of workers in 2003 were Louisiana, Colorado, Nevada, Mississippi, and Alaska.

Apprenticeships

Apprenticeships in plumbing give students a thorough knowledge of the trade. Most plumbers learn their jobs through apprenticeship training. Plumbing apprenticeships take four to five years, depending on the area of specialty. As an apprentice you will begin by learning basic skills, such as identifying different types of pipe, using the tools of the trade, and understanding safety considerations. As you master these skills you will begin working with the pipe, installing plumbing systems and fixtures under the supervision of a trained plumber.

In addition to the on-the-job training, you will study courses that will help you in the trade. As with all apprenticeships, the classroom work will be specifically related to your job. You may study mathematics applicable to pipework, physics (with an emphasis on liquids and gases), elements of hydraulics and heat, mechanical drawing, drafting and blueprint reading, and plumbing theory. In the theoretical classes, you will learn about the materials of the trade, sanitation, bacteriology, and piping systems. You will also study local plumbing codes and regulations.

Pipe fitter/steamfitter/sprinklerfitter course work could include related math, science, computer courses, safety regulations and programs, hazardous waste operations, National Fire Protection Safety Codes, soldering, brazing, testing, and maintenance. Most apprenticeships in the plumbing trade require at least 144 hours of classroom study each year.

Apprentices start at a percentage of a journeyperson's wages. Generally, apprentices are reviewed every six months and receive increases at that time.

Apprenticeship programs may be administered by local union-management committees that include members of the United Association of Journeymen and Apprentices of the Plumbing and Pipefitting Industry of the United States and Canada, and local employers who are members of either the Mechanical Contractors Association of America, the National Association of Plumbing-Heating-Cooling Contractors, or the National Fire Sprinkler Association.

Related Skills

The Plumbing-Heating-Cooling Contractors Association recommends that high school students emphasize certain courses during the junior and senior year. Algebra, geometry, chemistry, English, and speech can all provide excellent background if you are interested in entering the plumbing industry. Courses in shop, drafting, blueprint reading, computers, and physics can help you as well.

Plumbers need good visualization skills, giving them the ability to imagine how things will look once they are moved around. Manual and finger dexterity are important as plumbers manipulate and assemble many small objects. They need good information-ordering skills, the ability to put the pieces of a project in the proper order.

Those interested in learning the plumbing trade need to be in good shape. Much of the work requires working overhead and requires strength and stamina as well as manual dexterity.

Resources

For more information about apprenticeships or work opportunities in this trade, contact your local state apprenticeship agency or a local affiliate of one the organizations listed below.

Information about this trade can be found at:

United Association of Journeymen and Apprentices
   of the Plumbing and Pipefitting Industry
901 Massachusetts Ave., NW
Washington, DC 20001
Internet: http://www.ua.org/

Associated Builders and Contractors (ABC)
4250 N. Fairfax Dr., 9th Floor
Arlington, VA 22203-1607
Phone: 703-812-2000
E-mail: gotquestions@abc.org or CraftTraining@abc.org
Internet: http://www.abc.org

Home Builders Institute
1201 15th St., NW, 6th Floor
Washington, DC 20005-2800
Phone: (800) 795-7955
Internet: http://www.hbi.org

National Association of
   Plumbing-Heating-Cooling Contractors
180 S. Washington St.
P.O. Box 6808
Falls Church, VA 22040
Phone: (800) 533-7694
Internet: http://www.phccweb.org

For more information about sprinklerfitters:

American Fire Sprinkler Association, Inc.
9696 Skillman St., Suite 300
Dallas, TX 75243-8264
Phone: (214) 349-5965
Internet: http://www.firesprinkler.org

National Fire Sprinkler Association
P.O. Box 1000
Patterson, NY 12563
Phone: (845) 878-4200, ext. 133
Internet: http://www.nfsa.org

Roofer

Roofer	*O*NET/SOC*	*47-2181.00*
	DOT	*866.381-010*
	RAIS	*0480*

Want to get to the top? The top of the building project, that is. More than 118,390 workers in the United States work installing or repairing roofs. Because the roof protects everything inside a building, the importance of this trade can't be minimized or underestimated. Without an adequate roof, water damage can destroy ceilings, walls, and the contents of buildings.

Roofers work on all types of roofs from flat to pitched. Most commercial, industrial, and apartment buildings have flatter roof surfaces. Many residential properties have more pitched roofs. Roofers may work in the commercial/industrial industry, or they may specialize in residential work. Some do both.

Roofers use materials made of tar or asphalt and gravel; rubber, thermoplastic, or metal; shingles (asphalt, slate, fiberglass, wood, tile, or other materials); or a layered combination of materials to create the protective roofing surface. They may begin with a layer of insulation, cover it with a tarlike substance, add roofing felt in overlapping layers, and then spread hot bitumen to seal the seams, making the surface watertight. This process may be repeated several times, building up layers. The final layer is glazed to create a smooth surface or finished with gravel embedded into it for a rough surface. Today, some roofs are covered with a single-ply membrane of waterproof material that is applied in sheets and sealed with adhesives.

Most homes have shingled roofs. Roofers cover the surface with roofing felt and then they nail or staples shingles to the roof in overlapping rows to create the protective surface.

Job Outlook and Wages

The average salary for roofers in 2003 was $32,820, with the highest-paid workers earning wages in the upper $40,000 level. The top paying states for roofers were Alaska, Illinois, Nevada, New Jersey, and Hawaii. States with the highest concentrations of workers included Idaho, Oregon, Vermont, Nevada, and Florida. Most roofers work for building foundation and exterior contractors.

Jobs in the roofing trade are expected to grow about as fast as average—up 18.6 percent through 2012. Jobs should be plentiful during that time, because there is a very high turnover rate in the roofing trade. Although roofing work, like all construction work, can be subject to weather conditions, there is always repair work to be done. Repair and replacement jobs continue, even during poor economic times. People might be able to put off a bathroom upgrade, or a painting project, but when a roof needs repair, it must be taken care of.

Apprenticeships

Although most roofers learn their trade by informal on-the-job training, working as helpers, there are registered apprenticeships available in the trade. These programs are administered by local union-management committees made up of roofing contractors and locals of the United Union of Roofers, Waterproofers, and Allied workers. The Associated Builders and Contractors also sponsor apprenticeship programs in some states. Roofing apprenticeships are generally three-year programs requiring a minimum of 144 hours of classroom instruction in trade-related course work. Course work might include programs such as safety and first aid; nails, fasteners and adhesives; concrete and reinforcement materials; tools of the trade; hangers and supports; layout, sheet-metal process, soldering, gutters, and downspouts; flashing, trade tools, roof installation systems, coating materials, and reroofing.

Related Skills

Roofers need to be comfortable working on ladders and scaffolds, and they need to be comfortable working in high places. Strength, balance, and manual dexterity are important. This is a messy job, and many workers leave the trade because they don't like the heat and dirt associated with roofing. You need to think about that before considering this trade.

High school classes in mechanical drawing, general shop courses, carpentry, and mathematics are helpful in preparing for this apprenticeship.

Resources

You can get information on local apprenticeship programs at your local apprenticeship agency or from:

Associated Builders and Contractors (ABC)
Workforce Development Department
4250 N. Fairfax Dr., 9th Floor
Arlington, VA 22203-1607
E-mail: CraftTraining@abc.org
Internet: http://www.abc.org

National Roofing Contractors Association
10255 W. Higging Rd., Suite 600
Rosemont, IL 60018-5607
Phone: (888) ROOF-321 for a free brochure about
    opportunities in roofing
Internet: http://www.nrca.net
Using links on the left side of the home page, you can find a
    local contractor and more information about
    apprenticeship training.

United Union of Roofers, Waterproofers,
    and Allied Workers
1660 L St., NW, Suite 800
Washington, DC 20036
Internet: http://www.unionroofers.org

Sheet Metal Worker

Sheet Metal Worker	*O*NET/SOC*	*47-2211.00*
	DOT	*804.281-010*
	RAIS	*0510*

More than 189,000 people worked as sheet metal workers in
2003, and nearly two-thirds of them worked in the
construction industry. Most construction sheet metal workers
work in the plumbing, heating or air-conditioning fields and
other sheet metal workers also work for roofing and sheet
metal contractors. Some sheet metal workers also work in the
architectural sheet metal area, where they work with brass and
copper to produce ornamentation, columns, skylights, signs,
and metal ceilings and downspouts. These workers may also
design and install kitchen work areas.

Matt Whitlock works on his project, a copper bird feeder, during the 2004 Annual Sheet Metal Apprenticeship Contest. Matt won the fourth-year apprentice division that tested his skills in shop fabrication, sheet metal drafting, and welding, as well as his interpretation of architectural and mechanical drawings. Photo courtesy of the Sheet Metal and Air Conditioning Contractors' National Association (SMACNA).

MATT WHITLOCK EXPLAINS THE APPRENTICESHIP PROCESS

"The first thing you need to do is decide where you want to go with your life," says Matt. At eighteen, he didn't want to spend another four years in a traditional classroom, and he knew he didn't want to spend the rest of his life sitting at a desk in front of a computer all day. He enjoyed working with his hands and was looking for a career path that would allow him to enjoy that kind of work. Fortunately, he didn't have to look far. With a brother in the sheet metal trade, he knew someone who could answer his questions, like how do I get started?

Matt says the way to get started is to go to your local union hall. "Whether you want to be a carpenter, or an electrician, or a plumber, go in and ask them if they are taking applications." (Some unions accept applicants year-round; others take applications during specific times of year.) "They will tell you what to do from there." Expect some competition. "There could be 100 people in line for an apprenticeship."

Matt took an aptitude test. He says taking the test just after completing high school has its advantages. All the school work

(*continued*)

and math are still fresh in your mind and it is easy to apply what you know. Then, he had an interview. What could be a nerve-wracking experience is a really a way to show them who you are, to let them get to know you, and to tell them about the kind of experience you have. Matt says he thinks it helped that he had work experience. "I worked for a concrete guy all through high school. They knew I had been out working and that I wasn't afraid to work," he says.

Once his application and interview process were complete, the interview committee tallied Matt's score, and he was one of the highly qualified applicants to be selected for apprentice training.

But apprentice training means more classroom work, right? Well, yes, says Matt, but the classroom work is very different from the kind of work you do in high school. Never do you ask, "Where am I going to use this? What you learn in the classroom is what you will be using the next day on the job. One night you might be welding, and another night you might learn how to service a furnace or an air conditioner. Safety training is an important part of it," according to Matt.

Just because the classes are relevant doesn't make the process easy, he says. After long days on the job, it isn't always easy to spend another three hours in the classroom. It makes for very long days. "On school nights, I leave for work at 6 a.m. and I get home at 10 p.m. But, if you want to get somewhere, you have to work for it."

Matt says he loves the on-the-job training. "When you first start, they really don't expect you to know anything. They give you the easier jobs or you work directly with a journeyman. If you have questions, someone is always there to help you." Now entering his fifth year as an apprentice, Matt says he just "jumps right in" with everyone else.

Working as an apprentice in sheet metal provides great variety, and he likes that. Sometimes it can be a different job every day or a job can last a year. "One day you might be replacing just one piece of a gutter or a piece of a furnace in a house. Another day you might be assigned to a weeklong job installing at a Walgreen's or a Mobil station. You might be working with little pieces, or you could be working with three-foot wide sheets of metal that run the length of a roof."

As a sheet metal worker specializing in heating, ventilation, air conditioning, and refrigeration (HVACR), Matt says that is one of the best parts of working in the trade. "You might get tired of a job if you work on it too long." The other advantage is the quality of the training. "You get to learn from

(*continued*)

a lot of different people. At every job site, you get to learn from someone else . . . you take a little bit from each journeyman. Eventually, you come up with your own way."

That variety can be a relief when you are on a job site you don't particularly enjoy, he says. "You might be on a job you hate, crawling around in grease all day. Some days are dirty and some days are clean. There are definitely some bad days, but there are a lot of good days."

Matt earned his way to an especially good day during the 32nd Annual Sheet Metal Apprenticeship Contest in Las Vegas, Nevada, in May 2004. Every local has a competition and the winners earn the chance to compete in the nationals. Matt won the preliminary competition, and with all expenses paid by his local union, headed off to Las Vegas where all his hard work paid off.

Each apprentice was given a detailed drawing of the project and the raw materials necessary to complete it. In 2004, it was a copper bird feeder. With just four and a half hours to complete the job, apprentices are pushed to do their best work in a short period of time. Matt's project was the winner. He says his speed and his welding skills probably helped him take the top honors and top prizes—$2,500 provided by the International Union, a $5,000 mutual fund (provided by Invesco Mutual Funds), and a Lincoln Electric 500-mig welding machine.

All in all, his apprenticeship experience has been a terrific one, but would he recommend apprenticeship to others? "If you don't like to get dirty and don't like working hard, don't do it," he says. "For the people who know they don't want to go through college, for those who love building things and seeing the things they have built, yes!"

Sheet metal workers build, install, and repair and maintain metal building parts used in construction. They may also work with fiberglass and plastic materials. They install many types of duct systems and are sometimes trained in the installation of the heating or air conditioning systems as well. As HVACR technicians, they fabricate, install, and maintain heating, air conditioning, and ventilation systems. (There is more about HVACR workers in Chapter 6). Sheet metal workers may also build roofs, siding, rain gutters, skylights, and other objects made of metal. In addition they make and install many types of duct systems. Sheet metal workers may work both indoors in a fabrication environment and indoors or outdoors during installation. As part of the job, they:

- Study blueprints or other specifications to determine materials needed
- Convert blueprints into shop drawings to be followed in the construction and assembly of sheet metal products
- Determine project requirements, including scope, assembly sequences, and required methods and materials, according to blueprints, drawings, and written or verbal instructions
- Set up and operate fabricating machines to cut, bend, and straighten sheet metal
- Set up and operate soldering and welding equipment to join parts
- Measure cut, bend, shape, and fasten pieces of sheet metal to make ductwork or other products, using shears, hammers, punches, and drills
- May use computerized metalworking equipment
- Cut, drill, and form parts with computer-controlled saws, lasers, shears, and presses
- Trim, file, deburr, buff, and smooth surfaces, seams, and joints of assembled parts, using hand tools and portable power tools
- Check finished parts for proper measurements
- Use hand tools and power tools to install assemblies at the work site
- May fabricate, install, and service heating, air conditioning, and ventilation systems (See also HVACR technicians in the Installation chapter)

Job Outlook and Wages

Job opportunities should be good for sheet metal workers in the construction industry and related fields. Both a growth in employment and openings in jobs resulting from experienced sheet metal workers leaving the occupation will provide many opportunities for sheet metal workers. The Bureau of Labor Statistics projects the trade to grow about as fast as average through 2012 due to the expected growth in the demand for sheet metal installations as more industrial, commercial, and residential structures are built. Older buildings will need to be upgraded with energy-efficient air conditioning, heating, and ventilation systems as well. Sheet metal workers who enter manufacturing jobs, however, may not be as fortunate. Slower-than-average job growth is expected in that area.

As with other jobs in the construction industry, periods of unemployment may occur when individual projects end. On the plus side, many sheet metal projects are completed indoors, so there is less down time during bad weather.

The average annual income for sheet metal workers in 2003 was $37,780, with the highest-paid and most experienced workers earning just over $60,000. Remember, salaries can vary widely across the country. Although the national annual average salary was $37,780 in 2003, workers in Cape May, New Jersey, earned an average salary of $61,160. The top-paying states for this job were the District of Columbia, Hawaii, Alaska, New Jersey, and Nevada. The states with the largest number of workers in the sheet metal trade in 2003 were Indiana, Maryland, Kansas, Oklahoma, and Nevada.

Apprenticeships

Apprenticeship is the best way to learn this trade. Apprenticeship programs run from four to five years of on-the-job training and require an average of 200 hours per year of classroom instruction. Apprenticeships include instruction in both fabrication and installation of sheet metal. The Sheet Metal Workers' International Association and local chapters of the Sheet Metal and Air Conditioning Contractors National Association (SMACNA) form joint committees to help administer apprenticeships in this field. The Associated Builders and Contractors Association also offers apprenticeship programs. Combined apprenticeships in sheet metal and HVACR are now available as well.

According to Rosalind Raymond of the Sheet Metal and Air Conditioner Contractors National Association (SMACNA), one of the major benefits of becoming a sheet metal apprentice is "pride in doing this type of work."

"Las Vegas would be nothing but a desert without air conditioning. There would be no computer plants without air conditioning. They need clean rooms where everything must be sterile, and without HVAC, they couldn't produce those computer chips. It is incredibly valuable work.

"Some people believe that apprenticeship is blue-collar work and may not be prestigious, but the service that this offers to society is phenomenal. . . . It is worthwhile work to be commended."

On top of that, young people get an education, receive health benefits, and, because they begin their training at such a young age, they can retire while they are still young, with a nice retirement package, says Raymond.

For many, the training is state of the art. Many sheet metal classroom programs are designed by the International Training Institute for the Sheet Metal and Air Conditioning Industry (ITI). They have just updated all of their program materials for apprentices, and today classroom instruction not only specializes in providing an industry-specific curriculum, but personal skills classes as well, including time management, personal finance, study skills, and communication skills.

ITI-designed programs provide a core curriculum for the first two years that includes personal skills as well as drafting, layout and fabrication, and trade materials. Much of the material is presented in a DVD format, so students can review as necessary or move ahead to more advanced material, if they are looking for more.

In the second two years, specific modules are presented. For those interested in going into the HVAC trade, they offer HVAC-specific materials. For those who want to work with architectural metals, the modules will offer those courses. The modules are industry driven in that they provide the training that area contractors are looking for. Depending on the modules, courses might include CAD design and specifications, drafting, blueprint reading, trigonometry and geometry applicable to the job, welding, soldering, clean room training, sheet metal fabrication, computer applications, air conditioning, heating, and refrigeration principles, and duct design. Because this job can result in injuries, a special emphasis is placed on safety.

Related Skills

Because work in this field requires both mechanical and mathematical aptitude, high school programs strong in mathematics, algebra, trigonometry, and geometry help prepare young people for apprenticeship programs. Shop courses in metal work can also help get you ready. Computer classes, especially those in computerized design, can be especially beneficial. Because this job requires much sequential work, information-ordering skills (the ability to arrange things or actions in a certain order or sequence according to related rules) are very important.

On the physical side, this trade requires good manual dexterity and eye-hand coordination. Good balance is also important because there is much climbing, walking, stooping, and moving from one area to another during installations.

Resources

For more information about sheet metal work and apprenticeship, contact your local apprenticeship agency, a local of the Sheet Metal Workers International Association (see below), or a local sheet metal or heating, refrigeration, and/or air-conditioning contractor in your area.

For more information about sheet metal work, contact:

International Training Institute for Sheet Metal
    and Air-Conditioning Industry
601 North Fairfax St., Suite 240
Alexandria, VA 22314
Internet: http://www.sheetmetal-iti.org

Sheet Metal and Air-Conditioning Contractors
    National Association (SMACNA)
4201 Lafayette Center Dr.
Chantilly, VA 20151-1209
Phone: 703-803-2980
Internet: http://www.smacna.org

Sheet Metal Workers International Association
1750 New York Ave., NW
Washington, DC 20006
Internet: http://www.smwia.org
Click the "Locals" link on this site to find a sheet metal local
    in your area.

Structural and Reinforcing Iron and Metal Workers (Ironworkers)

Structural and reinforcing metal workers, called
ironworkers, use iron or steel materials to build buildings,
bridges and other structures. They also reinforce the concrete
used in building highways, buildings, bridges, tunnels, and
other structures by installing steel bars or mesh into concrete.
The metal work reinforces the concrete, making it strong
enough to use as a major building material.

Although we associate their work with the road building and
skyscraper projects we see in the urban landscape, they do a
variety of other work as well. Ironworkers may do ornamental
work, rig machinery, make bank vaults, build jail cells,
fabricate metal doors, install metal or reinforced concrete
columns, install elevator shafts, and construct amusement park
equipment and rides. Think about that the next time you take a
roller coaster ride.

Occupational Specialties

Structural Iron and	*O*NET/SOC*	*47-2221*
Steel Workers	*DOT*	*801.361-014*
	RAIS	*0669*

MOHAWK SKYWALKERS SPAN NEW YORK SKYLINE

Mohawk ironworkers have provided the skeletal structure for all of the historically important buildings and bridges in Manhattan. From the bridges across the Hudson River to the record-breaking towers of the World Trade Center, Native Americans have brought their skills to the heights of New York City's skyline.

These descendants of one of the main tribes of the historic Iroquois Confederacy got their start in 1886 when the St. Lawrence River Bridge was built on their land in Kahnawake, just outside Montreal. In exchange for allowing one side of the railway bridge to be constructed on Iroquois land, the construction company agreed to hire the Native American workers on the construction project. Dominion Bridge Company foremen watched as these new workers walked casually across the construction beams high across the river. Recognizing their natural talent, they began training the first Mohawk apprentice ironworkers.

Another project 21 years later would take the lives of 75 ironworkers, including 33 Mohawks, when a bridge they were constructing in Quebec City collapsed due to a design flaw. Distressed that the lives of so many from one tribe had been lost, the Mohawk ironworkers began to seek jobs working on a variety of projects in New York. Some relocated to the area to work on construction projects. Others commuted from their reservations in upstate New York and southern Quebec.

Beginning with the construction of the Hell's Gate Bridge on the East River in 1916, Mohawk ironworkers have worked on every major building project in New York City. Called "skywalkers," these experienced construction workers have helped build the George Washington Bridge, the bridges that span the Verrazano Narrows, the Empire State Building, Madison Square Garden, the RCA Tower in Rockefeller Plaza, the Waldorf Astoria Hotel, and the United Nations Assembly Building.

In the future, they will certainly work to reconstruct the area on and around the site of the World Trade Center Twin Towers disaster, rebuilding on the site of one of their most highly acclaimed and now most hallowed construction projects in the nation.

Looking up, way up, at a construction site, you see them. They are walking with confidence across those beams—maybe sitting on them having lunch. They are the fearless ironworkers, often called the "cowboys of the skies."

Before the actual construction even begins, structural ironworkers are there on the site erecting the steel frames and assembling the cranes that will move structural steel and other building materials around the construction site. They construct steel beams, columns, and girders to form the structural skeleton of the building project. They unload, erect, and bolt together or weld the prefabricated iron or steel to form the skeleton of a structure. They work on towers, bridges, stadiums, as well as large residential and commercial buildings. They also erect and install precast beams, columns, and panels.

In addition to forming the skeleton of the building, some workers specialize in ornamental work. Ornamental ironworkers install metal windows into masonry or wooden openings of buildings. They also install the nonstructural walls and window frames, called curtain walls, in large commercial, industrial, and residential buildings. They also install elevator shafts, stairs, catwalks, gratings, ladders, doors, railings, fencing, gates, metal screens, elevator fronts, platforms, and entranceways. These workers are sometimes called "finishers" in the trade.

Job Outlook and Wages

The Bureau of Labor Statistics predicts jobs in structural ironwork to grow about as fast as average—close to 16 percent through 2012. Industrial and commercial construction is expected to grow during that time, and as older factories, power plants, roads, and bridges are replaced there will be increased job opportunities. Because much of the work is done at great heights, work is halted in bad weather. Rain, winds, or icy conditions can make an ironworker's job extremely hazardous, so much of the work is done in good weather months. Periods of unemployment are often part of the job. In addition, major construction projects can vary widely from one area to another. Workers may have to relocate in order to find work.

The average salary for a structural ironworker in 2003 was $42,610, with the highest-paid workers in the country averaging more than $78,000. Many ironworkers are members of the International Association of Bridge, Structural, Ornamental, and Reinforcing Ironworkers. According to the union, average hourly earnings with benefits for full-time union workers were 34 percent higher than non-union workers.

In 2003, the states offering the highest wages were New York, New Jersey, Minnesota, Hawaii, and Alaska. The highest concentrations of ironworkers were in Mississippi, Missouri, South Dakota, Arkansas, and Alaska. As might be expected, much of the work of structural ironworkers is found in major metropolitan areas.

Reinforcing Iron and	*O*NET/SOC*	*47-2171*
Rebar Workers	*DOT*	*801.168-026*
	RAIS	*0471*

Many ironworkers start by doing reinforcing ironwork. Reinforcing ironworkers fabricate and place steel (or composite) reinforcing rods called rebar in concrete forms to reinforce the concrete. Some materials are reinforced with welded metal fabric. This reinforced material is widely used in construction projects. They may also install cables, called post tensioning tendons, in concrete forms, along with the reinforcing steel. Once the concrete is poured, the ends of these cables are left exposed. After the concrete hardens, the ironworkers tighten the cables with specially designed jacking equipment. This reinforcement allows structures to span great distances between supporting columns and is commonly used in arenas and parking garages. Reinforcing ironworkers help build highways, drainage channels, bridges, stadiums, airports, and buildings.

Job Outlook and Wages

Jobs for reinforcing ironworkers are expected to grow about 16.7 percent through 2012. As with structural ironworkers, growth is expected to come as construction, maintenance, and rehabilitation projects grow. This work, too, can be highly

IRONWORKER APPRENTICES MUST "RISE" TO THE OCCASION

Neil McKelligan supervises ironworker apprentices in the Boston area and says those who are interested in ironwork are a special breed. As with all apprentices, they must have a strong work ethic, be responsible, show up on time (both on the job and for classes), and have a good attitude. In addition, they must be prepared for periods of down time. Ironwork is an extremely weather- and economy-dependent craft and there may be extensive periods when an apprentice will not be able to find on-the-job assignments or may have to work short hours.

Jobs can vary widely from area to area. During the height of Boston's construction projects, McKelligan had as many as 776 active apprentices. This year, as the major construction is coming to an end, the graduating class was 130. Next year, only 50 new apprentices will be accepted to the program.

When work slows down, contractors are looking for the more experienced apprentices. Until they get some experience, finding regular work is difficult. Even journeymen experience periods of unemployment. "When work is good, it is tremendous," he says. "But until apprentices establish themselves, they will need to be prepared for the down times."

Once their apprenticeships are completed, they need to be flexible about where they will work and where they will live. McKelligan, who started as an apprentice himself, worked 30 different jobs one year and has worked all over the United States. Ironworkers need to be willing to go where the work is.

On top of all that, the working conditions are severe. Ironworkers are exposed to both extreme heat and extreme cold, and besides that, they might be more than twenty floors up.

"Watch for the reactions of people. How many times have you seen someone walk by a construction site, look up at the workers, and say, 'I could never do that.' Well, many people can't. I say apprentices in this job must *rise* to the occasion. . . . It is a unique individual who can stick with it. Safety and sanitary conditions are better today than they were 30 years ago, but it is still a harsh environment." In addition, most workers start out doing reinforcing work. They carry bundles of steel on their shoulders and work bent over tying it and placing it up to eight hours a day. It is physically demanding.

(*continued*)

> But, some people are just called to the work. They see it as a challenge. They love the freedom of it. They are the ones who are dedicated to the work. They are usually very independent sorts and have a confidence that allows them to do the work. Confidence can't be confused with cockiness, however. Contractors don't want workers who are unreliable or those who like to mouth off. It is a unique combination of personality traits that makes a young worker successful in the business.
>
> "Those who are willing to work hard, be respectful of their supervisors, and have a strong work ethic have the best chances of working. A contractor will find ways to keep them employed," says McKelligan.
>
> Rodney, one of his apprentices, agrees. "The best way to stay employed is to be reliable. Your reputation is all you have. Your name is your name. You don't want a contractor saying 'Well, Rodney doesn't like to get up every morning.' Out of the 17 months on a job, I went to work every day. The contractors know that."
>
> When a job is finished and ironworkers go back to the union hall looking for work, they need to show up ready for the job. Rodney says he has seen workers show up looking like they were ready to play basketball. "If you want a job, show up with your tools, ready to work."
>
> If you are going to succeed, you have to be reliable. He started out with 25 or 30 in his apprenticeship class. By the second year, it was down to 17. He says apprenticeship supervisors are strict and they need to be strict. "The work is dangerous and you want to go home to your family at the end of the day."

regional and seasonal. The average annual wages for rebar workers was $39,330 in 2003, with the highest-paid and most experienced workers averaging up to $80,000 a year. Wages in this trade vary widely according to location and the economy. The highest-paid workers were in New York, New Jersey, Oregon, Indiana, and Montana. The highest concentrations of workers were in Nevada, Texas, Louisiana, California, and Florida.

Apprenticeships

Most apprenticeship programs for ironworkers are three years. The classroom component of the program runs about 200 hours each year. In some programs, the course work is transferable to community college programs and earns college credit.

Classes may include trade orientation, trade history, union organization, related mathematics, rigging, reinforcing, post tensioning, trade agreements, welding, fabrication, ornamental erection, structural work, and instruments. Because of the hazards of the job, an emphasis is placed on safety and first aid training. Apprentices start at 50–60 percent of a journeyman's wage and receive regular increases in pay during the apprenticeship period.

Related Skills

This work requires excellent physical condition and stamina. The materials used for ironworking are heavy and bulky so above average physical strength is necessary. Balance, agility, and excellent eyesight, including peripheral vision and depth perception, are essential. If you are considering this trade, you must be comfortable working high above the ground.

Preparation for an apprenticeship in ironwork may include high school courses in blueprint reading, general math, and mechanical drawing.

Resources

For information about apprenticeships in ironworking, contact your local apprenticeship organization. The following can provide further information about ironworking apprenticeships.

Associated Builders and Contractors (ABC)
Workforce Development Department
4250 N. Fairfax Dr., 9th Floor
Arlington, VA 22203-1607
Phone: (703) 812-2000
E-mail: gotquestions@abc.org or CraftTraining@abc.org
Internet: http://www.abc.org

Associated General Contractors of America
333 John Carlyle St., Suite 200
Alexandria, VA 22314
Phone: (703) 548-3118
Internet: http://www.agc.org

International Association of Bridge, Structural,
    Ornamental, and Reinforcing Ironworkers
Apprenticeship Department
1750 New York Ave., NW
Washington, DC 20006
http://www.ironworkers.org
Use the link to "IW Locals" to find a local in your state

Women in the Trades

Although the "Rosie the Riveter" workers of World War II took on major construction and production jobs during the war, often with excellent support services like day care and meals programs, they were sent home and forgotten once the war was over. Opportunities for women were extremely limited until equal rights legislation started opening doors.

Job opportunities for women in the trades opened up with changes in the law during the 1970s. Affirmative action programs sought to bring more women into jobs previously identified as "nontraditional." Most of these jobs provide wages and benefits well above those traditionally filled by women.

The Department of Labor describes nontraditional jobs for women as jobs where less that 25 percent of the workforce is female. That makes construction work one of the most nontraditional job sectors in the country. Women represent between 2 and just under 6 percent of the workers in individual construction jobs. Today, women apprentices in construction make up just 3 percent of the total apprentices in the field.

Although things have improved since affirmative action legislation, the construction industry has yet to meet the 1981 goal of 6.9 percent. Contractors and union representatives say there are too few qualified applicants.

Women carpenters set a door jamb during a construction demonstration project. Photo courtesy of NYC District Council of Carpenters.

EMPLOYMENT FOR WOMEN IN CONSTRUCTION

All Construction Jobs	3 percent
Glaziers	5.7 percent
Sheet Metal Workers	4.8 percent
Highway Maintenance Workers	3.8 percent
Crane and Tower Operators	3.3 percent
Construction Laborers	3 percent
Floor Installers and Finishers	2.6 percent
Cement Masons, Concrete Finishers, and Terrazzo Workers	2.3 percent
Electricians	2.1 percent
Drywall Installers and Tapers	1.9 percent
Plasterers and Stucco Masons	1.9 percent
Carpenters	1.6 percent
Operating Engineers	1.3 percent
Roofers	1.3 percent
Plumbers, Pipe Fitters, and Steamfitters	1 percent
Brickmasons, Blockmasons, and Stonemasons	.9 percent
HVAC Installers	.6 percent
Structural Iron and Steelworkers	0 percent

Source: Nontraditional Occupations for Women in 2003, U.S. Department of Labor, Women's Bureau, June 10, 2004.

"That fries me," says Maura Russell of Boston's Women in the Building Trades. "We have tons of women coming in all the time, but they have a hard time getting those jobs." She says she isn't sure the discrimination is intentional, but it is there. When young women apply for apprenticeship programs, program overseers may be trying to find women to fit the program, but they have this arbitrary number in their heads. They may think if they take in one or two women applicants, they are doing a good job. Even if they have ten good women applicants and take one or two, they think what they have done is sufficient.

Once on the job, these women represent the entire gender, but the comparisons are one-sided. If they perform poorly, they hurt the chances for the next woman in line. If they perform well, it doesn't seem to make a positive difference.

Organizations like Women in the Trades are trying to make a difference (see Resources section below). Many sponsor outreach programs hoping to attract young women to the trades, some sponsor pre-apprenticeship programs that can sometimes provide women applicants with a few extra points in the application process, some offer support for women already on the job, and some offer scholarship programs. Those organizations are there to support young women who are interested in working construction.

Sure, there are obstacles for women. There is still discrimination and harassment in some cases, but for the young woman who wants a good job with good pay, the benefits are well worth the struggle.

"The trades are a great career and the work is very satisfying. I tell young women they can make a difference in people's lives," says Russell. "When people have no heat, and they are calling you, and you can go in and make that situation better, you are the expert. It is satisfying work. You also get good benefits and wages that can support a family. If you want a job where women receive equal pay for equal work, the trades give you that."

If you want to work in the trades, you have to be strong in both body and spirit. Construction work requires everyone be physically fit. For women entering the workforce, they must also be determined.

"Don't let people discourage you. Not your family; not your friends" says Russell. "Women have to be very persistent and strong in themselves. It takes someone pretty secure in themselves and quite committed to the choice."

For more information about women working in the trades and for further information about apprenticeship programs in the trades, the following resources will help. If there is no organization in your state, contact one of the national organizations for support and referrals. The Chicago Women in the Trades site is especially good.

Resources
National Organizations
Coalition of Labor Union Women
1925 K St., NW, Suite 402
Washington, DC 20006
Phone: (202) 223-8360
Internet: www.cluw.org

Tradeswomen Now and Tomorrow (TNT)
c/o CWIT, 1455 S. Michigan Ave., Suite 210
Chicago, IL 60605
Internet: http://www.tradeswomennow.org

National Association of Women in Construction (NAWIC)
327 S. Adams St.
Fort Worth, TX 76104
Phone (800) 552-3506
E-mail: nawic@nawic.org
Internet: http://www.nawic.org

Working Women—AFL/CIO
Internet: http://www.aflcio.org/issuespolitics/women/

Wider Opportunities for Women (WOW)
815 15th St., NW, Suite 916
Washington, DC 20005
Phone: (202) 638-3143
Internet: http://www.work4women.org

State Organizations
Chicago Women in Trades
1455 S. Michigan Ave., Suite 210
Chicago, IL 60605
Phone: (312) 942-1444
E-mail: cwitinfo@cwit2.org
Internet: www.chicagowomenintrades.org

Hard Hatted Women
3043 Superior Ave.
Cleveland, OH 44114
Phone: (218) 861-6500
E-mail: info@hardhattedwomen.org
Internet: http://www.hardhattedwomen.org

Nontraditional Employment for Women (NEW)
243 W. 20th St.
New York, NY 10011
E-mail: new@new-nyc.org
Internet: http://www.new-nyc.org

Northern New England Tradeswomen
51 Park St.
Essex Junction, VT 05452
Phone: (802) 878-0004
E-mail: info@nnetw.org
Internet: http://www.nnetw.org/

Oregon Tradeswomen, Inc.
1714 NE Alberta St.
Portland, OR 97211
Phone: (503) 335-8200
Internet: http://www.tradeswomen.net

Tradeswomen, Inc.
1433 Webster St.
Oakland, CA 94612
Phone: (510) 891-8733, ext. 313
Internet: http://www.tradeswomen.org

Washington Women in Trades
P.O. Box 837
Seattle, WA 98111-0857
Phone: (206) 903-9508
Internet: http://www.wawomenintrades.com

Women in Construction Company, LLC
114 North First Ave. West
Duluth, MN 55802
Phone: (218) 733-1451
E-mail: admin@womenworking.org
Internet: www.womenworking.org

Recommended Reading
   Eisenberg, Susan. *We'll Call You If We Need You:*
   Experiences of Women Working Construction.
   Ithaca: ILR Press, 1988.

Other Jobs in Construction

To find out more about other jobs in construction, consult
Appendix C in the back of the book to select a trade. Then, use
the information presented in the final chapter to find out more.

4 Entertainment and the Arts

ENTERTAINMENT

There are hundreds of different jobs in the entertainment industry. Most require at least a bachelor's degree in the arts or in a technical field. Although the Department of Labor lists several entertainment- and arts-related registered apprenticeship programs, most are inactive. There are currently three active registered apprenticeship programs—actor, stage technician, and wardrobe supervisor.

Actor

Actor	O*NET/SOC	27-2011.00
	DOT	150.027.010
	RAIS	0862

Actors may perform on stage, in videos, in motion pictures, and on the radio. Although those who work on Broadway, in the motion picture industry, or for national television are the most recognizable, most find employment doing local, small-scale theatrical, film, or advertising projects. Some work in nightclubs, in amusement parks, or in industrial training films. The numbers of talented people in this field far outnumber the jobs available, and actors often have to find additional jobs to help pay the bills. Of course, we all know the success stories, and maybe you will be one of them. Most overnight success stories, however, have years of previous work experience behind them.

Job Outlook and Wages

Competition for jobs in acting is fierce. Although jobs in this area are expected to grow about as fast as average—up about 18 percent, the numbers of people trained in the field will grow at least as fast.

The average annual salary for actors in the United States was $48,940 in 2003. This figure can be misleading, however, because a few actors with extremely high salaries can throw averages way out of whack. Members of the Actor's Equity Association, which represents stage actors, received a minimum salary of $1,354 each week as of June 2003 when working on Broadway. Those in off-Broadway productions earned between $479 and $557 a week as of October 2003. Equity actors performing in regional and touring companies earned between $531 and $800 a week in 2003. (Those with touring companies receive additional funds for living expenses.)

Members of the Screen Actors Guild (SAG) and the American Federation of Television and Radio Artists received a minimum of $2,352 each week for speaking parts as of July 2003, putting them in the six-figure salary category. That, of course, assumes they work 52 weeks a year. The average annual salary for SAG members was less than $5,000 a year!

Here are some surprising statistics. In 2003, New York and California were not the top-paying states, although they are in the top five—the District of Columbia, Arizona, Virginia, California, and New York. As might be expected, the highest concentrations of workers were in New York and California, followed by Nevada, Florida, and Virginia.

Apprenticeships

Acting apprenticeships are available across the country, most often with regional or community-based theater companies. Many programs include related studies, including acting workshops. Apprentices appear in regional productions and many are paid or at least receive stipends and housing. Most of these apprenticeships are highly competitive, and applicants must have previous acting experience and win positions through auditions. Some well-established theater companies, like the

Williamstown (Massachusetts) Theatre Festival, offer apprenticeships to promising students in a fee-based program. Here, students may take master classes and dialogue sessions with notable professionals. They learn about running a professional theater company working in the technical departments. Apprentices may audition for small parts in the theater's productions and are guaranteed an audition appointment for the following year's Act I/Non-Equity Company. Other theater companies across the country offer similar fee-based programs.

Related Skills

Young people interested in acting should take advantage of every opportunity they have to perform. High school productions and local theater productions can help prepare students for apprenticeships and careers in acting. Summer opportunities in local, regional, summer stock, theme park, or cruise line performances can help earn qualifying credits toward an actor's union membership.

Those interested in film and television work can gain experience at local cable stations or small production companies. Many local cable companies are required to provide local programming opportunities. You may get some training as the host of a local program.

Most, but not all, actors graduate from colleges and universities with degrees in theater, liberal arts, or fine arts. Many receive formal dramatic training in college or through an acting conservatory program.

Resources

For more information about apprenticeships, contact your local apprenticeship organization, a local or regional theater company, or your local cable company. For more information about educational programs for actors, contact:

National Association of Schools of Theatre
11250 Roger Bacon Dr., Suite 21
Reston, VA 20190
Internet: http://nast.arts-accredit.org

For information about actors unions

Actors Equity Association
165 West 46th St.
New York, NY 10036
Phone: (703) 437-0700
E-mail: info@arts-accredit.org
Internet: http://www.actorsequity.org

American Federation of Television and Radio Artists
New York National Office
260 Madison Ave.
New York, NY 10016
Phone: (212) 532-0800

Los Angeles National Office
5757 Wilshire Blvd., 9th Floor
Los Angeles, CA 90036-3689
Phone: (323) 634-8100
Internet: http://www.aftra.org/aftra/aftra.htm

Screen Actors Guild—Hollywood
5757 Wilshire Blvd.
Los Angeles, CA 90036
Phone: (323) 954-1600 (main switchboard)
(800) SAG-0767 (for SAG Members outside Los Angeles)

Screen Actors Guild—New York
360 Madison Ave., 12th Floor
New York, NY 10017
Phone: (212) 944-1030
Internet: http://www.sag.org

Stage Technician

Stage Technician	O*NET/SOC	27-4011.00
	DOT	962.226-014
	RAIS	0521

Maybe acting isn't the career you are interested in, but you would still like to be involved in the entertainment industry.

Maybe your skills are more hand-on than dramatic. Maybe you are the kind of person who likes to build things. Or maybe you are interested in sound or lighting. No matter what the technical skill, there is a job to be done onstage.

Stage technicians, sometimes called stage hands, are responsible for almost everything that goes on behind the scenes at concerts, plays, and opera productions. They may be skilled carpenters, building the sets. They may specialize in lighting, making sure the audience can not only see the performer, but also see them in the light that the director and lighting designer imagined. Some technicians specialize in sound work. Jobs for technicians can be broad, taking on the entire production, or they can be as specialized as handling the sound for one performer. They may set up and take down all of the sets and props needed for a production and take care of any necessary maintenance as well.

Workers in this field are often on-the-go. Their work comes and goes along with touring and performance companies. Technicians sometimes work for a particular theater or performance center, where the job comes to them, and sometimes they work for a particular production company, and they travel along. Stage technicians are not 9-to-5 workers. When they are working, they can work long hours getting everything ready for an evening production. In fact, most of the work is in the evening or on weekends.

Job Outlook and Wages

This is a specialized field, and the Bureau of Labor Statistics does not provide detailed information for this job. Salaries for stage technicians vary widely, depending on the venue, the geographical location, and the size of the production. Those who are members of a union usually earn higher wages. The work for stage technicians is often interrupted, and they seldom work a full-week, full-year job. The Department of Labor classifies this apprenticeship program with audio and video equipment technicians, where the average annual wage is $35,110.

According to 2004 reports from a local community college specializing in educating stage technicians, the average wage for a beginning journeyperson in the field was between $28,000 and $32,000 in a medium-sized market, and $40,000+ annually in a large market. Those working regularly for large touring companies can earn more than $80,000 a year.

Job growth in this area is expected to be better than average—up over 26 percent through 2012. Live entertainment, such as Broadway and off-Broadway theaters, touring productions and repertory theaters in many major metropolitan areas, theme parks, and resorts are expected to offer many job opportunities.

Apprenticeships

Many stage technicians get technical degrees from colleges or universities with specialized theatrical departments. Because they need such a broad background, they may study electricity, carpentry, sound, lighting, video production, audio production, and other technical courses. Some schools provide the related training required for registered apprenticeship programs.

Apprenticeship programs may be sponsored by employers, employer associations, or joint employer/union partnerships. The International Alliance of Theatrical Stage Employees, Moving Picture Technicians, Artists and Allied Crafts of the United States, Its Territories and Canada (IATSE) sponsors apprenticeship programs for stage technicians. In some cases, apprenticeship course work qualifies for college credit and may be applied toward associate's or bachelor's degrees in the field. Stage technician programs are usually three-year programs requiring a minimum of 144 hours of related training each year. Related training may include course work at a local college or university, including courses such as introduction to theater, occupational health and safety, scenery construction, stage properties, stage lighting, stage rigging, costumes, makeup, wardrobe, stage audio, audio-visual, and special effects. The costs of the related training are often, but not always, paid by the sponsoring organization.

Apprentices are often expected to bring their own tools, including an adjustable wrench, a mag light, a tape measure, a multitip screwdriver, leather gloves, safety goggles, protective earplugs or headphones, steel-toed boots, and a tool belt.

Related Skills

As with all careers in the theater, high school productions offer an excellent introduction to the jobs that must be done to make a performance successful. Summer work in theatrical productions also provides excellent experience. High school classes in carpentry and electronics are also useful in this field. Consider volunteering at a local or regional theater to get additional experience.

Resources

For more information about apprenticeship programs, contact your local apprenticeship organization, local and regional theater companies, and your IATSE local (see below).

IATSE International
1430 Broadway, 20th Floor
New York, NY 10018
Phone: (212) 730-1770
Internet: http://www.iatse-intl.org
Includes a directory of local union sites.

For more information about theatre technology:

United States Institute for Theatre Technology
6443 Ridings Rd.
Syracuse, NY 13206
Phone: (800) 938-7488 or (315) 463-6463
E-mail: info@office.usitt.org
Internet: http://www.usitt.org

For more information about jobs in the theater, check out Theatrejobs.com, http://www.theatrejobs.com.

Wardrobe Supervisor

Wardrobe Supervisor	O*NET/SOC	39-3092.00
	DOT	346-361-010
	RAIS	0494

Ever wonder how an actress can be on stage one minute wearing a long evening gown, leave the stage, and just a moment or two later appear in a totally different outfit, maybe with a different hairstyle? Ever wonder how those dancers on stage can leap and spin and roll on the floor and come up with the costume still intact? Ever wonder who keeps those costumes looking fresh each night?

All of this is handled by workers in the costume and wardrobe department of theatrical and film productions. Wardrobe supervisors are ultimately responsible for all aspects of managing the clothing, including wigs, worn by actors, actresses, and sometimes models.

They may begin by analyzing the script to learn the details of the costume work. They may be involved in the design and production of the costumes as well. They arrange costumes in order of appearance, so actors and actresses can make quick changes. They work with the designers, helping to create and adjust the details of the designs. They measure the performers and make the necessary alterations to ensure a good fit. They also make sure they look good on stage, keeping the costumes clean, repaired, and pressed.

The complexity of the wardrobe supervisor's job is directly related to the scale of the production. In some instances, wardrobe specialists do all the jobs of creating and maintaining the clothing and related fabric items (tablecloths, draperies, flags, etc.) for an entire production. In larger productions, they may work with a large staff of designers, sewers, dressers, and other specialists to be sure the wardrobe is in order.

When production companies rent costumes for the production, the wardrobe supervisor is responsible for picking up and returning the costumes, in addition to keeping them in good condition during the performance.

In some cases, wardrobe supervisors are involved in making budget recommendations and seeing that the wardrobe part of the production stays within budget.

Workers in this field must research the time period of the production, making sure the costumes reflect the historical era or mood called for.

Job Outlook and Wages

As you might expect, wages in this field can vary widely. People in this field work for small, local theatrical production companies and they work on major theatrical productions on Broadway and film productions in Hollywood. Most of the work is temporary or seasonal—lasting for the length of a production. Some dance and theatrical companies in larger cities require that workers be members of the United Screen Artists' Union, where wages are higher and benefits are regulated. Community theaters don't usually require that their costume workers be in the union. Many workers in the field work part time or freelance, supplementing their income with other jobs.

In 2003, the average annual salary for a costume attendant was $28,700. As might be expected, the highest annual salaries were paid in New York, followed by Massachusetts, Illinois, Michigan, and Washington. The highest concentration of workers, however, was in Nevada, where there are a large number of stage productions. New York came in second, with Florida, Missouri, and Mississippi following behind.

This is an extremely competitive business with few workers in the field. With an expected increase in the entertainment industry in general, jobs in this area are expected to grow just slightly faster than average—up 25.1 percent through 2012. However, that translates into only 2,000 job openings across the country during that time.

Apprenticeships

Apprenticeships for those with just a high school diploma are just about unheard of. Sometimes local theater companies will work with young people just starting out, but for the most part these are volunteer opportunities. Some established regional theatrical companies do offer apprenticeship programs, both for high school and college students. Some smaller ones offer stipends and housing in exchange for work, but registered apprenticeship programs pay their apprentices a salary and may or may not assist with related classroom instruction.

For the most part, those who get apprenticeships have a degree in theater arts or design, or are near the completion of a degree.

Locals of the United Scenic Artists, Local 829 labor union offer designer apprentice programs. Programs and qualifications vary, but in general these are not entry-level positions. They are looking for apprentices with degrees in a related field or are near completion of a degree, and those who have some experience with stock theater, regional theater, or low-budget films. They also require initiation fees. See the resources section below for more information.

Related Skills

Workers in this field have multidimensional backgrounds in theater, dance, and design combined with the technical skills of production. Those still in high school can prepare for jobs in the industry by taking part in high school productions, working with the costumes. Courses that include sewing, art history, dance appreciation, performance opportunities, textiles, photography, film, and videotape will be helpful.

Local and regional theaters are often looking for volunteers to help with production. You can get some experience working with these groups.

Still, most people in this field start with at least an associate's degree in design or other theater-related program. Most have a bachelor's degree in theater arts, design, technology, or fine arts, and many have advanced degrees in costume design. If you are really serious about working in this field, think about going to college.

Resources

For information about apprenticeships, contact your local apprenticeship organization, local and regional theater or dance companies, or a United Scenic Artists, Local 829, affiliate.

United Scenic Artists, Local 829, is a labor union representing designers and artists in the entertainment industry. It is a nationwide, autonomous local of the International Alliance of Theatrical Stage Employees (IATSE).

Links to locals in New York, Chicago, Los Angeles, Miami, and New England (including phone numbers, addresses, and e-mail addresses) can be found at the USA homepage, http://www.usa829.org.

A fascinating resource with links to a wide variety of information about costumes is the Costumer's Manifesto, http://www.costumes.org.

For background information about costume design, see The Costume Designer's Guild, http://www .costumedesignersguild.com.

ARTS

Folk and Traditional Arts Apprenticeship Programs

Across the country, folk and traditional artists and artisans practice arts that have been handed down from generation to generation. In order to see that these arts survive, folk and traditional arts apprenticeship programs are available across the country. These programs are not DOL-registered apprenticeship programs, but rather grants given to artists. The sponsors are not local businesses, but cultural arts councils across the country. These programs are as varied as the cultures they represent. Some programs offer apprenticeships focusing on worldwide cultures. Others provide master/apprentice matches designed to help pass along regional arts and crafts from very specific areas in the United States.

These programs match a skilled and respected artist in the field with an apprentice who is knowledgeable in the area but looking to improve his or her skills. Most often the programs provide funds to the master and a stipend to help the apprentice pay for materials and travel. Apprenticeship funding in this area varies from $1,000 up to about $5,000, so these don't provide a living wage for either the master or the apprentice. They do, however, supplement incomes enough to help the folk art practitioners continue their work. A list of the programs available across the country is included with the State Arts Organizations listing in Appendix A.

To give you an idea of just how varied these programs can be, a list of some of the programs funded in the past few years is in the sidebar "Arts and Crafts Encouraged Through Folk and

ARTS AND CRAFTS ENCOURAGED THROUGH FOLK AND TRADITIONAL ARTS APPRENTICESHIP PROGRAMS

Here are some of the traditional arts and crafts that are being protected through apprenticeship programs across the country:

Chinese knot tying
Jewish klezmer music
Irish ceili dancing
Scottish Highland piping
Brown ash basketmaking
Orthodox icon painting
Fly tying
Canoe building
Ox yolk making
Porcupine quill work
Star quilt making
Red River cart construction
Beadwork
Cradleboard making
Buckskin tanning
Japanese koto music
Mexican folk dancing
Metal casting
Pauite songs
Native American Church stack (medicine) boxes
Horsehair weaving
Thai flower arranging
Polish paper cutting
Stone carving
Appalachian fiddling
Irish step dancing
Woodcarving
Chicano corrido singing
Tamburitza music and polka
Hawaiian gourd growing, decorating, and dying
Lauhala weaving
Hawaiian quilting
Hulu (feather)
Japanese classical dance

Okinawn uta-sanshin (classical singing)
Cantonese opera and related instruments
Traditional blues and jazz
Hmong community ceremonial wedding songs
Laotian dance
Gospel music
Cape Verdean dance
Bookbinding
Finnish poppano weaving
Cuatros, tiples, bordanuas—Puerto Rican stringed instruments
Byzantine iconography
Folk tales from Benin
Peruvian folkloric dance
French-Canadian social dancing
Norwegian rosemaler painting
Irish traditional flute playing
Traditional boat construction techniques
Armenian fiddle (kamancha) playing
Laotian khene (mouth organ) playing
Storytelling
Rya rug making
Metal engraving
Yakama salmon preparation
Hawaiian guitar
Ukranian beaded necklaces
Indian drumming
Yugoslavian folk guitar
Korean salpuri dance
Hispanic ironwork
Eritrean music
Klickitat basketry
Totem carving
Mexican singing
Inupiaq Eskimo dancing

(*continued*)

Makah cooking and food preparation	Yakama hats and sally bags
Khmer dance	Kathak dance
Latvian embroidery	Hoh paddle songs
Tsimshian design and carving	Waashat culture and language
Korean kayagum	Lummi family stories
Korean poongmul nori	Chilkat and ravens-tail blanket weaving
Conjunto accordion	Afro-Cuban dancing and singing
Twana dances and songs	Philippine folk dance and music
Longhouse songs	Haida and Nishga weaving
Yakama wedding veils	Ukrainian pysanky
Mexican American harp	Egyptian oud
Suquamish basketweaving	Northwest coastal Indian art
Tlingit carving	Croatian lijerica music

Traditional Arts Apprenticeship Programs." If you look at some of the arts on this list and think, "What on earth is that?" you begin to know why these apprenticeships have been established. Without them, these arts would die, and no one would know what they were.

Glassblower

Glassblower	O*NET/SOC	51-9195.04
	DOT	772.381.022
	RAIS	0219

Humans have blown glass to make both decorative and practical objects from as early as 250 B.C. By 79 B.C., Pliny the Elder wrote that that glass cups had begun to replace precious metals as a status symbol among the rich. The art and craft of glassblowing has been passed down through generations, and today, glassblowers still create both artistic and functional objects from glass.

Glassblowers gather the melted glass onto a long blowpipe and begin shaping it by blowing air through the pipe and into the glass. As the glass expands, they rotate the pipe and spin the glass to prevent the object from becoming lopsided. Then, they may pinch the glass with tongs to create indentations and

Don Parkinson lost a hockey scholarship after an injury and wasn't able to go to college. Instead, he "talked his way" into an apprenticeship program through the Pairpoint Glass Works Company in Bourne, Massachusetts. Today he creates glass beads for his own gallery and is employed as a glassblowing and glass pressing demonstrator at the Sandwich Glass Museum in Sandwich, Massachusetts. Photo by Penny Hutchins Paquette.

GLASSBLOWING TRADITION CONTINUES WITH APPRENTICESHIP PROGRAMS

David McDermott, Don Parkinson, and Carolyn Stokes-Walker have all learned the art of glassblowing while on the job at the Pairpoint Glass Works, America's oldest glassworks. Glassblowing master Robbie Mason has taught all three while they served apprenticeships there.

David, now an artist and teacher with works on display at the Metropolitan Museum of Art and the Museum of Fine Arts in Boston, says he learned by watching and listening and "becoming putty with eyes and ears." He began working as an apprentice engraver and then "begged" to begin blowing glass. "Finally, Robbie let me try one thing, and of course, I couldn't do it. I waited several weeks and tried again. I would make it; he would smash it. Then, he would let me try another. The only way I would know if I was doing it right is he didn't say anything." Eventually David mastered the craft and then helped Robbie pass the gift along to Don Parkinson. Don now creates glass beads for his own business, works with David in his gallery, and gives glassblowing demonstrations at the Sandwich Glass Museum.

Carolyn is the newest apprentice. She got interested in glassblowing during a semester apprenticeship while she was in college. She did all the grunt work, cleaning up in exchange for learning to work with glass. Then, she became the next in line to learn the trade from Robbie Mason when she was hired as an apprentice at Pairpoint.

"He teaches until you get it," she says. "He teaches us to let the glass work for you, using gravity and centrifugal force. If we don't need a tool, we don't use it. . . . This is true-and-true glassblowing, Old World–style. Here, they pay you to learn, and that is a privilege."

To see some of the work created at Pairpoint Glass, visit its website, http://www.pairpoint.com/.

desired shapes. Once the shape is complete, they must break the object away from the pipe, without damaging the product. Glassblowers sometimes use glass molds or presses to shape the final object. Some glassblowers produce products we use every day, like bowls and glasses, and some create works of art, sometimes functional as well as artistic.

Job Outlook and Wages

The Bureau of Labor Statistics includes this work along with that of molders, shapers, and casters and doesn't offer specific information about glassblowers in particular. Because glassblowing can be both a production job and an artistic job, the job outlook may be different depending on the category. Production jobs are expected to grow more slowly than average, and automation may reduce the need for glassblowers. On the other hand, jobs for fine artists are expected to grow faster than average. Glassblowers who work in the arts can probably expect to see job growth at a similar rate. As with all artistic endeavors, competition is strong when trying to place work in art galleries.

In the Department of Labor occupational classification that includes other molders and shapers of clay, glass, plaster, concrete, and stone, the average salary was $26,420 in 2003. These, however, are manufacturing jobs and not jobs in the arts. Those who work for colleges and universities and are more likely teaching the craft as both an art form and a trade averaged $49,810 a year.

Apprenticeships

Glassblowing is a trade and art that has been passed down from generation to generation through apprenticeship, and apprenticeship continues to be one of the best methods for learning today. Training programs with glass companies and with individual journeymen are available. Programs last from three to four years and usually include 144 hours of related training. In addition to registered apprenticeship programs leading to jobs in industry and the arts, arts councils across the country sponsor artisan apprenticeship programs intended to supplement the artisan's income and see that the art is passed along to the next generation.

Those working in the production area generally begin their apprenticeships right out of high school. Those working in the arts may get basic training the same way, but may also have a background in arts education.

Related Skills

Those interested in working in this field need to be able to take the heat. The ovens and furnaces used in the production of glass materials are extremely hot. While in high school, courses in chemistry, blueprint reading, and the arts can help prepare you for a career in glass-blowing.

According to Carolyn Stokes-Walker, an apprentice at Pairpoint Glass (see sidebar on page 126), those interested in working with glass need to have a positive attitude and enjoy working with other people. They also have to be willing to ask questions in order to learn.

GLASS ARTISAN DIES TRYING

During the reign of Tiberius (13-47 A.D.), a glassmaker discovered how to make unbreakable glass. He astonished the rulers by dropping a beautiful transparent vase to the ground. Although it dented, it didn't break. Tiberius quizzed the glassmaker and found that he had not shared the recipe for his success with anyone. Was he celebrated for his discovery? No. Tiberius had him put to death and had his workshop destroyed for fear this new discovery would reduce the value of imperial gold and silver.

Resources

For more information about apprenticeships in your state, contact your local apprenticeship organization or local arts council. For more information about glass production:

The Corning Museum of Glass
One Museum Way
Corning, NY 14830
Phone: (800) 732-6845
Internet: http://www.cmog.org/

International Guild of Glass Artists
Internet: http://www.igga.org

Historic Trades Apprenticeship

Because this apprenticeship program provides a unique combination of talents and skills, it doesn't fit into a particular DOT category. These specialists are actors, teachers, historical interpreters, and tradespeople in Colonial Williamsburg, the only site in the United States where you can complete a formal apprenticeship in an 18th-century trade.

Costumed historical interpreters help teach visitors how colonial Americans actually lived at sites throughout Williamsburg. Among them are 90 skilled artisans working in trades just as they did 300 years ago. They are masters, journeymen,

A milliner (left) helps adjust a new dress with the help of her apprentice (right). Photo courtesy of the Colonial Williamsburg Foundation.

and apprentices demonstrating their crafts and teaching visitors. Among these workers are milliners, sawyers, coopers, blacksmiths, founders, tailors, weavers, wheelwrights, shoemakers, silversmiths, wigmakers, cabinetmakers, carpenters, engravers, joiners, and printers.

Preserving the skills and techniques of the 18th century, these costumed interpreters and craftspeople use the same materials and methods as the original workers.

Like most historical sites, Williamsburg caters to the tourist industry and schedules its hours to be most accommodating to visitors. That means interpreters must be willing to work weekends and holidays, when many travelers can visit the site.

Job Outlook and Wages

The Bureau of Labor Statistics does not collect data on historic interpreters, but employment ads in 2004 suggested beginning earnings at about $8 to $10 an hour, or between $18,000 and $30,000 annually. In the Williamsburg apprenticeship programs, salaries increased with experience and knowledge of the trade. Obviously, the market for historic interpreters is limited. Living history museums and farms, historic homes, travel companies, and the National Park Service use historic interpreters.

Apprenticeships

Although a variety of museums and history sites and the National Park Service offer training programs for historic interpreters, Colonial Williamsburg is the only historical site that offers apprenticeship programs in the historic trades. The development of these highly trained interpreters of history can take many years—usually between six and seven years for an apprentice to reach the journeyman level. In addition to their on-the-job training, apprentices also study the original objects they are expected to produce. When an apprentice is hired for a particular trade or to work in a particular trade shop, he or she is accepted for a trial period of 45–60 days. During that time, the apprentice must demonstrate an aptitude for the trade as well as the communication skills necessary to present the work and the trade to visitors. Costumes and historic research materials are provided. Interpreters at Colonial Williamsburg spend several months in the classroom learning and reviewing history, 18th-century language, and acting skills, including improvisation.

Related Skills

A love of history, a love of performing, and an aptitude for the specific trade is an essential part of this job. High school students should take as many courses in history, particularly American history, as possible. Courses in industrial arts, including carpentry and sewing, can provide background for colonial trades.

Several colleges across the country offer degrees in historic interpretation, but a degree in this field isn't necessarily a requirement. Many interpreters start their careers by volunteering at a historic site or museum. Here, opportunities to learn more about history and opportunities to practice performance skills can help develop the special talents needed in this field. The National Association for Interpretation offers certification in historic interpretation and offers workshops and conferences. The Association for Living History, Farm and Agricultural Museums also offers programs.

Those looking for apprenticeships will need basic knowledge and proficiency in the trade they hope to enter. They will also need the ability to perform research and to interpret the information.

Resources

The Colonial Williamsburg Foundation
P. O. Box 1776
Williamsburg, VA 23187-1776
Phone: (757) 229-1000
Internet: http://www.history.org/

Living History, Association for Agricultural Farm,
    and Museums
Internet: http://www.alhfam.org
Includes links to living history sites

The National Association for Interpretation
P.O. Box 2246
Fort Collins, CO 80522
Phone: (970) 484-8283
Internet: http://www.interpnet.com/home.htm

OTHER ARTISTS AND ARTISANS

Although there are no formal, registered apprenticeship programs for individual artists and artisans, painters, sculptors, potters, performance artists, and all variety of artists and artisans can qualify for support from national and state cultural organizations. Most often this comes in the form of funding for individual artists. These funds go to the most experienced and gifted artists across the country. Individual artist's fellowships funded by state arts councils are included in the State Arts Organizations listing in Appendix C. Some states sponsor a Youth Employment in the Arts Program. These programs provide funds to not-for-profit organizations so they can provide employment opportunities for high school students. The program provides for paid, on-the-job training to enhance the personal development of young people. Contact your local arts organization for further information.

5 Health Care Careers

Interested in health care? Always wanted to find a career that will help you help others? You couldn't pick a better time to enter the heath care industry. Whether you want to be involved directly with patients or prefer to help on a technical support services team, jobs will be there for you. Careers in health care will be among the fastest-growing job opportunities for the next ten years and beyond. According to the Bureau of Labor Statistics, the number of people in older age groups with much greater than average heath care needs will grow faster than the total population. New technologies and treatments will help severely ill or injured people survive, and they will need extensive therapy and care. The need for medical assistants and home health care practitioners will sky rocket in response.

Information about apprenticeships in specific health care jobs follows. For more information about health care professions in general:

American Medical Association
Health Professions Career and Education Directory
515 North State St.
Chicago, IL 60610
Internet: http://www.ama-assn.org/ama/pub/category/
  2322.html

Artificial Eye Makers

| Artificial | O*NET/SOC | 51-9195.04 (glass) |
| Eye Makers | | 51-9082.00 (plastic) |

Ocularist	DOT	*713-261.010 (glass)*
		713-261.014 (plastic)
	RAIS	*0011 and 0012*

One of the most competitive and unusual apprenticeable occupations is the artificial eye maker or ocularist. There are only about 300 ocularists in the United States. There are no schools for this specialty and there is no way to get this training without working directly with someone highly qualified in the field. An ocularist is a carefully trained technician skilled in the arts of fitting, shaping, and painting artificial eyes, or ocular prostheses. Not only does the ocularist create the prosthesis, but he or she instructs the patient on how to care for the prosthesis and provides long-term patient care. In the past, artificial eyes were made of glass. Today, most are acrylic.

Ocularists must not only be skilled technicians, but they must have excellent people skills as well. The loss of eye,

A HISTORY OF PROSTHETIC DEVICES

ARTIFICIAL EYES

Roman and Egyptian priests fabricated artificial eyes as early as 4 B.C. In ancient times, artificial eyes were made of pieces of painted clay that were attached to pieces of fabric to be worn over the eye socket. Hundreds of years passed before the first eye was made to fit within the eye socket. The earliest artificial eyes were made of gold and were colored with enamel. The highly skilled glassmakers of Venice first started making artificial eyes in the early part of the 16th century. Not only were these early replacements crude and uncomfortable, they were fragile as well.

By the mid-19th century, German glassblowers developed superior techniques and Germany became the center of artificial eye production. German ocularists began to tour the United States, making glass artificial eyes in one area and then moving on to another.

During World War II, the German products were boycotted, and the United States government in conjunction with American companies began mass-producing artificial eyes from acrylic plastic. These ready-made or stock eyes were not made for a particular individual, and didn't fit a particular individual. They could even be ordered by mail!

(continued)

Today, high-quality acrylics are used to create the artificial eyes that are custom fit and custom colored for an individual patient. These eyes not only match the patient's remaining eye, but can move as well.

ARTIFICIAL LIMBS

The first written history of an artificial limb dates back to Herodotus' *The Histories* (484 B.C.). In his writings, he relates the story of an imprisoned soldier who cut off part of his foot to escape from the stocks and later wore a wooden replacement. The oldest known prosthesis was discovered in a tomb in Capua, Italy. The artificial leg made of copper and wood dates to 300 B.C.

During the Middle Ages, many prostheses were made from iron and were created by the same craftsmen who made armor.

In the early 1500s, Ambroise Pare, who learned his surgical skills as an apprentice barber-surgeon, designed an iron leg that was the first to use an articulated knee joint.

During the 19th century, there were many improvements in artificial limbs, with wood replacing iron. James Potts created artificial tendons in his design that lifted the toe when the knee was bent. Around the same time, an arm prosthesis was created that could produce movement in the hand and arm through a series of straps attached to the opposite shoulder.

Unfortunately, it is war that brings about even more improvements in prosthetic devices. During the Civil War, many soldiers lost limbs. Improvements in anesthesia (ether and chloroform) allowed for longer surgeries and stumps could be shaped to improve the fit of prosthetic devices. The government funded prosthetic devices for veterans. World War II left many amputated soldiers, and the National Academy of Sciences established the Artificial Limb program in 1945. Doctors and engineers worked together to improve both the appearance and function of limb replacements.

In 1985, Ernest Burgess helped develop a prosthetic device called the "Seattle Foot." Burgess studied the running motions of amputees and with newer and stronger lightweight materials created a foot with springiness that helped achieve a more natural gait. Lighter-weight materials make today's prosthetic devices more comfortable, and myoelectric upper limbs now give patients the ability to open and close their hands. State-of-the-art improvements have been made while treating soldiers injured in the war in Iraq. Experts at the Walter Reed Army Medical Center help create and fit prosthetic devices that can cost as much as $150,000 each. Returning soldiers with arm injuries may be fitted with a prosthetic device that has interchangeable, task-oriented hand parts—one for shaking hands, another with a hook, another with a plierslike grip. An amputee may receive a hand that helps him write, play golf, or go fishing. Funds for these sophisticated devices come from the federal government. Between 2001 and 2004, Congress gave Walter Reed $6.6 million for the costs of treating amputees.

Research on prosthetic devices is ongoing. Today, research at Stanford University Medical Center is looking at the possibility of creating an implant capable of bridging severed nerve connections. This research may prove beneficial to those with both limb and eye injuries.

whether due to disease, injury, or birth defect is a highly emotional experience for the patient, and the ocularist must be skilled in helping. Ocularists treat people of all ages from the youngest of children to senior citizens.

An ocularist begins by making an impression of the eye socket, using the same materials a dentist might use to make an impression of your teeth. Then, an acrylic model is made and fitted to the individual patient, ensuring a good fit. The ocularist then hand paints the prosthesis to create a natural-looking eye. Ocularists create the pupil, iris, and white of the eye and sometimes use fine cotton or silk threads to create the blood vessels of the artificial eye. Most often, the ocularist is making an ideal match to the remaining eye of the patient.

Job Outlook and Wages

The Department of Labor classifies ocularists with other medical appliance technicians, so it is difficult to get information specific to this highly specialized area. The general field is expected to grow about as fast as average—16 percent. There are no specific salary ranges for this field, but in 2003, other prosthetic technician salaries ranged from an average of $27,890 to $46,910. Since many in this field own their own businesses, salaries are probably much higher.

Apprenticeships

First, you must find a board-certified ocularist willing to train an apprentice. That is the only way you can be trained in this field. That can be pretty daunting, but if this is a career you are truly interested in, you can find lists of the 230 ocularists across the United States at the American Society of Ocularists website. The ASO recommends that you contact one in your area and, if you are able to relocate, that you attend one of their annual conventions. Conventions provide excellent opportunities to meet ocularists from across the country and around the world.

Apprenticeships for ocularists include 10,000 hours of on-the-job training and last five to seven years. Unlike other apprenticeships, classroom training happens only twice each year at American Society of Ocularists' (ASO) conferences. The

ASO provides educational courses for those preparing to take the National Examining Board of Ocularists exams. Lectures and workshops are presented for those preparing for the exam, including hands-on opportunities and visual presentations. Some programs are followed by exams. There is no formal school for this training.

The ASO expects apprentices to be involved 100 percent of their time in the on-the-job training aspect of the job. Apprentices learn to fit and fabricate the ocular prosthesis under the direction of a "board-approved diplomate ocularist." The apprentice receives a handbook with established guidelines for each level of training. Apprentices are tested during regular intervals to evaluate the on-the-job skills learned. The ocularist curriculum includes fitting theory, materials, processing and fabrication techniques, iris and sclera tinting techniques, orbital anatomy and physiology, patient care and office hygiene, and office management and communication techniques.

Wages for ocularist apprentices are negotiated directly with the training ocularist.

Related Skills

The job of an ocularist requires a unique combination of science and art. Ocularists must have a thorough understanding of human anatomy and be able to hand-craft and paint a synthetic eye that is an identical match to the patient's remaining eye. Courses in science and courses in the arts can help prepare a young person for this apprenticeship. Apprentices must have a high school diploma or GED and many have related experience or some college background.

Because this is such a competitive apprenticeship, high school students could benefit from volunteer opportunities in the field—maybe a summer job doing clerical work in an ocularist's office or other health-related volunteer work.

Resources

For more information about apprenticeships in your area, contact your local apprenticeship organization. For more information about ocularists and for a list of ocularists in the United States:

American Society of Ocularists
P.O. Box 7342
Charlottesville, VA 22906-7342
E-mail: info@ocularist.org
Internet: http://www.ocularist.org

Dental Assistant

Dental Assistant	O*NET/SOC	31-9091.00
	DOT	079-361.018
	RAIS	0101

Dental assistants are involved in many activities in the dentist's office, including patient care, clerical activities, and laboratory duties. For young people interested in comforting others, this can be a very rewarding job. Most people are nervous when they sit in a dentist's chair, and one of the most important roles of the dental assistant is to help the patient feel comfortable.

Assistants provide an extra set of hands for the dentist when he or she is working on a patient, handing the dentist instruments and suctioning the patient's mouth to keep it clear and dry. They may assist the dentist by applying anesthetics or cavity prevention materials to the teeth. Assistants also have the job of keeping all of the instruments and equipment sterile. As a dental assistant, you may have instructional duties as well, teaching patients how to care for their teeth or giving postoperative instruction when patients have had teeth removed.

In some areas, dental assistants take dental X-rays and process the film. In some areas, assistants also take on laboratory duties, making casts of teeth from impressions. They may clean and polish removable appliances and make temporary crowns.

In some offices, dental assistants do clerical work as well— scheduling appointments, sending bills, crediting payments, keeping dental records, and ordering supplies.

There were about 266,000 dental assistants in 2002, and one-third of them worked part time. If you are looking for a job that will allow part-time work, this may be right for you.

Job Outlook and Wages

The outlook for those looking for jobs as dental assistants is excellent, as growth in this area is expected to grow much faster than average—up a whopping 42 percent through 2012! It is one of the fastest-growing occupations. Today's older population of baby boomers have kept their natural teeth, unlike the generations before them. This large population will provide a need for additional services in dentist's offices across the country. As the workload of dentists increases, more and more will hire assistants to help them with routine tasks.

The average annual salary for a dental assistant was $28,230 in 2003, with the most experienced workers averaging about $40,000. The largest number of dental assistants works in dentist's offices. The largest concentration of dental assistants was found in Washington, Utah, Oregon, California, and Alaska. The top-paying states were the District of Columbia, Nevada, Colorado, Connecticut, and Massachusetts.

Apprenticeships

Most dental assistants receive their training through informal on-the-job programs. Today, however, many are taking part in apprenticeship programs that allow them to earn a salary while they are enrolled in educational programs that may provide a certificate or, in some cases, an associate's degree. The typical program is one to two years with an additional 144 hours of classroom study each year. Course work for dental assistants may include dental theory, chairside assistance, clinical science, dental anatomy, clinical procedures, dental emergency training, dental pharmacology, dental radiology, and preventive dentistry. Community and technical schools across the country offer dental assistant programs, and some even allow high school students to begin their studies before graduation. In some programs, the course work will be paid for by the sponsor; in others, you may have to pay for your classes yourself. But in either case, you will be paid for the on-the-job portion of your training. Pay varies and will be negotiated with your employer.

If you are interested in working in this field, you may want to consider volunteering in a dentist's office to gain some experience and to get your foot in the door. As with all programs, apprenticeships in dental assistance look for young people who are eager to work and who demonstrate a good work ethic.

Related Skills

Dental assistants need good people skills because one of their primary roles is to comfort the patient. Because you will be handling dental tools, good manual dexterity is important as well.

The work of an assistant is so varied, a variety of high school courses can help prepare you for the job. Both general math and business math can help with the accounting component of the job; science classes, including biology and first aid, are also good preparation.

Resources

To find out more about the availability of dental assistant apprenticeships in your area, contact your local apprenticeship organization. Talk to your own dentist, dental hygienist, and dental assistant about the job. You might be surprised to learn your own dentist is looking for help.

For more information about dental assistants, contact:

Commission on Dental Accreditation
American Dental Association
211 East Chicago Ave., Suite 1814
Chicago, IL 60611
Internet: http://www.ada.org
Type "dental assistant" in the search box.

Dental Assisting National Board, Inc.
676 North Saint Clair, Suite 1880
Chicago, IL 60611
Internet: http://www.danb.org

American Dental Assistants Association
35 East Wacker Dr., Suite 1730
Chicago, IL 60601
Internet: http://www.dentalassisting.org

National Association of Dental Assistants
900 South Washington St., Suite G-13
Falls Church, VA 22046

Dispensing Opticians

Dispensing Opticians	*O*NET/SOC*	*29-2081.00*
	DOT	*299-361.010*
	RIAS	*0089*

Most people who wear glasses or contact lenses have visited with a dispensing optician. There were 63,000 of them working in 2002. Basically, they help people see better. People in this job have close contact with their clients or patients. They fit the eyeglasses and contact lenses prescribed by ophthalmologists or optometrists. They begin by translating the written prescriptions into the required specifications of the lenses. Then, they make precise measurements to ensure the patient's lenses align with his or her eyes. In addition to the medical side of the job, dispensing opticians must also have an eye for fashion, helping customers select appropriate lenses.

Some also fit contact lenses, measuring the shape and size of the eye and selecting the type of contact lens material.

In addition to the work of fitting eyeglasses and lenses, they must also keep records on prescriptions, work orders, and payments. They may perform other administrative duties as well.

DISPENSING OPTICIAN LEARNS THROUGH APPRENTICESHIP

Jill Fries has been working in optical shops since she was in high school. She says she saw an ad in school and applied for the job, as simple as that. She hadn't really thought about being an optician. In fact, she started out as a receptionist, but after a few years at a local optical shop, Jill applied for an apprenticeship at a national optical chain store.

Jill displays a pupilometer used to fit lenses. Photo by Penny Hutchins Paquette.

Jill says it is unusual for them to hire someone as an apprentice from the outside. National optical chains usually fill those positions from within their own company, looking for young people who have potential.

Because Jill already had a few years of experience in the field, they were willing to hire her. The program she completed is a 6,000-hour program that usually takes about three years to complete. The related training is also done on the job. The company provides a series of training DVDs that supplement the hands-on training.

Jill says it takes more than an interest in optics to become a dispensing optician. "You definitely have to be tolerant and patient. You have to be able to work with the public. . . . Some people are cut out to do that and some people aren't. . . . It is a sales-driven environment, too. You are selling a product, so you have to be good at sales as well."

You also have to be willing to work nights and weekends. A typical week for Jill includes two evenings and a weekend. She gets one weekend off each month.

Apprenticeship has given her the opportunity to secure what she calls "another degree"—one that will provide her with job security as she works on her master's degree.

Job Outlook and Wages

As the baby boomers reach middle age, more and more people will need vision correction. Jobs for dispensing opticians are expected to grow about as fast as average—up just over 18 percent through 2012. That will mean an additional 23,000 jobs nationwide. Although the increase is significant, the number of actual jobs overall is limited.

The average wage for a dispensing optician in 2003 was $28,570, with the best paid averaging about $44,000 a year. The top-paying states were Connecticut, New Jersey, Massachusetts, New York, and Rhode Island. The highest concentrations of workers were in Nebraska, North Dakota, South Dakota, Indiana, and Montana.

Apprenticeships

Apprenticeships for dispensing opticians run between two and three years, with a minimum of 144 hours of additional classroom training each year. Related training hours may be offered at local community colleges, through home-study programs, or through DVD programming provided by the employer. The training may include anatomy of the eye, optical lab techniques, frame fitting and selection, lens dispensing, office management, sales, and ophthalmic optics. Most programs are sponsored by large employers of dispensing opticians. In some cases, classroom training leads to an associate's degree. Dispensing opticians are licensed in some states.

Related Skills

High school programs that provide good preparation include physics, basic anatomy, geometry, and mechanical drawing. Manual dexterity is important in forming and fitting the lenses, and a good sense of fashion in also helpful. Those interested in working as dispensing opticians must have good people skills as well. In some cases, apprentices are hired from within the company. For example, someone working as a frame fitter may express an interest in the apprenticeship program and may be hired.

Resources

For more information about apprenticeship programs in your area, contact your local apprenticeship agency. For more information about dispensing opticians, contact:

National Academy of Opticianry
8401 Corporate Dr., Suite 605
Landover, MD 20785
Phone: (800) 229-4828
E-mail: info@nao.org
Internet: http://www.nao.org
Includes information on home-study courses.

Commission on Opticianry Accreditation
P.O. Box 3073
Merrifield, VA 22116-3073
Internet: http://www.coaccreditation.com/

Medical Laboratory Technician

Medical Laboratory Technician	*O*NET/SOC*	*29-2012*
	DOT	*078-381.014*
	RAIS	*0323*

If you have always wanted to work inside a laboratory in a hospital or university research center, this might be the entry-level job for you. Clinical laboratory technicians work with lab technologists, performing supportive services. Under the supervision of a technologist, lab technicians may analyze body fluids looking for bacteria, parasites, microorganisms, or abnormalities. They prepare specimens for examination and operate automated systems that analyze the specimen. They assist in the diagnostic area by hunting for clues to the absence, presence, extent, and cause of diseases. Histotechnicians specialize in blood work, cutting and staining tissue samples for microscopic examination by pathologists. Phlebotomists work directly with patients, collecting blood samples.

Job Outlook and Wages

According to Department of Labor estimates, jobs in this area will exceed the number of job seekers. Growth in this area is expected to be about average—up 18 percent by 2012, but as the population ages and more health issues can be diagnosed through blood work, increases in the numbers of diagnostic tests will create the need for more jobs. In addition, workers will be needed to replace retiring workers and those who leave to do other jobs.

The average salary for a medical technician in 2003 was $30,940, with the most-experienced workers averaging more than $44,000 a year. Most technicians work in hospitals, but a large number also work in doctor's offices and medical laboratories. Insurance carriers also hire laboratory technicians, and those working in that area were among the highest paid. States with the highest salaries for lab technicians included Rhode Island, Connecticut, Alaska, New Jersey, and New York. The highest concentrations of workers were in Arizona, Missouri, Tennessee, Pennsylvania, and Massachusetts.

Apprenticeships

Many lab technicians learn their jobs through informal on-the-job programs. There are formal registered apprenticeships, however, and they usually run about two to three years, with a minimum of 144 hours of classroom study each year. Some programs earn college credit toward an associate's degree. Typical classes would include hematology, health care, general and biological chemistry, immunology, human physiology, clinical chemistry, and microbiology. Most classroom components are offered at local community colleges. For those who want to advance their careers, continued education to become a clinical laboratory technologist will increase responsibilities and pay.

Hospitals, blood banks, for-profit laboratories, nursing homes, public health facilities, doctor's offices, and private businesses hire lab technicians and may sponsor apprenticeship programs. In many hospitals, they recruit for apprenticeship programs from within the hospital's employees first. If you volunteer at a local hospital, you may receive priority when apprenticeships become available.

Sponsoring organizations may pay the costs of the educational component of the apprenticeship, or they may have scholarships available to fund the program.

Related Skills

High school courses in the sciences, especially biology, can be good preparation for lab technicians. People who do well in this job enjoy problem solving. They pay great attention to detail and are accurate and reliable. They need good communication skills, both spoken and written. If you have an interest in medicine and are fascinated by laboratory tests, you should excel.

Resources

For information about apprenticeship opportunities in your area, contact your local apprenticeship organization. For more information about laboratory technicians, contact:

American Association of Blood Banks
8101 Glenbrook Rd.
Bethesda, MD 20814-2749
Internet: http://www.aabb.org

American Society for Clinical Laboratory Science
6701 Democracy Blvd., Suite 300
Bethesda, MD 20817
Internet: http://www.ascls.org

American Society for Clinical Pathology
2100 West Harrison St.
Chicago, IL 60612
Internet: http://www.ascp.org

American Society for Cytopathology
400 West 9th St., Suite 201
Wilmington, DE 19801
Internet: http://www.cytopathology.org
Includes information about new clinical testing procedures.

Clinical Laboratory Management Association
989 Old Eagle Rd.
Wayne, PA 19087
Internet: http://www.clma.org

Orthotic-Prosthetic Technician

Orthotic-Prosthetic	*O*NET/SOC*	*51-9082.00*
Technician	*DOT*	*712-381.034*
		(orthotic)
		712-381.030
		(prosthetic)
	RAIS	*0911 and 0377*

Orthotic and prosthetic technicians have jobs that bring
together hearts and hands. It is a job for the young person
more interested in the production aspects of health care. This
is a job that helps those who are disabled lead normal lives,
and it requires excellent hand work to create the appliances
that improve the patient's life. Orthotic technicians fabricate
arm and leg braces and other corrective devices for those who
have disabling conditions. Prosthetic technicians fabricate
artificial limbs.

Job Outlook and Wages

Jobs for orthotic and prosthetic technicians are expected to
grow about as fast as average—up 16 percent through 2012,
with a growth of 5,000 jobs over the same period. In 2003, the
average annual salary for appliance technicians was $27,890,
with experienced workers averaging up to $46,910 a year.
Technicians who were certified usually earned higher salaries.
Those who worked in the offices of health care practitioners
earned the highest salaries. In 2003, the top-paying states were
Washington, New Jersey, Connecticut, Rhode Island, and Idaho.
The highest concentration of workers was found in Kansas,
Pennsylvania, North Carolina, Colorado, and Arkansas.

Work as a technician can provide an entry-level position for
the prosthetist and orthotist professions. These jobs require a

bachelor's degree and a 12-month residency program, but prerequisite courses for the job may be included in the technician's training. In 2003, salaries for these professional-level jobs could range from $45,000 to $90,000 a year.

Apprenticeships

Apprenticeships for technicians average two years with a minimum of 144 hours each year of related classroom study. On-the-job training is supervised by a registered technician or a certified prothetist or orthotist. Under the direction of the professional, the apprentice learns to fabricate, repair, and maintain orthotic and/or prosthetic devices. Related course work may take place at a local community college or other approved educational setting, and may include anatomy, prosthetic tools and materials, kinesiology, fabrication theory, fabrication application, psychology, related computer skills, and biomechanics.

Related Skills

Technicians need good manual dexterity and visualization skills. High school courses than can help prepare for this job include the sciences—biology and anatomy as well as mathematics, including algebra. Shop classes can also be helpful.

Those interested in apprenticeships might try volunteering in an orthotist's or prosthetist's office or in a hospital or rehabilitation setting where patients needing orthotic or prosthetic devices may be treated.

Resources

For information about apprenticeships, contact your local apprenticeship organization. For more information about orthotic and prosthetic careers and education, contact:

American Academy of Orthotists and Prosthetists
1650 King St., Suite 201
Alexandria, VA 22314
E-mail: academy@oandp.org
Internet: www.oandp.org

Orthotics and Prosthetics Careers
Internet: www.opcareers.org

National Commission on Orthotic and Prosthetic Education
   (NCOPE)
330 John Carlyle St., Suite 200
Alexandria, VA 22314
Phone: (703) 836-7114
E-mail: info@ncope.org
Internet: http://www.ncope.org

Pharmacy Technicians

Pharmacy Technicians	*O*NET/SOC*	*29-2052*
	DOT	*074-381.010*
	RIAS	*0844*

Pharmacy technicians, also called pharmacy assistants, help
pharmacists provide medication and other health care products
to patients. They work under a pharmacist's supervision,
counting tablets and labeling bottles in a retail or mail-order
pharmacy. Technicians may receive written prescriptions,
including refills, from patients, as well as electronic
prescriptions sent from doctors' offices. In some cases, they may
weigh, measure, and mix medication. They are also responsible
for pricing the prescription. Prescriptions must be checked by a
pharmacist before they are handed over to a patient.

In hospitals, nursing homes, and assisted-living facilities,
pharmacy technicians may also assemble a 24-hour supply of
medicine for every patient, packaging and labeling each dose
separately. A pharmacist must check the work for accuracy
before the medicine is given to a patient.

Technicians may be certified by taking the National
Pharmacy Technician Certification Exam that confirms the
competency of the worker.

Job Outlook and Wages
There were 211,000 pharmacy technicians in 2002, and the
number of jobs is expected to grow faster than average—almost

29 percent through 2012. The aging population will have greater pharmaceutical needs and as more medications are prescribed to this aging population, the need for pharmacy technicians will continue to grow.

Most technicians work in retail pharmacies, including drugstore chains, grocery stores, and department stores. About 22 percent worked in hospital settings in 2002. A small number worked in mail-order and Internet pharmacies.

The average annual wage for a pharmacy technician was $23,860 in 2003, with the highest-paid technicians averaging $33,780. Workers in pharmaceutical and medicine manufacturing were among the highest paid. The states with the best incomes for pharmacy assistants were California, Alaska, Washington, the District of Columbia, and Oregon. The highest concentrations of workers were in West Virginia, Minnesota, Missouri, Alabama, and Rhode Island.

Apprenticeships

The pharmacy assistant apprenticeship is one to two years, with at least 144 hours of related classroom work each year. Related course work may include pharmaceutical terminology, pharmaceutical calculations, classification of drugs, pharmaceutical dosage forms, administration routes, record keeping, pharmaceutical techniques, pharmacy law, and pharmacy ethics. Apprenticeships require a high school diploma or GED and no felony convictions. In some programs, related training programs may be applied to an associate's degree.

If you are interested in working as a pharmacy apprentice, get some additional experience by volunteering in a hospital or other health care setting.

Related Skills

High school classes in the sciences, mathematics, and health are good preparation for pharmacy technician apprentices. As with many entry-level jobs in the health field, volunteer work can give you an edge when looking for an apprenticeship.

Pharmacy assistants need to have good written and spoken comprehension skills and a facility with numbers.

Resources

Apprenticeships for pharmacy technicians are not available in all states. Check with your local apprenticeship organization for more information. For more information about pharmacy technicians, contact:

American Society of Health-System Pharmacists
7272 Wisconsin Ave.
Bethesda, MD 20814
Phone: (301) 657-3000
Internet: http://www.ashp.org/

Pharmacy Technician Certification Board
2215 Constitution Ave., NW
Washington, DC 20037
Internet: http://www.ptcb.org

New and Growing

Across the country, health care organizations and apprenticeship agencies have been looking for opportunities to bring people into the health care sector and, just as important, to keep them there. Innovative programs, like the Health Care Apprenticeship Initiative in Wisconsin, are providing flexible learning options for health care education and professional development. Started in summer/fall 2004, apprenticeship programs were available in the medical coder, mammography technologist, CT technologist, and MRI technologist fields. It is likely states across the nation will also open new health care career options through apprenticeship training. For more information about the Wisconsin programs, call 608-261-8487.

Another health care initiative hopes to address the nursing shortage with an innovative program being implemented in five areas. If you are interested in entering the health care field, have a sincere desire to help others, and want a good start on an exciting and rewarding career path, read more about it below.

Certified Nurse Assistant (CNA)

Certified Nurse Assistant	O*NETSOC	31-1012.00
	DOT	355-674.014
	RAIS	0824

CNAs help care for the physically or mentally ill, injured, disabled, or infirm individuals in hospitals, nursing care facilities, long-term care facilities, or other health provider facilities. Nurse assistants may answer patient calls, deliver messages, serve meals, make beds, and help patients eat, dress, bathe, and get into or out of bed. They may also take temperatures, pulse rates, respiration rates, and blood pressures. CNAs are aware of a patient's physical, mental, and emotional condition and report changes to the nursing staff. In many health care settings, they are the first line of defense and the person who knows the patient best. CNAs, like all health care professionals, must maintain patient records and critical notes.

CNA is often the entry-level position for more advanced positions in health care.

Job Outlook and Wages

Across the country, the job outlook for nurse assistants is excellent. The Department of Labor estimates job growth of nearly 25 percent through 2012, with a total of 365,000 job openings. The increasing emphasis on rehabilitation and the long-term needs of the growing elderly population will present job opportunities for those entering the nursing career.

Unfortunately, in 2003 the salary for an entry-level nursing position was below the national average for high school graduates. The average annual salary for nurse assistants was $21,050, with the most experienced averaging about $28,570. The highest-paid CNAs worked in Alaska, Connecticut, New York, Massachusetts, and Maryland. The highest concentrations of assistants were in North Dakota, South Dakota, Rhode Island, Kansas, and Nebraska. Still, if you want to enter the health care field, this could be a good place to start. Opportunities for CNAs to continue their educations and advance in the health care industry are improving (see apprenticeships below), and with increased education levels, salary levels increase as well.

In addition, CNAs have the opportunity to be entrepreneurs as well. As the baby boomer generation ages, more will need help with the activities of daily living, what the health profession calls ADLs. CNAs are trained to fill that need and are starting up their own home health care businesses or working with community organizations to provide private duty care.

Licensed Practical Nurse (LPN) or Licensed Vocational Nurse (LVN)

Licensed Practical	O*NET SOC	29-2061.00
Nurse or Licensed	DOT	079-374.014
Vocational Nurse	RAIS	08373

LPNs, also called LVNs in some states, do much of the direct nursing care for patients today. Under the supervision of a registered nurse or physician, they may take vital signs, prepare and give injections, apply dressings, collect samples, perform routine lab tests, and assist patients with personal hygiene. In long-term care facilities, they may help evaluate a patient's needs, develop plans for patient care, and help supervise certified nurse assistants (CNAs). They maintain patient records and critical notes related to the health care plan. LPNs may also work in doctors' offices and in private homes. In the doctor's office, a LPN may be responsible for clerical duties as well as nursing duties, and in private homes, LPNs may help prepare meals and train family members in simple nursing tasks.

Most of the 682,500 LPNs work in hospitals or long-term care facilities. Other top industries include doctors' offices and home health care services.

Job Outlook and Wages

With the severe nursing shortage, job opportunities for LPNs are excellent. Jobs will be up about 20 percent through 2012, with the greatest growth coming in long-term care facilities and in the home health care field. As the population ages, more Americans will need long-term care, whether in a health care facility or at home. The DOL estimates there will be 295,000 job openings for LPNs through 2012.

LPNs are better paid than CNAs. The average annual salary was $33,210 in 2003, with the most-experienced LPNs earning an average of $44,740. LPNs received the best pay in the District of Columbia, Connecticut, Rhode Island, Massachusetts, and Delaware. The highest concentrations of nurses were in Arkansas, West Virginia, Louisiana, Oklahoma, and North Dakota. LPNs who choose to advance their careers and become registered nurses can earn much more. The average salary for registered nurses nationally was $51,230 in 2003, with the highest paid and most experienced averaging $71,210. That's a substantial increase in salary. Those who can work while they advance their careers can usually better afford this career change. The job outlook for registered nurses is excellent. Nursing jobs will be up 27.3 percent through 2012, with more than a million job openings during that time. The difficulty will come in finding a nursing school. With such a shortage of nurses, there is also a serious shortage in teaching professionals, limiting the numbers of young people who can enter nursing school.

Apprenticeships

There are developing opportunities for apprenticeships in nursing. A new health care initiative hopes to reverse the nursing shortage by providing new opportunities for training through apprenticeship. The CAEL/DOL Nursing Career Lattice Program helps both incumbent and newly hired workers enter and advance in health care careers. The program is being implemented by the Council for Adult and Experiential Learning (CAEL) in collaboration with the Employment and Training Administration of the U.S. Department of Labor. The goal of the program is to increase the number of CNAs, LPNs and RNs, while helping sponsoring organizations maintain a stable workforce.

According to Pamela Tate, president and CEO of CAEL, the program will use "innovative models for the delivery of clinical and didactic training to make it easier for participants to earn nursing credentials while continuing to work." The new program is being implemented in five sites currently: Chicago, Houston, Washington state, Sioux Falls, and Maryland.

Melissa Kahn, site coordinator for the Chicago program, says, "the CAEL/U.S. DOL Nursing Career Lattice Program is customized based on the needs of the hospital or skilled-care facility and varies from site to site based on the shortages they face. Each facility or hospital may implement a different apprenticeship model and provide several opportunities to their incumbent workers. The goal is to create greater opportunities in the field of nursing, so the DOL sets the basic apprenticeship competency standards, but the employers can modify them to meet their specific needs." Current DOL requirements for CNAs include 2,000 hours of on-the-job training combined with a minimum of 144 hours of related training.

The program hopes to bring new workers into nursing. In many cases, the employer will offer the apprenticeships first to current employees. The goal is to help retain those employees and give them an opportunity to advance their careers. Once current employees have had opportunities to enter the program, apprenticeships may be available to new employees. In some programs, the employers will be hospitals. In others, long-term care health facilities and other health service providers will act as program sponsors.

Individual programs may offer specialization opportunities in geriatric, dementia, pediatric, and restorative care. Young people who choose to enter this field do some of the most important work in the health care industry, providing intimate care to people when they are unable to care for themselves.

Once the initial CNA apprenticeship is complete, the assistants will have an opportunity to move on to the next level, the licensed practical nurse (LPN), or make lateral moves to other fields such as lab technicians. LPN apprentices will take part in competency-based training programs and will prepare for the licensing exam. Once apprentices have completed the LPN portion of the program, they may continue to work in that field, move laterally to other health care positions, or they may have the opportunity to go on to a web-based LPN-to-RN degree program. In this program, local community colleges oversee the program.

Depending on the program sponsor, funding for the classroom portion of the program may or may not be provided. If not, funds may be available through local workforce offices, through nursing associations, or through other health scholarship programs.

Opportunities for nurses will not only be in hospital and extended, skilled-care settings, but in public health departments, in the public service industry, in corporate settings, in schools, and for the food industry as well.

Related Skills

High school classes in the sciences and math will help prepare you for a nursing career. The new apprenticeship program looks to draw workers from the sponsor's current workforce, so those already working in sponsoring facilities will have the first opportunities

If you are hoping to enter the nursing field, volunteer opportunities can help you get the experience you will need to enter the field or to apply for an apprenticeship. Help deliver hot meals for your local meals program, work at your local hospital's information desk, be a friendly visitor. Contact your local hospital or your own pediatrician's office for work opportunities. Reach out. You will find work than can help prepare you for this career.

Resources

For apprenticeship opportunities, contact your local apprenticeship agency for information. For further information, contact:

CAEL
55 E. Monroe St., Suite 1930
Chicago, IL 60603
Phone: (312) 499-2600
Internet: http://www.cael.org

National Federation of Licensed Practical Nurses, Inc.
605 Poole Dr.
Garner, NC 27529
Internet: http://www.nflpn.org/

National Association for Practical Nurse Education
    and Service
P.O. Box 25647
Alexandria, VA 22313
Phone: (703) 933-1003
Internet: http://www.napnes.org

6 Installation, Maintenance, and Repair

From the workers we look to every day, like those who install and repair our cable systems or the highly trained specialists who repair race cars, workers in charge of installation, maintenance, and repair help keep both industrial and consumer systems and products up and running. Installation, maintenance, and repair work is as varied as the products these workers service. In general, they are the specialists that industry owners and personal consumers are grateful to see, whether the air conditioner is broken on an especially hot day or a manufacturing plant is on hold because of a faulty machine. If you enjoy making things work, these jobs might be right for you.

Automotive Workers

Automotive Body	*O*NET/SOC*	*49-3021*
and Related Repairs	*DOT*	*807.381-010*
	RAIS	*0024*

The people who repair our damaged automobiles are often called autobody technicians. If you enjoy working with your hands, have a creative side, and appreciate the beauty of automobile design, this could be just right for you. And as long as people drive, there will be work for you. According to *Collision Repair Industry Insight* online magazine, collision repair is a $33.9 billion a year industry.

Autobody technicians straighten out, repair, and replace those broken bits of our cars, restoring them to their former glory. When necessary, they straighten bent frames by chaining or clamping the frames and sections to special alignment machines that use hydraulic pressure to straighten and align the damaged area.

When portions of the car body are badly damaged, they may cut away the dented parts with a pneumatic metal-cutting gun and then weld in the replacement area. Small dents and dings can be hammered out or popped out with special jacks and hammers. They may also fill small dents and then smooth the filler to a finished surface.

Newer plastic body parts can be repaired as well. When these areas need to be repaired, autobody technicians can reform them using a hot-air welding gun or by placing them in hot water and then hand-shaping the plastic back to its original form.

Large repair shops produce assembly-line repairs with workers specializing in one type of work, whether it is straightening a frame or filling dents. In small shops, one worker may do all of the work, including doing the finish painting. In larger shops, specialists in automotive painting complete the job.

Job Outlook and Wages

The job outlook for repair workers is mixed. Job growth in this sector is expected to be about average—up about 13.2 percent through 2012. As the population grows, the need for new cars goes up. As the number of cars on the road increases, the numbers of accidents will go up as well. As accidents go up, the numbers of people needed to do the repairs should grow as well. In addition to the new workers needed in the field, retiring workers will create openings as well.

Larger body shops, using the assembly-line approach to repairs, can increase productivity, reducing repair time and expanding the number of cars they can repair. New lighter-weight materials can mean more damage to cars during accidents, resulting in the vehicle being declared a total loss. Also damage to the newer electronic components in automobiles can be very expensive to repair, also leading to total loss estimates. This means the demand for repairs will decrease as the number of cars declared a total loss increases.

Opportunities will be best for highly skilled workers who have had formal training, like the training available in apprenticeship programs. Workers certified by the National Institute of Automotive Service Excellence can reach the top classification as an ASE Master Collision Repair and Refinish Technician.

The average annual wage for autobody technicians was $35,760 in 2003. The top wage earners in this field averaged close to $60,000 a year. The highest-paid workers were in Colorado, Alaska, Nevada, Maryland, and Virginia. The highest concentrations of workers were in Montana, Michigan, North Dakota, South Dakota, and Pennsylvania. There were 173,590 workers in this field in 2003.

Apprenticeships

Autobody repair apprenticeships are four years, with a minimum of 144 hours of related training. Most apprentices work full time during the day and attend community college programs two nights each week. In most programs, applicants must be high school graduates and at least 18 years old. Those with technical high school training have an advantage, but it is not required.

Related course work may include welding, body shop management and estimating, technical math, refinishing, structural repair, nonstructural repair, industrial safety, preparing metal, fiberglass, and plastic for painting; removing, repairing, and replacing trim; metal finishing, grinding and shaping; and polishing/detailing.

In some areas, employers and the International Association of Machinists and Aerospace Workers form joint apprenticeship committees to sponsor apprenticeship programs. In other areas, they may be sponsored by the local apprenticeship organization and area employers.

Related Skills

Those with both mechanical and artistic abilities will do well in this field. Manual dexterity is essential. Those who have the opportunity to take auto body courses while still in high school will be well prepared for apprenticeship opportunities. Those in traditional high school should take classes in body shop, design, art, and mathematics.

Resources

For more information about apprenticeships, contact your local apprenticeship organization. For more information about educational programs and careers in auto body repair, contact:

Accrediting Commission of Career Schools and Colleges
    of Technology
2101 Wilson Blvd., Suite 302
Arlington, VA 22201
Internet: http://www.accsct.org

Autobody Repair News
Internet: www.abrn.com/

Inter-Industry Conference on Auto Collision Repair
    Education Foundation
3701 Algonquin Rd., Suite 400
Rolling Meadow, IL 60008
Phone: (800) 422-7872

National Automobile Dealers Association
8400 Westpark Dr.
McLean, VA 22101
Internet: http://www.nada.org

International Association of Machinists and
    Aerospace Workers
9000 Machinists Place
Upper Marloro, MD 20772
Phone: (301) 967-4500
E-mail: websteward@goiam.org
Internet: http://www.goiam.org/visit.asp?c=3894

National Institute For Automotive Service Excellence
101 Blue Seal Dr., SE, Suite 101
Leesburg, VA 20175
Internet: http://www.asecert.org

Automotive Service	*O*NET/SOC*	*49-3023*
Technicians and	*DOT*	*620.261-010*
Mechanics	*RAIS*	*0023*

Do you just love tinkering with cars? Do you always want to know how things work? Are you interested in electronics as well? You may be right for a career as an automotive service technician.

What used to be a greasy-hands and dirty-clothes job has been transformed into a high-tech job diagnosing and repairing both mechanical and electrical problems in today's automobiles. Not only does today's automobile mechanic use traditional hand tools to repair problems, he or she is also using electronic diagnostic equipment and computer-based technical manuals to do the job.

These technicians work closely with the automobile owner to find out what problems the owner is having with the car. Then, they begin diagnosing the problem, testing the related systems to see if they are in good working order. Once the source of a problem has been identified, the technicians may compare electronic diagnostic readouts with normal readings supplied by the manufacturer.

Some workers specialize and only work with transmissions, electrical problems, or hydraulic problems. Some tune-up specialists make the necessary adjustments to ensure the engine runs properly. Some work exclusively on the new alternative-fuel vehicles that are becoming more popular.

Most automobile mechanics work for automotive repair and maintenance shops or automobile dealers.

Job Outlook and Wages

Jobs in this area are expected to grow about as fast as average—up about 12.5 percent through 2012. The number of cars on the road will increase as the population grows, creating an increased demand for maintenance and repair services. With an increase in dual-worker households, the number of families with two cars has grown. However the Bureau of Labor Statistics expects a slowdown in the growth of the driving-age population, as the smaller, post-baby boom generation comes of age. They expect this will curb demand for both cars and trucks. In addition, improved vehicle quality and durability will mean a reduction in necessary repairs.

Still, the job outlook will be good for workers with formal technical and mechanical training—the kind of training supplied by apprenticeships.

The average annual wage for an automotive service technician or mechanic was $31,130 in 2003. The top 10 percent of workers in the field averaged $53,120. Alaska, Delaware, the District of Columbia, Colorado, and New Jersey were among the top-paying states. The highest concentrations of workers were in Delaware, North Dakota, New Hampshire, Vermont, and Arizona.

In December 2003, the *Boston Globe* reported that the auto industry is paying salaries of up to $60,000—and in some cases six figures—in addition to the free training it provided. Some were giving signing bonuses or helping students with loans from earlier educational programs.

Apprenticeships

Four-year apprenticeships are necessary in this field. Related technical studies of at least 144 hours each year are also included in the program. Many apprentices work a full day on the job and then continue their studies at approved technical schools or community colleges at night. Most programs require applicants to be a minimum of 18, with at least a high school education. Many applicants have some vocational school or postsecondary course work in automobile repair.

In some areas, programs are jointly sponsored by employers and the International Association of Machinists and Aerospace Workers. In others, automobile dealerships or repair shops may sponsor programs.

In some areas, high school students can get a head start by working in automotive technology through the Automotive Youth Educational Systems (AYES), a collaborative effort between selected high schools, technical schools, and automobile manufacturers. Audi, BMW, DaimlerChrysler, General Motors, Honda, Hyundai, Kia, Mercedes-Benz, Mitsubishi, Nissan, Subaru, Toyota, and Volkswagen are among the manufacturers who offer technical instruction to select high school students in order to encourage young people to enter the automotive fields. You can find out more information about this program in the resources section below.

Related Skills

The new technologies require that those in this field be not only good with their hands, but with electronics and computer technologies as well. Any programs you can take in high school to help you gain knowledge in those areas will help improve your chances of finding an apprenticeship. Shop courses in auto mechanics and electronics are obvious choices, but good communications skills are necessary as well. To see what experienced master technicians suggest, see the sidebar, "Top Ten Tips."

Resources

To find information about apprenticeships in your area, contact your local apprenticeship organization. For more information about automotive technology, see the resources listed below:

Accrediting Commission of Career Schools
    and Colleges of Technology
2101 Wilson Blvd., Suite 302
Arlington, VA 22201
Internet: http://www.accsct.org

Automotive Service Association
P.O. Box 929
Bedford, TX 76095
Internet: www.asashop.org

TOP TEN TIPS FOR AUTO TECHNOLOGY STUDENTS
FROM ASE-CERTIFIED MASTER TECHNICIANS

ASE-certified master technicians were surveyed for their advice to students who want to become automotive service professionals. The following tips are a compilation of the responses.

1. *Education, education, education*—Continue your education and develop strong math, reading, study skills, and computer skills. A strong background in electronics is essential.
2. *Take advantage of on-the-job training, co-op, or apprenticeship opportunities*—Get all the training you can and start in a work environment that caters to service and excellence.
3. *Keep abreast of new technology*—Make a commitment to lifelong learning. There is constant change in technology so take advantage of additional training whenever it is available.
4. *Learn a systems approach*—Vehicles today are complex so it is necessary to understand the interaction of electrical and mechanical components within the total system. Learn how to understand the whole system and you can apply this knowledge across the spectrum of vehicles.
5. *Develop good communication skills*—Learn not only the professional and technical skills but also communication and people skills. Your credibility is linked to your perceived competence.
6. *Keep a positive attitude*—Develop a positive outlook so that you perform proper repairs. Apply yourself—you get exactly as much out of your job as you put into it.
7. *Take pride in your work*—Work on every car as if it were your own. Whatever you do—do it well, it's your signature.
8. *Be honest and ethical*—Stay focused on what is most important, practice good work ethics, be dependable and honest, and fix it right the first time.
9. *Cultivate professionalism in yourself and others*—Act professionally and take pride in your appearance as well as in the shop area. Be a positive role model for others. Show up for work every day and always be on time.
10. *Become ASE-certified*—Certification gives you an edge when you are seeking employment. Your confidence, sense of self-worth, and ability to get a job almost anywhere are improved once you become certified. ASE certification shows your employer that you have proven your technical expertise and that you are among a group of the very best technicians.

Reprinted with permission from the National Automotive Technicians Education Foundation.

Automotive Youth Educational Systems (AYES)
50 West Big Beaver, Suite 145
Troy, MI 48084
Internet: http://www.ayes.org

National Automobile Dealers Association
8400 Westpark Dr.
McLean, VA 22101
Internet: http://www.nada.org

National Automotive Technicians Education Foundation
101 Blue Seal Dr., SE, Suite 101
Leesburg, VA 20175
Internet: www.natef.org/

National Institute For Automotive Service Excellence
101 Blue Seal Dr., SE, Suite 101
Leesburg, VA 20175
Internet: http://www.asecert.org

Avionics Technicians,	*O*NET/SOC*	*49-2091also*
also called Aircraft	*DOT*	*825.261-018*
Electricians	*RAIS*	*0160*

All of us sometimes wonder what keeps airplanes in the air. Of course, we know about the physics of it—the Bernoulli Effect—the difference in pressure between the top and bottom of the wing results in a net upward force, or lift, on the wing. But what about the mechanical and human side of the equation? Who makes sure the pilot gets the information he or she needs to keep that plane in the air?

Avionics (a combination of *airplane* and *electronics*) technicians are among those people who keep the electronics in the airplane operating safely. The radar systems, the radio systems, the electrical controls and switches and junction boxes, the cockpit and light data recorders, the navigation systems, automatic flight control systems, the communications systems, and the lighting and antiskid systems are all installed and maintained by avionics technicians.

These highly specialized electricians begin by reviewing blueprints and wiring diagrams to lay out the installation of aircraft assemblies. They assemble the necessary components and install switches, electrical controls, and junction boxes, using hand tools and soldering irons. Then they test all the components to be sure they are working. They may set up and operate the ground support and test equipment to perform functional flight tests of electrical and electronic systems. They are also responsible for inspecting and maintaining these systems and diagnosing any problems. They make adjustments and repairs and replace parts as necessary. Avionics technicians must be licensed by the United States Federal Communications Commission (FCC).

Job Outlook and Wages

Job growth for avionics technicians is expected to be slower than average—up only 3.4 percent through 2012. The Bureau of Labor Statistics estimates there will be only 6,000 job openings in this field during that time. The numbers are small. The September 11, 2001, attacks forced airlines to cut back flights and as a result, airplanes have been taken out of service. Still, few people choose to train in this field, making opportunities for those who can find and complete apprenticeship programs very good. Right now the best opportunities are with small commuter, regional, and new economy airlines as these are the fastest-growing areas of the aviation industry.

The average annual salary for an avionics technician in 2003 was $43,630. Salary levels were highest in Hawaii, $56,170, followed by Washington, Delaware, Alaska, and Oregon. The highest concentrations of workers were in Kansas, Oklahoma, Utah, Washington, and Alaska.

Many workers in this area are members of the International Association of Machinists and Aerospace Workers and the Transport Workers Union of America.

Apprenticeships

Apprenticeships for avionic technicians average 8,000 hours of on-the-job training, or about four years. Apprentices must also complete at least 144 hours of related instruction. The course work may include aviation electricity, communications, electrical distribution systems, nondestructive inspection techniques, electrical charging systems, landing gear, aircraft electronics, aircraft inspection, avionics digital systems, and maintenance. In some programs, course work may be applied to an associate's degree at a local community college or technical school. Sponsors may include aircraft and parts manufacturers, airline companies, defense services, equipment manufacturers, and air transport service companies.

Related Skills

Those who succeed in this area have good mechanical skills and excellent problem-solving skills. People in this career must have excellent reading comprehension skills because much of the work is presented in writing. Electrical work on airplanes also requires good manual dexterity and good visualization skills.

High school courses that will be helpful in this area include English, algebra, trigonometry, physics, computers, and electronics. People in this field must be willing to check and double-check to ensure safety.

Resources

For more information about apprenticeships in your area, contact your local apprenticeship organization. For more information about avionics technicians, contact:

Professional Aviation Maintenance Association
717 Princess St.
Alexandria, VA 22314
Internet: http://www.pama.org

Diesel Service Technicians	*O*NET/SOC*	*49-3031*
and Mechanics	*DOT*	*625.281-010*
	RAIS	*0124*

Do you love trucks? Their size, their power, all the chrome? Have you ever been amazed at the number of trucks and buses on the road when you make a long car trip? Sometimes there seem to be more trucks than cars. This creates an excellent job opportunity for people in love with those huge machines.

Trucks and buses are powered with diesel engines that are more powerful and more durable than the gasoline-burning engines found in most cars. Diesel service technicians, sometimes called bus and truck mechanics or diesel engine specialists, keep those trucks and buses in good operating order by repairing and maintaining their engines. Some also work on heavy equipment like bulldozers and cranes and diesel electric locomotives. As with automobiles, truck and bus systems have become more complex, and include electronic components that control the operation of the diesel engine.

Diesel technicians use a variety of equipment to repair and maintain these systems. They use the hand tools we are all familiar with like screwdrivers and pliers, but they also use machine tools like lathes and grinding machines and welding and flame-cutting equipment to make repairs. As with the auto technician, diesel technicians also use computerized testing equipment to help diagnose problems with the electrical systems.

Many diesel technicians belong to labor unions, including the International Association of Machinists and Aerospace Workers; the Amalgamated Transit Union; the International Union—United Automobile, Aerospace and Agricultural Implement Workers of America; the Transport Workers Union of America; the Sheet Metal Workers' International Association; and the International Brotherhood of Teamsters.

Job Outlook and Wages

Nearly 250,000 diesel engine specialists were working in the field in 2003. They earned an average wage of $34,970 a year. Most worked for general freight trucking companies, local governments, automotive repair and maintenance shops, motor vehicle parts merchants, and for elementary and secondary schools. As you might expect, many of those industries need a staff of diesel mechanics just to keep their fleets operational.

The National Institute for Automotive Service Excellence (ASE) offers certifications as master truck technicians, or in specific areas of truck repair. Diesel technicians can be certified in more than one specialty. They may also be certified as master school bus technicians or master truck equipment technicians. Certified diesel technicians have the skills and training that transport companies look for.

In 2003, the top-paying states for diesel technicians were Hawaii, Alaska, Massachusetts, Washington, and New Jersey. The highest concentrations of workers were in Wyoming, Arkansas, Iowa, Utah, and Kansas.

Employment in this area is expected to grow about as fast as average—up 14.2 percent through 2012. Job opportunities will increase as freight transportation by truck increases. In addition to being the primary form of transport, truckers also do intermediary service for other forms of transportation, such as train and air. Because diesel engines are more durable and economical than gasoline engines, buses and trucks of all types will increasingly be powered by diesel engines.

Job prospects will be good for well-trained technicians such as those who complete apprenticeship programs or other types of formal training at community colleges or other vocational/technical schools.

Apprenticeships

Apprenticeships for diesel mechanics are 8,000 hours or about four years. As with most apprenticeships, an additional 144 hours of related training is also required each year. Community college and vocational schools can provide the related training. Typical course work would include diesel engine fuel systems, air brake systems, heavy-duty suspension, power transmission, electrical systems, fluid mechanics, wheels and tires, steering, and preventative maintenance inspection.

The International Association of Machinists and Aerospace Workers, United Autoworkers, and the Amalgamated Transit Union offer apprenticeship programs for diesel technicians. Transit companies, school districts, and trucking companies in your area may sponsor apprenticeships as well.

Related Skills

As with all jobs in the automotive area, good mechanical skills and manual dexterity are important. Those who can gain experience in engine repair or other types of automotive and electrical programs while still in high school will have an advantage. A solid background in mathematics and physics provides good preparation as those courses can help with the understanding of force, friction, hydraulics, and electrical circuits. Good problem-solving skills are an asset in this industry, and computer skills are becoming increasingly important. Those with good communication skills, both spoken and written, will be able to deal with drivers and coworkers and write the necessary work orders associated with the job.

Resources

For information about apprenticeships in your area, contact your local apprenticeship organization. For more information about diesel engine repair, contact:

Detroit Diesel
13400 West Outer Dr.
Detroit, MI 48239

National Institute for Automotive Excellence
101 Blue Seal Dr., SE, Suite 101
Leesburg, VA 20175
Internet: http://www.asecert.org

National Automotive Technicians Education Foundation
Same address as above
Internet: http://www.natef.org

Locksmith

Locksmith	O*NET/SOC	49-9094
	DOT	709.281.010
	RAIS	0289

Locksmiths install locks, deadbolts, and other locking devices in homes and businesses. They may go to homes or businesses to unlock doors or automobiles that have been accidentally locked or where locks have malfunctioned. They also repair locks and make replacement keys, using key-duplicating machines. They help customers decide which locks are best for their purposes.

Locksmiths may also sell and service home or business safes. Some install and maintain electronic alarm and surveillance systems as well as access control systems. Some service locks on vault doors, safe deposit boxes, and teller equipment at banks.

Some locksmiths work for hotels and motels, apartment complexes, or college and universities providing master key systems, resetting combinations, and rekeying door locks on a regular basis.

Some states require that locksmiths be licensed.

Job Outlook and Wages

The Department of Labor estimates jobs for locksmiths will grow faster than average—up 21 percent through 2012. Growing concern about security in the United States will mean an increase in jobs for locksmiths. Additionally, the need to replace retiring workers will provide new opportunities as well. This is not a job category with huge numbers in the workforce. There are only 19,340 people employed as locksmiths in the United States today, so the actual number of new jobs will be small.

The average annual wage for locksmiths was $28,760 in 2003, with those working in the automotive repair and maintenance specialty averaging $46,230 a year. Jobs working for the federal government and for schools paid well also. Workers in the District of Columbia, Delaware, Connecticut, Nevada, and Minnesota were among the best paid, and the largest concentrations of workers were found in Nevada, Alaska, Virginia, Idaho, and Utah.

Apprenticeships

Most locksmiths learn their jobs through on-the-job training. Some complete formal apprenticeship programs lasting up to four years, with a minimum of 144 hours of related training. Course work might include the history and development of security products, locksmith's tools, assembly and disassembly of door hardware, picking and shimming, key cutting equipment operation, master key systems, impression production, core cylinders, access control systems, codes and code cutting equipment, and automobile servicing. Some universities offer locksmith apprenticeships to train locksmiths for their own facilities. Individual companies and individual locksmiths may sponsor apprenticeships as well.

Related Skills

According to the Associated Locksmiths of America, high school students should take courses in mathematics, mechanical drawing, metalworking, basic electronics, and business education. Good communication skills are useful as well.

Resources

For information about apprenticeships in your area, contact your local apprenticeship agency. For more information about locksmiths, contact:

Associated Locksmiths of America
3003 Live Oak St.
Dallas, TX 75204
Phone: (800) 532-2562
Internet: http://www.aloa.org
Includes a list of schools for locksmiths.

Meter Technician and Meter Mechanic

Meter Technician and Meter Mechanic	O*NET/SOC	49-9012.
	DOT	Varies
	RAIS	0332

Meter technicians (sometimes called field service representatives) install, maintain, and repair electromechanical and electronic meters and allied equipment that measure customer consumption of gas, electricity, or water. They turn meters on or off to establish or close service. They rebuild, remove, inspect, clean, repair, adjust, or change meters and regulators. They are responsible for verifying the accuracy of meters and look for causes and solutions for customer complaints. They may also investigate situations of illegally tapping into gas, water, or other service lines.

Job Outlook and Wages

Jobs in this area are expected to grow as fast as average—up just over 14 percent through 2012. These are essential services, so there is not much downward fluctuation. Most job openings will come as older workers retire. Because these are high-paying jobs that usually include excellent benefits, there are often waiting lists of perspective employees.

The average annual wage for meter technicians and mechanics was $42,540 in 2003. The majority worked for power generation and gas distribution utilities where salaries averaged between $48,000 and $51,000. The highest-paid workers were in Illinois, New York, California, Alaska, and Connecticut. The highest concentrations of workers were found in Oklahoma, New Mexico, Utah, Texas, and New York

Apprenticeships

Apprenticeships for meter technicians and mechanics are between three and four years, with a minimum of 144 hours of related classroom work. Course work varies according to utility.

Applicants must be high school graduates and some utility experience or some related postsecondary education is preferred. The International Brotherhood of Electrical Workers and employers sponsor apprenticeships for electrical workers. Local utility companies may sponsor programs for gas and water field representatives.

Related Skills

A strong background in mathematics is helpful, and electrical shop courses can be most beneficial. Mechanical drawing and blueprint reading are also useful programs for this field. Because these workers often deal directly with customers, employers will look for those with good interpersonal skills. In some areas, bilingual candidates will have an edge.

International Brotherhood of Electrical Workers
900 7th St., NW
Washington, DC 20001
Internet: http://www.ibew.org

Heating and Air Conditioning Mechanics

HVACR Workers	*O*NET/SOC*	*49-9021.01*
	DOT	*637.261-014*
	RIAS	*0637*

Heating specialists solder plumbing joints when installing a new residential heating system. Photo by Penny Hutchins Paquette.

Heating and air conditioning mechanics install, service, and repair heating and air conditioning systems. As the names imply, heating mechanics work on heating systems, and air conditioning mechanics work on cooling systems.

Heating mechanics may also be called furnace installers or heating equipment technicians. They are responsible for installing and maintaining oil, gas, electric, solid-fuel, and multiple-fuel heating systems. As mentioned above, workers may be responsible for all aspects of the installation process or may work with other trade specialists to get the job done. When responsible for the entire job, workers install the heating system, cut the necessary holes in floors, walls, and roof necessary for the ductwork. Some heating mechanics also fabricate, assemble, and install the necessary duct-work and install the necessary pipe or tubing for fuel and water lines. They are also responsible for installing, connecting, and adjusting the thermostats and humidistats. These technicians may also lay out and connect the electrical wiring between the controls and the equipment. In addition to performing the tasks necessary to install the system, they also work to maintain and repair the heating system.

Heating systems need routine maintenance that may include replacing filters, ducts, or other parts. HVACR workers may adjust the burners or blowers during these routine maintenance visits. When the system fails, they must diagnose and repair the problem.

Air conditioning specialists install and service central air conditioning systems. They install the necessary motors, compressors, piping, fuel and water supply lines, and other parts of air conditioning systems. Once the equipment is installed, they connect it to ductwork that is often already in place for the heating system. Then, they must connect the equipment to the electrical source, and add the refrigerant necessary to make the system operational.

Once installed, air conditioning mechanics make sure the system is maintained and repaired, when necessary. The importance of this job can't be underestimated. While we may be uncomfortable when an air conditioner breaks down, equipment and supplies can be damaged or destroyed when temperatures rise above controlled levels. Those involved in the repair of cooling systems are also responsible for helping protect the environment. When working on cooling systems, technicians must use care not to let the chemicals release into the atmosphere. Air conditioning and refrigeration (see below) specialists must take care to conserve, recover, and recycle chlorofluorocarbon (CFC) and hydrochlorofluorocarbon (HCFC) refrigerants. The release of these chemicals can contribute to the depletion of the ozone layer.

Refrigeration Mechanics	*O*NET/SOC*	*49-9021.02*
	DOT	*637.261-026*
	RIAS	*0666*

Refrigeration mechanics install, service, and repair industrial and commercial refrigeration systems and equipment. Again, technicians in this field may specialize in installation or repair. These technicians work on commercial properties that could include supermarkets, pharmaceutical companies, blood banks, or any other business or industry where products or spaces need to be refrigerated.

When your home air conditioner or refrigerator breaks down, an appliance repair person can handle that task, but these refrigeration systems specialists actually install motors, compressors, condensing units, evaporators, piping, and other components. This equipment is then connected to ductwork, refrigerant lines, and electrical power sources. Those who specialize in service and repair must keep these systems running. As with air conditioning specialists, they must be fully trained in managing the coolants that keep these systems operational. All technicians who purchase or work with refrigerants must be certified in the handling of these materials. The tests are administered by organizations approved by the Environmental Protection Agency.

Job Outlook and Wages

The job outlook for HVACR workers is excellent—with available jobs expected to be up by more than 30 percent between 2002 and 2012. As business and home owners look for more efficient ways to manage the heating and cooling of their buildings, there will be an increased demand for system upgrades and system replacements. In addition, new environmental standards that became effective in 2000 will cause an increased demand for new systems or system modifications that allow newer and safer refrigerants to be used.

The increased demand for new construction will mean an increased demand for heating and cooling systems. As more businesses rely on an environmentally controlled environment, the importance of having workers to keep the systems in working order will mean more jobs in this area.

Indoor air quality has come under increased scrutiny during the past decade, and both home owners and businesses are eager to have systems that ensure good air in homes, schools, factories, and businesses.

The Department of Labor predicts that the growth of business establishments that use refrigerated equipment like supermarkets and convenience stores will create a growth in the need for refrigeration technicians. In addition to all of the new openings created by job growth, there is always a need to replace workers who leave the field.

In 2003, the average salary for HVACR technicians was $36,790 with experienced workers averaging more than $55,000. Highly skilled and specialized workers earned even more. Florida employed significantly more workers in this field than any other state. Maryland, Maine, Alabama, and South Dakota were also among the states with the highest concentration of workers in the HVACR field. The best-paying states in 2003 were Alaska, Hawaii, the District of Columbia, Massachusetts, and Connecticut.

Although we think of cooling and heating as seasonal jobs and might expect there to be significant periods of unemployment in the off-season, many companies work at both installation and maintenance, balancing the work year with off-season repair and maintenance.

Apprenticeships

Apprenticeship programs in HVACR run between three and five years and may require more than 200 hours of classroom study in addition to on-the-job training. Many apprentices in this field are already experienced plumbers or sheet metal workers.

Apprentices with less experience start at 50 percent of the journeyman's wage for the specific job and get regular salary increases as they become more proficient.

Because HVACR technicians often require multiple skills, apprenticeship programs are sponsored by a wide variety of organizations including joint committees representing local chapters of the Air-Conditioning Contractors of America, the Mechanical Contractors Association of America, the National Association of Plumbing-Heating-Cooling Contractors, and locals of the Sheet Metal Workers' International Association or the United Association of Journeymen and Apprentices of the Plumbing and Pipefitting Industry of the United States and Canada. Local chapters of the Associated Builders and Contractors and the National Association of Home Builders also sponsor apprenticeships.

In addition to the hands-on skills acquired during the on-site portion of the apprenticeship, classroom studies might include industrial math and measurements, safety, tools, preventive maintenance techniques, blueprint and electrical symbol reading, electrical codes, wiring methods, chemistry, mechanics, electronics, spec writing, air conditioning systems, refrigerating systems, electric heating, gas heating and appliances, plumbing, and refrigeration theory.

Related Skills

If you are interested in a HVACR career, you can begin your preparations in high school. Blueprint reading, math (including both algebra and geometry), computer applications, computer-aided design (CAD), and business courses are all beneficial. If you are in a vocational school environment and have the opportunity to also take courses in sheet metal, air conditioning, or electronics, you will be even better prepared.

You need steady hands and arms to perform many of the tasks associated with these jobs, and manual and finger dexterity are important. You need strength to lift and move many of the components of HVACR systems. You also need good communication skills. Because HVACR workers often work with other trades specialists, it is important to be able to understand directions and be able to make yourself understood. The diverse tasks that are combined in these jobs require good reasoning skills.

Resources

Again, because so many trades are involved in this career, there are many trade organizations that have general information on HVACR and on apprenticeships. For information about apprenticeship programs, you can also contact your local apprenticeship agency.

Air-Conditioning Contractors of America (ACCA)
2800 Shirlington Rd., Suite 300
Arlington, VA 22206
Phone: (703) 575-4477
Internet: http://www.acca.org

Air Conditioning-Refrigeration Institute
4100 North Fairfax Dr., Suite 200
Arlington, VA 22203
Phone: (703) 524-8000
Internet: http://www.ari.org

Associated Builders and Contactors
Workforce Development Department
4250 North Fairfax Dr., 9th Floor
Arlington, VA 22203
Phone: (703) 812-2000
Internet: http://www.abc.org
E-mail: CraftTraining@abc.org

Home Builders Institute
1201 15th St., NW, 6th Floor
Washington, DC 20005-2800
Phone: (800) 795-7955
Internet: http://www.hbi.org

Mechanical Contractors Association of America
1385 Piccard Dr.
Rockville, MD 20850-4329
Phone: (301) 869-5800
Internet: http://www.mcaa.org

National Association of
   Plumbing-Heating-Cooling Contractors
180 S. Washington St.
P.O. Box 6808
Falls Church, VA 22046
Phone: (703) 237-8100
Internet: http://www.phccweb.org

Refrigeration Service Engineers Society (RSES)
1666 Rand Rd.
Des Plaines, IL 60016-3552
Phone: (800) 297-5660
Internet: http://www.rses.org

Sheet Metal and Air-Conditioning Contractors'
    National Association
4201 Lafayette Center Dr.
Chantily, VA 20151-1209
Phone: (703) 803-2980
Internet: http://www.smacna.org

Industrial Machinery

Those who install, repair, and maintain industrial machinery are those who keep the production line running smoothly and correctly. There are dozens of highly specialized repair jobs in this area from keeping the equipment running in a bakery to repairing industrial sewing machines. In this highly technical field, industrial machinery mechanics and millwrights are responsible for keeping things running. The mechanics are most often responsible for repair and the millwrights are most responsible for installation, but in many cases the job descriptions overlap.

Industrial	*O*NET/SOC*	*49-9041*
Machinery	*DOT*	*May vary (see below)*
Mechanics	*RAIS*	*May vary (see below)*

Most industrial machinery mechanics specialize in repair, and as you can see in the apprenticeship section below, the repairs are usually focused on a very specific type of machinery. To keep equipment running smoothly, industrial machinery mechanics must be able to detect minor problems and repair them before they cause problems on the production line. They diagnose the problems and then take apart the machinery, repairing or replacing the necessary parts.

As more and more equipment includes electronic components, these specialty mechanics often have to have a strong background in electronics and computerized controls as well. Sometimes they work with electronics specialists in doing their jobs. Part of their job might include preventative maintenance as well, as they calibrate automated manufacturing equipment, like robots.

Some mechanics do machinery installation as well.

Job Outlook and Wages

There were 197,000 workers specializing in machinery mechanics in 2002. The average annual wage for these workers averages $39,640, with the top 10 percent averaging $57,060 in 2003. Power generation and supply companies employed the largest number of workers in this field, followed closely by machinery and supply merchant wholesalers, motor vehicle parts manufacturing, converted paper product manufacturing, and animal slaughtering and processing. The top-paying industry for machinists was power generation and supply, where workers averaged just over $53,000 a year. In 2003, the highest concentrations of workers were in Wyoming, Louisiana, South Carolina, Kentucky, and North Carolina. The top-paying state was Alaska, where workers averaged close to $53,000. Nevada, Wyoming, Michigan, and Washington were also among the top-paying states in the country.

The job outlook for industrial machinery mechanics is mixed. Jobs are expected to grow more slowly than the national average—up about 5.5 percent through 2012. Those with broad skills in machine repair should have favorable job prospects, however. Many of the mechanics are older and retirements will be creating job openings each year as workers leave the workforce.

Companies will be replacing older equipment with newer, more-automated equipment that is often capable of self-diagnosis. This may create a reduced need for repair mechanics.

On a more positive note, workers in this field work even when production slows. During this time, mechanics may overhaul and do routine repairs to equipment, so it will be up and running once production improves.

Apprenticeships

This job classification covers a broad range of industrial mechanics, and apprenticeships are available in 36 specific categories in this field including: automotive-maintenance-equipment servicer; aviation support equipment repairer; bakery-machine mechanic; canal-equipment mechanic; composing-room machinist; conveyor-maintenance mechanic; electronic-production-line-maintenance mechanic; forge-shop-machine repairer; fuel-System-maintenance worker; hydraulic repairer; hydraulic-press servicer; hydroelectric-machinery mechanic; industrial machine system technician; laundry-machine mechanic; machine fixer (carpet and rug); machine repairer, maintenance; machinist, linotype; maintenance mechanic; maintenance mechanic; maintenance mechanic, compressed-gas plant; overhauler (textile); pinsetter adjuster, automatic; pneumatic-tool repairer; pneumatic-tube repairer; powerhouse mechanic; pump erector (construction); pump servicer; repairer I; repairer, welding equipment; repairer, welding systems and equipment; rubberizing mechanic; scale mechanic; sewing-machine repairer; stoker erector-and-servicer; treatment-plant mechanic; cooling tower technician.

Whew! Obviously apprenticeship training would include on-the-job instruction specific to the particular industry or to a specific piece of equipment.

Apprenticeships can run from two to six years, depending on the area of specialty. As with most apprenticeships, 144 hours of related course work is also included each year.

Related Skills

No matter what type of machinery you plan to repair, certain skills are required. Obviously, jobs in this field require an understanding of mechanics and design. High school classes in mathematics, blueprint reading, and mechanical shop can help prepare you for this kind of job. As more equipment has electronics components, a background in electronics is also useful.

Millwrights	O*NET/SOC	49-9044
	DOT	638.281-018
	RAIS	0335

Millwrights install, repair, replace, and dismantle machinery and other heavy equipment used in industry. They need a wide range of skills, including the ability to read blueprints, pour concrete, and diagnose and repair mechanical problems.

Their primary responsibility is the installation of equipment. Because they are responsible for putting the equipment in place, they need to know how to use rigging and pulley devices to help place the machines. When equipment is too heavy for that type of installation, they need to work with hydraulic lift or crane operators to position the equipment. They decide how the equipment will be moved, so they need to understand how much weight the ropes, cables, hoists, and cranes can bear. Sometimes the machinery is so heavy that a new foundation must be installed to support it. In that case, they will either prepare the foundation themselves or supervise the work.

They not only have to move the machinery into place, but they also must know how to assemble it, fitting the bearings, aligning the gears and wheels, attaching motors, and connecting belts according to the manufacturer's plans. When the machine breaks down, they may work with other mechanics and maintenance workers to repair and maintain the equipment. In addition to working in production, some millwrights also work in the construction industry caring for the building equipment.

These workers are essential in production and construction. Without them, work couldn't even begin.

Job Outlook and Wages

There were 69,000 millwrights working in the United States in 2003. The average annual salary for all millwrights was $43,150. The top 10 percent of workers in this field earned over $63,000. Most worked for building equipment contractors or in motor vehicle parts manufacturing. Those who worked in car parts manufacturing were among the highest paid, averaging about $58,000 a year. Although millwrights work across the United States, employment is concentrated in highly industrialized areas. In 2003, the highest concentrations of workers were in Michigan, Indiana, Maine, Ohio, and Louisiana. Michigan also paid its employees the best, followed by New Jersey, Ohio, Indiana, and Wisconsin.

As with industrial machinery mechanics, the job outlook is mixed. New jobs in this area are expected to grow more slowly than average—up 5.3 percent through 2012. Because so many are employed in production facilities, much of the job outlook for millwrights is linked to the country's production. Although production can be cyclical, in order to remain competitive, U.S. manufacturers will need to purchase and install up-to-date machinery, keeping millwrights busy with dismantling and installation projects. Equipment that remains will need regular service.

Workers in this field tend to be older than average and will be leaving the workforce to retire. This will mean new openings for trained millwrights.

On the downside, highly trained electronics technicians and industrial machinery mechanics are beginning to assume some of the responsibilities of millwrights, reducing their numbers.

Apprenticeships

The standard apprenticeship for millwrights is 8,000 hours, or about four years. These programs provide on-the-job instruction in dismantling, moving, erecting, and replacing machinery. Generally, apprentices learn to work with concrete and are trained in carpentry, welding, and sheet metal work as well. Apprentices will need up to an additional 160 hours each year of related training, either through workshops, community college programs, or online training. Course work may include related mathematics, measurements (including programs in energy, force, and power), blueprint reading, related tools (hand and power), metal cutting, machine tooling, rigging, welding, vibration analysis, lubrication, and others.

Related Skills

This is a job for those who like to work with machines and tools—the mechanically inclined. A solid background in computer technology and mechanical drawing and machine shop will be helpful. Focus on math while in high school, including algebra and geometry. Millwrights must coordinate many activities and workers to get machines installed and keep them running, so good communications skills are essential. If you enjoy working with your hands, like to assemble things and take them apart, and are good in math, this may be a job worth exploring.

Resources

For information about apprenticeships for industrial machinery mechanics and for millwrights, contact your local apprenticeship organization. For more information about this work, contact:

Associated General Contractors of America
333 John Carlyle St., Suite 200
Alexandria, VA 22314
Internet: http://www.agc.org

National Tooling and Machining Association
9300 Livingston Rd.
Fort Washington, MD 20744
Internet: http://www.ntma.org

United Brotherhood of Carpenters and Joiners of America
Internet: http://www.Carpenters.org
For regional and local information, click on
    "Local Contacts"

Line Installers and Repairers

Electrical	*O*NET/SOC*	*49-9051.00*
	DOT	*821.361-026*
	RAIS	*0282*

Telecommunications O*NET/SOC *49-9052.00*
         DOT *822.381-014*
         RAIS *0056*

Get up in the morning, turn on the lights, have a little breakfast, check your e-mail, and call a friend. Sounds like a typical day, but there would be nothing typical about it without line installers and repairers. In order for us to have those services we take for granted, line installers begin by constructing utility poles, towers, and underground trenches to carry the wires and cables. Sometimes they install tubes within underground tunnels to carry wire below the ground.

Next, the line installers string the cable and attach it to the building. They are also responsible for setting up, servicing, and installing network equipment. They run the necessary lines from the building to the power poles, tower, or trenches. For electricity, workers install and replace transformers, circuit breakers, switches, or fuses that control and direct the electrical current.

These are also the workers who come to our homes to repair the system when things go wrong. They repair or replace defective cables, splicing together separate pieces of cable when necessary. Workers dealing with fine fiber optic cable use special equipment to slice, match, and align the individual glass fibers. Then they join them by welding or by using a mechanical fixture and a special glue.

Job Outlook and Wages

Electrical power-line installers and repairers earned an average of $47,460 a year in 2003, with the best-paid workers in the country averaging $66,870. Workers earned the highest wages in Alaska, New York, California, New Jersey, and Nevada. The highest concentrations of workers were in Wyoming, North Dakota, South Dakota, West Virginia, and Mississippi. In 2002, there were just over 100,000 workers in this field.

Those specializing in the telecommunications sector averaged $39,560 in 2003, with the highest-paid workers in the country averaging $55,290. Massachusetts, Alaska, New York, Rhode Island, and California were the top-paying states. The highest concentrations of workers were in Montana, New York, Texas, Massachusetts, and Oklahoma.

The job outlook for entry-level workers in the power-line sector is not good. Little growth is expected in this area. Industry deregulation has led to cost-cutting measures including cuts in maintenance, reducing employment opportunities. Although, like many industries, there will be a need to replace retiring workers, these jobs will be filled by experienced workers.

The prospects are better for those looking for work in the telecommunications field. Growth in this area will be about as fast as average—up 18.8 percent through 2012. Demand for high-speed Internet access and multiple telephone lines will mean jobs for workers to improve and expand local phone networks. Older telephone lines will need to be replaced to allow for this high-tech service, and new job openings will be available modernizing and maintaining the new telecommunications networks. In addition to this area of growth, workers will be needed to replace retiring workers.

This good news will be countered, however, by the increasing use of wireless telephones, as wireless systems do not require as many technicians to maintain and expand those services.

Apprenticeships

Apprenticeship programs for line installers and repairers require three to five years to complete, with electrical-line installation apprenticeships taking the most time. Both apprenticeships may be administered by the employer and a union representing the workers.

Government safety standards are very strict and regulate the training and education requirements for apprentice electrical-line installers. In addition to the four to five years of on-the-job training, apprentice line installers should expect to spend an additional 144–200 hours of related classroom work each year. Related courses may include wiring procedures, pole framing, circuit testing, transformer connections, DC circuitry, residential wiring, safety, related math, AC theory and transformer applications, commercial wiring, three-phase distribution and transmission lines, National Electric Safety Code, and substation equipment. Training programs are also offered at the International Brotherhood of Electrical Workers Training Institutes. Course work may apply to college credit in some states.

Applicants must have a high school diploma, and some states require an associate's degree in electrical technology or at least a year of experience in a related field. Many also require at least a year of high school algebra.

Apprenticeships in telecommunications installation and maintenance are usually a little shorter, three to four years, with a minimum of 144 hours of related study each year. Coursework may include basic AC and DC theory, conductor connections, pole climbing, pay stations, CATV distribution fundamentals, fiber optics, related systems and lines studies, area network protocols and transmission methods, phone installation, cable splicing, and transmission fundamentals.

Apprentices in these fields start at a percentage of the journeyman's pay and receive increases as they gain experience.

Related Skills

Algebra is often required, and geometry and physics can be useful as well. Electrical shop classes and blueprint reading can provide an introduction to the work. Because some installation work requires direct contact with customers, good interpersonal and communication skills are essential. Many workers need to work in high places, so you must be comfortable with that.

Resources

For information about apprenticeships in your area, contact your local apprenticeship organization. For more information about jobs in this field, contact:

Communications Workers of America
501 Third St., NW
Washington, DC 20001
http://www.cwa-union.org/

Society of Cable Telecommunications Engineers
140 Philips Rd.
Exton, PA 19341-1318
Internet: http://www.scte.org

International Brotherhood of Electrical Workers
Telecommunications Department
1125 15th St., NW
Washington, DC 20005

7 Personal Care and Service

Included in this unlikely combination of jobs are those that help us with hair and makeup, prepare our meals, and those who help us train our animals. Interestingly, it includes those who help us look good while we are living as well as those who attend to our needs after death. From animal trainer to embalmer, these jobs have one thing in common—personal care.

Animal Trainer/Horse Trainer

Animal Trainer/	O*NET/SOC	39-2011.00
Horse Trainer	DOT	159.224-010
	DOT	419.224-010 *(horses)*
	RAIS	0871
	RAIS	1001 *(horses)*

Animal trainers train animals for performance, obedience, security, and/or service. Horse trainers may train animals for riding, harness, and service, including carrying pack loads, controlling crowds, and working with people with disabilities.

The working environment depends on the type of animal the trainer is working with and the purpose of the training. Those who train dolphins, for example, spend time working in or near the water with the animals both during routine care and during performances. Marine mammal trainers train animals like seals, whales, and dolphins to perform at zoos, aquariums, or other marine facilities. All of the work is not glamorous. In addition to working with the animals, workers in this field must prepare food, maintain water quality, and monitor the health of the animals. Animal trainers can also work with other animals in zoos and other educational performance centers. They often take care of cleaning cages, feeding animals, and other routine maintenance issues as well.

Those who work with dogs can specialize in a several areas. The most common occupations in the field include dog obedience training and show dog training. Here the jobs may be as routine as teaching an animal good behavior and obedience. Show trainers teach animals to perform according to show regulations.

Some dog trainers work with dogs who will work in the law enforcement area, training dogs to attack intruders, recognize the smell of drugs or explosives, help with routine crowd control, assist in rescue situations, or locate the dead.

Some animal trainers focus in animal service areas, training guide dogs to help the visually impaired or otherwise disabled people with daily activities (see sidebar on page 195). In addition to teaching the dogs, these trainers also work with their future owners teaching them how to work with the animal.

Others work with horses who deliver services in rehabilitative areas, working with people who have a variety of impairments. Of course, horse trainers also work with race and show horses, but this is a highly specialized field, requiring years of experience with horse breeders.

Job Outlook and Wages

Workers in the animal training field face stiff competition for jobs, and salaries rarely go above a modest range. Most people in this field work with animals because they love the work. Some are even willing to work second jobs in order to continue to work with animals.

Jobs in this field will increase about as quickly as average—up 14.3 percent through 2012, but because very few people work in this area, there will only be about 9,000 openings across the country during that time.

GUIDE DOG TRAINING

Morris Frank and Buddy, the first Seeing Eye dog, training in Vevey, Switzerland in May 1920. Photo courtesy of The Seeing Eye.

An extremely specialized field in the animal training category is the job of training guide dogs. According to the Guide Dog Foundation for the Blind, Morris Frank was the first American to use a guide dog. After hearing that German veterans were being trained with guide dogs, he traveled to Switzerland to work with American dog training specialist Dorothy Harrison Eustis. After training Frank, she requested that he start a school in the United States. Frank founded The Seeing Eye in 1929.

Today, organizations across the United States specialize in training dogs to help blind and visually impaired, deaf, or wheelchair-bound people go about their everyday tasks. This job requires not only the ability to work closely with animals, but also the ability to help blind or visually impaired individuals learn to work with the dog. This job comes with the unattractive combination of long hours, hard work, and low pay. But, for those who want to work with animals and enjoy working with people, it may be the opportunity of a lifetime.

Unfortunately, there are few openings in guide dog programs. Many apprentices are hired from within the organization, so you can better your chances of obtaining an apprenticeship by working for the organization in another capacity first. Guide dog programs need people to work with puppies, to help in the kennels, and other entry-level jobs. Some programs recruit volunteers to help. If you are serious about becoming a guide dog instructor, you should inquire about all jobs available.

Programs in the dog training service industry require that those interested in becoming guide dog trainers or instructors serve an apprenticeship. Requirements vary from program to program, but in most cases, dog trainer apprentices must provide between two and a half and four years of apprenticeship work. Tasks also vary from school to school but most often require apprentices start by working with the dogs.

Apprentices in this field also need good communication skills. It is not enough to like animals or to feel confident training pets. Because these organizations are nonprofit organizations, they need people who can communicate their goals to others. Academic requirements vary from program to program as well. According to representatives from Guide Dogs for the Blind in California, students there are not required to attend specific classes, but they are required to do work-related readings, prepare book reports, and take written tests. The Guide Dog Foundation in Smithtown, New York, also requires written and oral tests and requires readings on subjects ranging from dog breeding to causes of blindness.

The Puppy Place, an Internet site providing information on guide dogs and guide dog training, includes a listing of guide dog programs in the United States. For more information, visit their site, www.thepuppyplace.org.

The average salary for an animal trainer in the United States in 2003 was $26,310. Although you might think those working in the spectator sports category would be making substantially more, they averaged $26,260. Those working in amusement parks and arcades earned slightly more, $32,870. The highest concentrations of animal workers were in New Hampshire, Delaware, South Carolina, Maryland, and Kentucky. Even here, the numbers of workers were very small, representing between .010 percent and .018 percent of employment in the state. Workers in Rhode Island, Nevada, Washington, Texas, and Missouri were among the highest paid with average salaries ranging from $31,430 to $40,790.

Apprenticeships

Apprenticeships for animal trainers are among the most competitive. Few programs are available, and competition for them is stiff. Many people entering the field have extensive backgrounds, including bachelor's degrees in related fields and years of related work in the area.

Apprenticeships average about 4,000 hours or about two years. Course work averages 144 hours each year, and varies widely according to the sponsoring business.

Related Skills

Most people who get apprenticeships in animal training have been working or volunteering in other related jobs. If you love animals and are seriously interested in working in this area, find a volunteer opportunity in your area while you are still in high school. Working at your local animal shelter, dog breeding or training facility, veterinary office, or local zoo will help you meet people in the field and give you some related experience.

Most animal trainers have a college-level background. Many have degrees in biology, animal behavior, environmental science, or zoology. Some dog trainers do not have college degrees but have spent years in related fields.

Resources

For information about apprenticeship programs, contact your local apprenticeship organization. For more information about animal training:

American Dog Trainers Network
Internet: www.inch.com/~dogs/protrainer.html
Includes a list of apprenticeship programs.

Leaders of the Pack: Guide Dog Instructors
Guide Dogs for the Blind
P.O. Box 15120
San Rafael, CA 94915-1200
Internet: http://www.guidedogs.com/career-training.html

National Association of Dog Obedience Instructors
PMB # 369
729 Grapevine Highway, Suite 369
Hurst, TX 76054-2085

How Do I Become a Dog Trainer and Obedience Instructor
Internet: http://www.nadoi.org/howdoi.htm

National Police Canine Association
P.O. Box 264
Robert, LA 70455
Internet: http://www.npca.net
Click on "trainer standards" link

The Seeing Eye
P.O. Box 375
Morristown, NJ 07963
Internet: http://www.seeingeye.org

United States Police Canine Association
P.O. Box 80
Springboro, OH 45066
Internet: http://www.uspcak9.com
Click on "So You Want to be a K9 Handler" link
http://www.uspcak9.com/training/K9handler.pdf

Animal trainers who train animals for films and the theater must belong to:

> The International Alliance of Theatrical State Employees,
>   Moving Picture Technicians, Artists, and Allied Crafts
>   of the United States, Its Territories and Canada
> IATSE General Office
> 1430 Broadway, 20th Floor
> New York, NY 10018
> Phone: (212) 730-1770
> Internet: www.iatse-intl.org

Baker

Baker	O*NET/SOC	51-3011.01 (hotel and restaurant)
		51-3011.02 (production)
	DOT	313.381.010 (hotel and restaurant)
		526.381.01 (production)
	RAIS	0076 (hotel and restaurant)
		0028 (production)

Those who bake the sweet-smelling goodies we all love—breads, cakes, pies, and cookies—can work in two areas. Some work for restaurants, grocery stores, specialty shops, or other areas where the treats can be eaten, or they work for production facilities where large quantities of baked products are made to be sold later on store shelves. Either way, it is a sweet job.

Those who prepare breads and pastries to be eaten on-site or for specialized take-out sections of bakeries or grocery stores mix ingredients according to recipes and bake the goodies for us to enjoy, usually the same day. They may also frost cakes, decorate cookies, or form dough for specialty breads.

Those who produce mass quantities of baked goods use high-volume mixers, ovens, and other equipment to produce the packaged foods we purchase at the grocery store.

Specialty bakers, called pastry chefs, manage the business, supervise a staff, develop dessert menus, purchase ingredients, and maintain business records. They are classified with chefs (below).

Job Outlook and Wages

The demand for bakers is expected to grow about as fast as average—up 11.2 percent, through 2012. The Department of Labor projects there will be 59,000 job openings during that time. Freshly baked artisan and specialty breads like focaccia, epis, and other whole and multigrain breads are becoming more popular among bread lovers. On the other side of the equation, trendy diets like the current low-carb eating plans may result in a reduction in overall bread consumption. Still, demand for workers in this category should remain steady.

The average salary for bakers in 2003 was $22,600. More than half of the workers in this category were employed by bakeries, tortilla manufacturing companies, and grocery stores. Many workers are also employed by specialty shops and full-service restaurants.

In 2003, the top-paying states for bakers were the District of Columbia, Alaska, New Jersey, Massachusetts, and Nevada. The highest concentrations of workers were in Vermont, Hawaii, North Dakota, Pennsylvania, and Connecticut.

Apprenticeships

The American Culinary Institute, individual restaurants, grocery stores, and specialty shops all sponsor apprenticeships for bakers. Three years (6,000 hours) of on-the-job training is combined with 144 hours each year in related training. Classroom work may include culinary foundations, baking theory, professional standards for food service, sanitation and safety, food microbiology, baking science, chemistry, nutrition, flour and dough testing, business operations, bakery layout and design, business writing, and management concepts.

One of the newest programs in baking is sponsored by the Wisconsin Bakers Association. The organization is looking for high school graduates, at least 18 years old, to begin training in association's own bakery lab. The program will total 6,016 hours, including related training. The Wisconsin Bakers Association will not only pay for all related training, but unlike most apprenticeship programs, they will pay you for the time you spend in the classroom as well!

If Wisconsin is looking for apprentices and hoping to improve the training of bakers, you can expect that similar organizations in your area will be offering programs in the near future.

Related Skills

First, you must be willing to get up early. Bakers start their days as early as 3 a.m. to ensure their bakery products will be ready for distribution or consumption by the start of the day.

In high school, courses in food preparation can come in handy. If you are in vocational school, you can begin to specialize right now. Good math skills and a background in chemistry are all good preparation. Most of all, you must enjoy cooking and baking.

Resources

American Culinary Federation
180 Center Place Way
St. Augustine, FL 32095
Phone: (904) 824-4468
Internet: http://www.acfchefs.org/apprwhat.html
   (apprenticeship fundamentals)
Includes a link to programs across the country.

Bread Bakers Guild of America
3203 Maryland Ave.
North Versailles, PA 15137-1629
Internet: http://www.bbga.org

The Retailer's Bakery Association (RBA)
14239 Park Center Dr.
Laurel, MD 20707
Phone: (800) 638-0924
Internet: http://www.rbanet.com

Cooks

Cooks—Restaurant	O*NET/SOC	35-2014.00
and Hotel	DOT	313.336-014
	RAIS	0663

Love the food channel? Can't get enough of Bobby Flay, Wolfgang Puck, the Barefoot Contessa, or Rachel Ray? Like to experiment in the kitchen, adding just the right ingredient to transform a recipe? This might be the career for you.

Cooks and chefs plan and prepare the meals we enjoy at hotels and restaurants. Cooks are involved in food preparation and may work in specialized areas within a kitchen—vegetable cook, fry cook, grill cook, etc. With experience, they may progress to work as head cooks, sous chefs, and chefs. Executive chefs direct the preparation of the food, from planning menus to supervising the kitchen staff. Sous chefs (under chefs) may assist executive chefs with these activities. Together, they plan and price menus, order supplies, maintain records and accounts, and supervise the staff of cooks and food preparation workers as they prepare and present the food. They may also be involved in food preparation as well. Pastry chefs, as the title implies, specialize in desserts and other baked products. Together these workers are responsible for providing us with the delicious meals we enjoy when we are away from home.

Job Outlook and Wages

Job growth for chefs and other supervisory-level cooks is expected to be about as fast as average—up about 15.8 percent through 2012. Sixty thousand job openings will be available for chefs during that time. Jobs for cooks in hotels and restaurants will also grow at about the same rate, with 341,000 job openings through 2012. The growth of two-income households, increases in leisure time, and increases in population and income will help contribute to growth in this field.

Cooks in hotels and restaurants averaged $20,020 in 2003. Those working in New York earned the highest wages, averaging $25,210. Hawaii, New Jersey, Connecticut, and

Nevada were also in the top five top-paying states for cooks. The highest concentrations of workers were in Hawaii, Nevada, Montana, Colorado, and Oregon.

Those with the highest qualifications, chefs and head cooks, earned an average of $32,620 in 2003.

Apprenticeships

Those with apprenticeship training can rise through the ranks of hotel and restaurant workers (see sidebar). In fact, most chefs got their start working as apprentices.

Culinary arts apprenticeship programs (including pastry) are sponsored across the country by members of the American Culinary Federation (ACF). Today, nearly 2,000 apprentices are learning and earning by participating in ACF apprenticeships in the United States. These apprenticeships are three-year programs with 6,000 hours of on-the-job training and 192 additional hours of related classroom training each year. Included in the related training are courses like an introduction to the hospitality industry, waitstaff training, business and professional writing, sanitation and safety, menu planning and design, food purchasing and storage, business math, beverage management, food marketing, and nutrition. Fees for related training are generally not provided with ACF apprenticeships, but scholarships or financial aid may be available. Apprentices are responsible for purchasing their own set of basic kitchen tools. They must also pay a $110 enrollment fee that includes a training log and the required text for the program. Meals are provided in many of these programs, and in some resort locations, housing may be provided as well. ACF has trained more than 17,000 apprentices in their program. After completing the apprenticeship, workers are certified as "Culinarians" with the AFC and are certified as journeymen chefs with the Department of Labor.

Other hotels and restaurants may also sponsor similar programs, and local vocational schools may have apprenticeship arrangements with area restaurants or other food service establishments.

Culinary apprentice and now sous chef* Rohan Brown (left) learns on the job while working under the direction of master chef Eric Baloy. Brown's apprenticeship is sponsored by the Anthony Spinazzola Foundation Culinary Apprenticeship Program. Apprentices are placed at area restaurants with a chef to mentor them, and their initial salary is paid through the foundation. The program requires students to complete 25 credit hours at a local community college (tuition and expenses paid for by the foundation), where, upon completion, they will receive a certificate in culinary arts. The student is then eligible to receive an associate of science degree in hospitality. Photo by Penny Hutchins Paquette.

APPRENTICESHIP IS JUST THE BEGINNING

After high school, Rohan Brown began an apprenticeship with Sebastian's Catering in Boston. He started by working with the waitstaff and shortly after asked for a transfer to the kitchen. Today he is in the number-two position of the prestigious Boston catering firm.

Now with the title and responsibilities of sous chef under chief executive chef Eric Baloy, Brown is adding business experience to his already-accomplished cooking skills.

*The sous chef is second in command in the kitchen and in large organizations may supervise all food production.

(*continued*)

Included in his new responsibilities are scheduling, paperwork, and supervising the staff. Rohan says it took patience and time to get where he is today. It didn't happen overnight.

When he started his apprenticeship, his goals were to get the feel of the place and to see what catering is all about. While learning to cook in his apprenticeship position, he attended night classes at a local community college.

According to his mentor, Brown's potential was obvious from the start. The executive chef observed him as he worked with a group of seven or eight other cooks for the special events staff. According to Baloy, it was obvious to him even then that Brown had what it takes to advance in the business. "He was always on time, he came in early if he knew we were going to be busy, he had his head down, and he was working. It was obvious that he cared about what he was doing," says Baloy. While those around him were chatting and fooling around, the apprentice was on task and at the same time he was developing into the kind of employee that Baloy respects.

When the opening of sous chef became available, Brown was the person Baloy recruited for the job. "It is great for me to have someone I know and that I can trust who is going to know what to do," says the executive chef.

Baloy says an apprenticeship helps develop young people. Those who start working just out of school sometimes don't even know how to use a knife. Apprenticeship gives them the on-site experience to develop good skills. He has three tips for those who consider entering a culinary apprenticeship program, "Be on time. Work hard. Be sure your uniform is clean."

Related Skills

Most apprenticeship programs require at least a high school diploma. Cooking classes in most high schools can provide background for work in this area. More specialized training at a vocational school can provide a background in much of the work that will be required in the related training courses. Part-time work in area restaurants can also help you get an understanding of what it is like to work in food service.

Nationally recognized chefs across the country say they look for young people with a good work ethic, a positive attitude, lots of energy, and a passion for cooking.

Resources

For more information about apprenticeship programs in your area, contact your local apprenticeship organization. For more information about apprenticeships and work in the food service industry, contact:

American Culinary Federation
180 Center Place Way
St. Augustine, FL 32095
Phone: (904) 824-4468
Internet: http://www.acfchefs.org/apprwhat.html
   (apprenticeship fundamentals)
Includes a link to programs across the country.

National Restaurant Association
1200 17th St., NW
Washington, DC 20036-3097
Internet: http://www.restaurant.org
Click on the "careers and education" link for background
   information about training in the field, and take a look at
   advice from nationally recognized chefs.

StarChefs Online
Internet: http://www.starchefs.com
Provides a wide variety of information about the business,
   including a listing of both star chefs and up-and-coming
   "rising stars."

Funeral Director and Embalmer

Funeral Director	*O*NET/SOC*	*11-9061.00*
	DOT	*187.167-030*
	RAIS	*0820*
Embalmer	*O*NET/SOC*	*39-4011.00*
	DOT	*338.281.010*
	RIAS	*0665*

With the popularity of the HBO television series *Six Feet Under*, interest in the funeral services business is on the rise. Funeral directors, sometimes called morticians or undertakers, arrange and direct the tasks associated with funeral practices. They provide bereavement support to the family and arrange and direct funeral ceremonies. They remove the body to the mortuary and prepare the remains according to the wishes of the survivors, following any legal requirements that may be necessary.

Most funeral directors are also trained embalmers and may prepare the body by replacing blood with embalming fluid to preserve the tissue. They are trained to make any reconstruction necessary in cases where the body has been disfigured and to apply cosmetics to create a natural appearance. Funeral directors then place the body in a casket for viewing. In most areas, burial in the casket it still the most common method of handling the remains.

More families are choosing cremation today, however. In some cases cremation follows funeral services, and in others cremation is followed by a memorial service. Cremated remains are placed in an urn or other receptacle that is usually buried or placed in a mausoleum or a special niche called a columbarium. The remains may be scattered or retained by a loved one as well.

While many people believe most funeral directors spend a great deal of time with embalming or preparing the body, that's not the case. According to Jacquelyn Taylor, executive director of the New England Institute at Mt. Ida College, of the 40 to 50 hours it takes to prepare for a typical funeral, only two or three hours are spent on technically preparing the body.

Funeral directors organize the logistics of the funeral, including scheduling the grave opening and closing, preparing the sites, and providing transportation for the remains, the family, and other mourners.

Today, more focus is on tributes. "The next wave of funeral service education is about personalization and meaningful tributes. That requires a whole new skill set. Today's ceremonies may include new technologies, including Power

Point presentations or DVD presentations, complete with music or video clips," says Taylor.

Funeral directors also handle all of the paperwork involved, including placing obituary notices, filing for death certificates, handling insurance matters, and other applications for burial benefits.

Because funeral customs can vary widely, workers in this field must be knowledgeable in the funeral and burial customs of many faiths, ethnic groups, and fraternal organizations. Funeral directors who own their own businesses are responsible for all of the business operations as well.

Those who start out in funeral services follow a career path into medical forensics, working as medical examiners.

Job Outlook and Wages

The average annual salary for a funeral director was $53,510 in 2003. Those who provide embalming services in funeral establishments averaged $36,360 a year. Funeral directors in Connecticut had the highest average earnings, $79,980, followed closely by New Jersey, Ohio, California, and Massachusetts. The highest concentrations of workers were in South Dakota, North Dakota, West Virginia, Arkansas, and South Carolina. In addition to variations across the country, salaries of funeral directors depend on the number of years of experience in the business, the number of services they perform, the number of facilities they operate, the size of community, and the level of formal education.

Although the Bureau of Labor Statistics predicts job grow in this area to be slower than average—up just 6.6 percent through 2012, employment opportunities are still expected to be good. This job isn't for everyone, and the number of people who choose to go into the profession is small. In addition, the number of older workers in the field is higher than for most jobs, and large numbers will retire in the next eight to ten years.

Apprenticeships

Funeral directors are licensed in all states. In most states, funeral director candidates must complete at least a two-year associate's degree program or a four-year bachelor's degree program. According to Dr. George P. Connick, executive director of the American Board of Funeral Service Education, the board requires that every graduate of an accredited program must be trained as an embalmer as well.

Course work may include anatomy, physiology, pathology, and restoration. In addition to programs in the sciences, programs in social services and legal and ethical issues are covered as well. Psychology and grief counseling courses are required as well as programs that prepare funeral directors for the business side of the job. Business management, accounting, and funeral home management are also part of the curriculum.

After completing college-level studies (and sometimes before or during college work), those who want to join the profession must serve at least a one-year apprenticeship and pass a qualifying exam. Apprenticeships must be completed under the direction of an experienced and licensed funeral director. Programs vary from state to state and may last from one to three years. Depending on state requirements, apprenticeships may be served before, during, or after studies are completed. During apprenticeships, workers receive hands-on training in all aspects of funeral work from embalming to bereavement support. Once all prerequisites are met, licensing is required in all states. Licensing exams may be written and oral and require a demonstration of practical skills as well.

What we often think of as a male-dominated business is changing rapidly. More and more women are entering this business, and today 51 percent of mortuary school graduates are women. Many believe this is because it is a business that requires the nurturing and comforting skills often associated with women. Others think it merely reflects the same percentages as other professional careers like physicians and lawyers.

Related Skills

Many people are uncomfortable discussing death. Most are uncomfortable being near dead bodies or even considering touching them. This is a job for a very special group of people who require a range of skills unlike any other profession.

Although much of the attention is spent on the preparation of bodies, workers in this field spend much more time working with the living than the dead. You will need excellent interpersonal skills to work in this field. This job calls for people who are sensitive, calm, and compassionate. These personal traits must be combined with an interest in the human biological sciences.

High school course work in biology, chemistry, and public speaking provide good preparatory work for this field. Often there are volunteer opportunities at funeral homes that can provide some exposure to the work involved. Young people often take on maintenance tasks at the facility, keeping the grounds manicured and the limousines polished.

Resources

Those interested in making a career in funeral services should first check the licensing requirements in the state or states in which they hope to practice.

For information about jobs in the funeral services industry, contact:

National Funeral Directors Association
13625 Bishop's Dr.
Brookfield, WI 53005
Internet: http://www.nfda.org

For information about college programs in mortuary science:

The American Board of Funeral Service Education
38 Florida Ave.
Portland, ME 04123
Internet: http://www.abfse.org

Personal Appearance Specialists

Barber	*O*NET/SOC*	*39-5011.00*
	DOT	*330.371-010*
	RAIS	*0030*

The barber profession has changed significantly over the years. In ancient times, some people believed that both good and bad spirits lived in the hair and that a haircut could drive the bad ones away. Did you know that during the Middle Ages the barbers not only cut hair, but pulled teeth, gave enemas, did bloodletting, and treated wounds as well? During that time, one of the earliest trade organizations was established, the Worshipful Company of Barbers. Barbers and surgeons continued to have dual roles until the end of the 18th century!

Today, barbers cut and style hair and trim beards or shave them away. At one time, barbers only worked on men. Today, they may cut and style hair for women and children as well. They must be licensed in all states.

Cosmetologist,	*O*NET/SOC*	*39-5012.00*
Hairdresser, and	*DOT*	*332.271-010*
Hair Stylist	*RAIS*	*0096*

In the recent past, cosmetologists, hairdressers, and hair stylists only worked on women. Today, women, men, and children benefit from the services of workers in this field. Cosmetologists may cut, style, and color hair. Some specialize as nail technicians, giving manicures, applying nail extensions, and giving pedicures. Others may specialize in skin care. These workers are sometimes called estheticians. They may clean and treat the skin, giving facials, full-body treatments, and head and neck massages. They may also perform hair removal, waxing eyebrows, bikini lines, and other areas of the body. Some also specialize in makeup application. Some are qualified to do work in all areas. Cosmetologists must be licensed in all states.

Job Outlook and Wages

In 2003, the average annual salary (including tips) for a barber was $23,210; cosmetologists averaged $21,810 (including tips). This difference in salaries may be related to the wider variety of jobs that cosmetologists may perform; the average includes workers that only perform manicures and pedicures, for example. The vast majority of barbers and cosmetologists work in the personal care field. Barbers working in the District of Columbia, Minnesota, Kentucky, North Carolina, and Kansas were among the highest paid. The highest concentrations of barbers were in Alaska, Connecticut, New Mexico, New Jersey, and West Virginia. Cosmetologists working in the District of Columbia averaged more than $46,000 a year. Hawaii, Washington, Alaska, and Connecticut were also among the top-paying states for cosmetologists. The highest concentrations of workers were found in New Jersey, North Dakota, Maryland, Pennsylvania, and Wisconsin.

Job growth for cosmetologists is expected to be about average—up 14.7 percent through 2012. Growth will be slower for barbers—up only 6.5 percent, as more and more men choose to have their hair cut, colored, and styled in hair salons rather than barber shops. Job opportunities will be good in the cosmetology field, but competition for jobs in the higher-paying salons will be intense. Those with the broadest training will have the best opportunities.

Apprenticeships

Apprenticeship programs vary widely from state to state. Most require about 2,000 to 3,600 hours of on-the-job training—about one to two years. Related instruction may take place at a community college, local technical school, or, in some cases, in distance learning programs. Course work may include professional ethics, bacteriology, decontamination and infection control, hair analysis, draping, shampooing, thermal hairstyling, permanent waving, hair coloring, chemical relaxing, thermal straightening, manicuring and pedicuring, anatomy and physiology, chemistry, and basic business practices. Some areas allow workers as young as 16 to work as apprentices.

Some vocational high schools offer certificates for barbers and cosmetologists as well. Many of these programs require a period of apprenticeship before licensing. Apprentices may also complete shorter programs in specialty areas like nail technicians and estheticians. All must be licensed, and licensing exams usually include both a written exam as well as a practical exam demonstrating ability. Check with your local licensing board for specific requirements in your area.

Related Skills

Although cosmetology and barber apprenticeships do not always require a high school diploma or GED, those with a high school education often have the skills necessary to advance in the field. Course work in anatomy can be useful for this career. Since many cosmetologists go on to start their own businesses, a background in business is also useful—accounting, business math, etc.

As important are communication skills. Workers in this field need to listen to the desires and ideas of their clients and be able to give them suggestions about cut, color, and cosmetics. Those with strengths in fashion, art, and technical design are often successful in this field.

For information about apprenticeships in your area, contact your local apprenticeship organization, a local vocational school, or your local community college.

A list of licensed training schools and licensing requirements for cosmetologists is available from:

National Accrediting Commission of Cosmetology Arts
   and Sciences
4401 Ford Ave., Suite 1300
Alexandria, VA 22301
Internet: http://www.naccas.org

For more information about cosmetology careers:

National Cosmetology Association
401 North Michigan Ave., 22nd Floor
Chicago, IL 60611
Internet: http://www.salonprofessionals.org

Production

Stop and think about the first ten things you touched today. An alarm clock? A faucet? The handle to your refrigerator door? The toaster? The knob on your stove? No matter how your day started, it is likely that many of the things you touched were produced in factories. Our cars come from factories. Our computers come from factories. In addition to all the common things we use every day, specialty items are produced as well. Whether it is a hand-tooled part for one of Jay Leno's cars or a pacifier to keep an infant quiet, workers all over the country help design and produce the products we need.

Metal and Plastics Production— Precision Machine Technology

Do you like to tinker? Do you like to work with your hands? Do you like to design things? Are you the one that gets handed the directions when a complicated toy needs to be assembled? Your skills might be just right for the precision machine technology field.

There were 16,429 registered apprentices designing, making, and tinkering in the production industry in 2002, and most of them were doing precision machine work. It takes a coordinated effort from design to finished product to make the consumer goods that we need each day. Someone not only has to design the product, but also design and make the machines and tools that will produce that product. Some workers in this field operate machines that mass produce

Apprentice Frank Roth IV makes adjustments during the National Tooling and Machining Association's annual apprenticeship contest. Photo provided by the National Tooling and Machining Association.

TOOL AND DIE APPRENTICE COMPETES IN PRECISION MACHINING COMPETITION

In 2004, Frank Roth of Hawk Point, Missouri, beat out the competition in the 32nd Annual National Apprentice Competition sponsored by the National Tooling and Machining Association. Fifteen winners of regional competitions met at the event that tests the skills and knowledge of fourth-year apprentices in the precision metal working industry. The intense two-day event included projects in lathe, mill, and precision grinding, as well as a competitive written exam.

The young competitors are among the highly skilled individuals trained to use sophisticated equipment to design and manufacture the metal and plastic parts that go into most things we use every day.

Roth says his apprenticeship training and his willingness to listen helped him win national recognition and prizes including a toolbox, precision measuring instruments, and other tools of the trade.

With an associate's degree from a technical college, Roth says he was well prepared for his entry-level apprenticeship

(*continued*)

job. "I had the basics. What I learned during the apprenticeship came from the older gentlemen who have been in the trade for a long time. Even though you learn the basics in school, there is more than one way to skin a cat. The experienced workers taught me how to do things faster and more easily than the ways we were taught in school. Apprenticeship training makes you efficient. You take what you know and with the guidance of the journeymen you become good, fast, and accurate."

Roth says apprentices should be prepared for a little good-natured teasing, but the experienced workers who taught him were always willing to answer questions and help him improve his skills. "I am always eager to learn," says Roth. "My mom said if you ever stop learning, the world is going to pass you by. I am willing to listen to how things can be done better and I tried to take in as much as I possibly could."

Roth says those good listening skills paid off during the competition—that and the ability to remain calm. "That may sound trivial, but with newspaper reporters watching and television cameras rolling, it is easy to get nervous," he said.

Now a journeyman himself, he operates computer numerically controlled (CNC) systems helping create specialty metal products for industries across the country.

individual pieces that will later be assembled into a finished product. Some workers create one-of-a-kind models that will be used as a template for production. Other workers hand tool parts that are so special that they may only be created once in a lifetime. Together these machine setters, operators, tenders, machinists, pattern makers, and model makers are among the precision machine workers that help make most things we use each day.

Machine Setters, Operators, and Tenders

In order to produce anything made of metal or plastic, these workers must be involved with the complex production machinery. With varying levels of skills and training, they keep the production line moving by setting up, operating, and looking after the machines used in production.

Those who set up the machines, called set-up workers, get the machines ready for production and make necessary adjustments as the project goes along. In the past, they have been the most highly skilled workers in this category. Today, however, newer automated production techniques allow less-skilled workers to take over some of the tasks.

Operators and tenders monitor the machinery during operation. They may load and unload the machine (although in some cases robots do this now) or make minor adjustments to controls.

Setters, operators, and tenders of metal products work with machinery that cuts and forms all types of metal parts. Those responsible for setting up the machines review the sequence of the project by reviewing blueprints, layouts, or other plans. They make the necessary adjustments to speed, feed, and other controls and take care of the cooling and lubricating to ensure the machine does not overheat. Operators and tenders then take care of the repetitive operations particular to the type of machine they are using (see below).

Two-liter soda bottles, baby pacifiers, rubber duckies, auto parts, and garden hoses are among the thousands of consumer products made of plastics. Plastics setters, operators, and tenders are the workers who deal with the machinery that turns plastic compounds into those consumer goods.

Workers in metal and workers in plastic do a variety of production operations with very specialized machines. Individual machines forge, roll, cut, punch, press, drill, bore, turn, mill, plane, cast, and mold metal or plastic. Workers may specialize in one type of machine or handle several types. Although there are about 15 specialized machine tool apprenticeships in production, the following were most often represented on the state apprenticeships page:

Occupational Specialties

Drilling and Boring	*O*NET/SOC*	*51-4032*
Machine Tool	*DOT*	*604-380.022*
	RAIS	*0502*

Set up, operate, or tend drilling machines to drill, bore, ream, mill, or countersink metal or plastic work pieces.

Lathe and Tuning	O*NET/SOC	51-4034
Machine Tool	DOT	604-380.022
(Screw Machine)	RAIS	0502

These machines turn, bore, thread, form, or face metal or plastics, such as wire, rod, or bar stock.

Multiple Machine Tool	O*NET/SOC	51-4081
	DOT	600-380.018
	RAIS	0958

These production machine tool operators can work with a variety of machines and robots.

Numerical Control	O*NET/SOC	5140-11.01
Machine Tool	DOT	609-362.010
	RAIS	0845

Operate computer-controlled machines or robots to perform one or more machine functions on metal or plastic work pieces.

Tool Grinders, Filers,	O*NET/SOC	51-4194
and Sharpeners	DOT	680-380.010
	RAIS	0898

These machine tools workers set up, operate, or tend grinding and related tools that remove excess material or burrs from surfaces, sharpen edges or corners, or buff, hone, or polish metal or plastic work pieces.

Welding Machine Tool	O*NET/SOC	51-4122.01
	DOT	810-382.010
	RAIS	0945

Workers in this category set up, operate, or tend machines that permanently join the metal components of products like car and airplane parts, brackets, and panels.

Job Outlook and Wages

Average annual wages for machine specialists in 2003 were between $26,000 and $30,000. Those who could operate multiple machines averaged about $31,000 a year. Setters made the highest wages in this category. Growth in jobs in this category will be slower than average. Multiple machine operators will have the most opportunities.

Computer-controlled machine tools and robots are replacing workers in the operating and tender jobs. Jobs in this area will diminish as more of the functions they perform become automated. In addition, foreign competition has U.S. producers moving their production facilities to other countries where labor is cheaper.

On the plus side, many workers are rapidly approaching retirement age, so there will be jobs in the future. Operators who can operate multiple machine tools and numerical control machine tools and have a good knowledge of the properties of metals and plastics will have the best opportunities in this changing job market.

Apprenticeships

Because of the varying complexity of the machines used in production, apprenticeships for set-up, operator, and tender apprenticeships vary in length, usually between two and four years, with 144 hours of classroom training required as well. Related instruction for these jobs may take place in vocational schools or community colleges and may include blueprint reading, related mathematics and measurement, industrial machining, welding, related computer classes, and maintenance. In some programs, apprentices may work on associate's degrees while doing their related classroom work.

Some apprenticeships in this category are now competency based and experienced workers may progress more quickly. Workers in this area may continue their training and become more-skilled workers called machinists (see below).

Related Skills

Machine tools setters, operators, and tenders should have a strong mechanical background. High school classes that provide experience with machines and tools as well as blueprint reading will be beneficial. A solid background in math is also important. Algebra, geometry, calculus, and statistics can help prepare workers to handle these complex machines. Computer skills are also beneficial. Good communication skills, both written and spoken, are also important.

Resources

In addition to finding information about apprenticeships from your local apprenticeship agency, you can find out more about jobs in production at the end of this section.

Machinists

Machinists	O*NET/SOC	51-4041.00
	DOT	600-280.22
	RAIS	9296

Machinists remind me of the old chicken-and-the-egg question. Because machinists use machines to produce precision parts that may be used to make the machines the machinist use, which came first, the machine, or the machine part? Something to think about.

Of course, machinists produce the metal parts of all kinds of things, not just machines. They make the parts that are needed in numbers too small to be mass-produced. They have made artificial tusks for an injured elephant and high-speed gears for Jay Leno's antique cars. If you can imagine it, they have probably made it.

They use machine tools like lathes, milling machines, and machining centers to produce the metal parts that are durable under a variety of operating conditions. Some produce large quantities of one part, and many produce one-of-kind parts or a small number of parts. The work requires precision and must meet exacting standards when producing precision parts.

Before they begin, they must review blueprints or specifications and then calculate where to cut or bore the metal. They need to know how fast to feed the metal into the machine, and how much metal to remove. They need to select the appropriate tools and materials for the job, plan the order of the production and finishing, and mark the material to show where cuts will be made. All of this before they even begin cutting!

They monitor and sometimes adjust the feed rate and the speed of the machine and make sure the systems do not overheat during the process. Once the project is complete, they must check the accuracy of their work.

Today, computer technology may also be used during the production process, and the machines may be computer numerically controlled (CNC). Some machinists work with CNC programmers to determine the best production method, and many are trained in CNC programming themselves and can write basic programs or modify programs during production, if necessary.

Some machinists specialize in maintenance work, repairing or making new parts for existing machines.

Job Outlook and Wages

There were more than 368,000 machinists working in 2003, with an average salary of $33,900. The best-paid and most-experienced workers averaged $48,590. Workers in the District of Columbia were the best paid in the country, averaging $54,980. Hawaii, Alaska, Delaware, and Washington were also among the top-paying areas of the country. The highest concentrations of workers were in Michigan, Ohio, Connecticut, Wisconsin, and Indiana.

Although job growth in this area is expected to be slower than average, up just over 8 percent through 2012, job prospects will be excellent. Because few young people choose to go into production jobs, there are not enough trained workers to fill both the new jobs and those created when workers retire or go into other fields.

Apprenticeships

Many machinists learn their jobs through apprenticeship programs lasting about three or four years. Some programs are competency based and allow apprentices to progress more quickly. Apprentice machinists work full time, getting on-the-job training, learning to use the machine tools under the supervision of an experienced machinist.

Related classroom work usually takes place in a community college or vocational college setting. Most training facilities use a curriculum that incorporates the national skills standards developed by the National Institute of Metalworking Skills. Those who complete these programs are certified and have better career opportunities. In addition, most schools using this curriculum provide college credit to apprentices, allowing them to work toward a degree as they work on their apprenticeship programs. Courses may include math, physics, materials science, blueprint reading, mechanical drawing, CNC operations, and CNC programming.

Most programs require a high school diploma or GED and applicants must be at least 18 years old.

Related Skills

Workers in this field must we willing to pay close attention to detail. This is precision work where 1/10,000th of an inch can mean the difference between a functioning part and a piece of worthless metal. Skill in math is essential. The Tooling and Manufacturing Association recommends students take at least two years of high school math, including algebra and geometry. Trigonometry, physics, and chemistry are also useful. They also suggest visiting a manufacturing facility in your area and talking with an industry representative about the work and related training. If you can work at a manufacturing company part time while going to high school, you will be even better prepared.

Resources

Because many of the resources provide information about several areas of production, a list of related resources is at the end of this section.

Model Makers, Metal and Plastic

Model Makers, Metal and Plastic	O*NET/SOC	51-4061.00
	DOT	Numbers vary according to product
	RAIS	Varies according to product

Model makers create the prototype to be used in the development of the actual product. These models are accurate down to the finest detail planned for the finished product. In fact, it is a finished product on its own—one that will be used to mass-produce the product. Because the models represent the final product, workers in this field must be knowledgeable in all areas, design through production. They take a designer's idea and turn it into a product. Designers think these are the most gifted people in industrial manufacturing.

Models may include something as small as a razor or as large as a full-size automobile. Model makers work in a wide variety of industrial settings, including the production of automobiles, jewelry, watches, airplanes, toys, appliances, and all kinds of consumer products. The models are crafted in the same material as the finished product. Model makers may specialize in plastic or metal. Some also specialize in wood.

Job Outlook and Wages

This is a highly specialized career, with the total number of workers in 2002 numbering only 9,000. The number of new jobs is expected to grow about as fast as average—up about 14.5 percent through 2012. Because workers is this field are older, on average, there will be job openings due to retirements over the next ten years, creating job opportunities for those with the right combinations of skills.

Model makers were among the highest paid in the precision production field. The average salary across the nation was $43,630 in 2003. Those working in the production of automobiles and household appliances were among the top earners, averaging more than $50,000 a year.

Experienced workers earned much more. The top-paying states for model makers were Connecticut, Ohio, Maryland, Indiana, and Mississippi. The highest concentrations of workers were in Rhode Island, New Hampshire, Indiana, Wisconsin, and Ohio.

Many model makers are member of the Pattern Makers League of North America

Apprenticeships

As you might expect, apprenticeships in this field are longer than any other in the industry. Apprentices need 10,000 hours (about five years) of on-the-job training, combined with related study of at least 144 hours a year. Because this job requires a background in all aspects of production, related studies include all aspects of production from related mathematics to the drafting interpretation of three-dimensional shapes. Studies in computer-aided design (CAD), blueprint patterns, molding and coremaking, assembly, machine practice and theory, and characteristics of ferrous metals may also be part of the program. As with many apprenticeship programs in precision production, course work can often be applied to degree programs.

Related Skills

Mechanical and mathematical skills, artistic talent, manual dexterity, and interpersonal and communications skills are all required in this field of design and production. A background in CAD and other computer design skills is helpful. Many people in this field have bachelor's degrees in design or other related field.

Resources

Call your local apprenticeship organization for information about apprenticeships in your area. The resources at the end of this section will help you learn more about jobs in the industry.

Pattern Makers

Pattern Makers	O*NET/SOC	51-4062.00
	DOT	Varies according to materials used
	RAIS	Varies by material

Pattern makers, like model makers, help in the developmental stage of production. They are involved in creating the patterns or the forms that will be used in creating the final product. They may use wood, plastic, metal, plaster of paris, or polystyrene to produce the precision castings—full-scale three-dimensional models that become the "patterns" for making molds used in the production process.

They also produce the core boxes used to make the cores that go inside a mold to allow an open space or cavity within the product. They provide the forms or castings used to produce all kinds of consumer products, from replacement joints for the medical industry to aircraft engines for aerospace. They help produce full-size cars and the small, scale-model cars you probably played with as a child. Almost any consumer product or a part of that consumer product needs a pattern maker to help in its production.

Job Outlook and Wages

There are even fewer pattern makers than model makers (see above). In 2002, there were only about 6,000 specialists in the field. Job growth is expected to be slower than average—up only 3.6 percent through 2012. Because, once created, patterns can be used over and over to create identical castings, the number of patterns for castings has dropped. Still, as with most jobs in the industry, many workers are reaching retirement age and openings will be available. The Bureau of Labor Statistics estimates that about 2,000 jobs will be available over the next ten years. Not a large number, but the number of people with the range of skills necessary for this field is small as well. If you think you might enjoy a career in the field, visit some of the resources at the end of this section to learn more about it.

Pattern makers averaged $36,290 in 2003. The top 10 percent of workers in the field averaged $61,000. The best-paid pattern makers worked in machinery manufacturing. Workers in Michigan, Ohio, Iowa, Massachusetts, and Washington were the best paid in the nation, and the highest concentrations of workers were in Wisconsin, Ohio, Indiana, Michigan, and Iowa.

Apprenticeships

Apprenticeships in this specialty are among the longest, four to five years. Because workers need skills in a wide variety of areas, the training takes a long time. Related course work is similar to training for model makers—related mathematics, including geometry and trigonometry, blueprint reading, related tools and machines, geometrical drawing, drafting, CAD, molding and core making, and other related courses of study. As with many of the apprenticeship programs in precision production, course work may be applied to a degree.

Related Skills

According to one Canadian trade school, "you must have the creative conception of a draftsperson-designer, the practical ability of a molder, the precise skills of a machinist, the analytical judgment of a metallurgist, and the specific exactness of a mathematician." Such diverse skills require a head start while in high school. Take all the math courses your high school offers. If your school offers courses in CAD or blueprint reading or mechanical drawing, take those as well.

Because this job requires that you work with a number of people who have different specialties, it is important that you have good communication skills as well.

Tool and Die Maker and Mold Maker

Tool and Die Maker	*O*NET/SOC*	*51-4111*
and Mold Maker	*DOT*	*601-260.010*
		(tool and die)
		601-128.030
		(mold)

225

RAIS   *0586*
                                         (tool and die)
                                         0116 (mold)

From the paper clips we use to hold our papers together to the airplanes that take us around the world, tool and die makers are the highly specialized machinists who make the tools and machines used by other machinists to produce these products. Toolmakers are responsible for crafting the tools and machines that cut, shape, and form metal and other materials. They also craft the equipment that holds the metal while it is bored, stamped, or drilled, as well as the measuring devices and gauges used to calibrate the process. Die makers make the metal forms, or dies, used to shape the metal during stamping and forging. Mold makers make metal molds for diecasting and molding plastics, ceramics, and other composite materials. Without them, there would be no cell phones, toothbrushes, or computer monitors, or any of the other products we take for granted.

These workers may be involved from the beginning of the manufacturing process, creating the prototypes of parts and determining how they will be made. They work from blueprints and plan the steps necessary to create the tool or die. They measure, mark, cut, bore, drill, file, grind, polish, and check for accuracy until the product is complete. They may use computer-aided design (CAD) during the development stage. The computer program can develop drawings for the tools and dies. Then computer-aided manufacturing programs can be used to convert the drawings into a computer program that gives instructions for the sequence of the cutting tool operations. Using these electronic programs, computer numerically controlled (CNC) machines can follow the directions and produce the tool or die. Tool and die makers can both write the programs and operate the machines.

Job Outlook and Wages

Although little growth is expected in this field (up only 0.4 percent through 2012), the outlook is excellent for anyone interested in becoming a tool and die maker. As with machinists (see above), not enough young people are interested in entering this manufacturing specialty, creating a shortage of trained workers. Although much of the work is now automated (resulting in the slow growth pattern), tool and die makers are still needed to build and maintain the new automated equipment. As older workers leave the field, there are not enough trained workers to replace them.

The high level of skill required to do this job is reflected in the wages. The average tool and die maker earned $43,900 in 2003. The top 10 percent of all workers earned $64,140. The highest-paid workers worked in architectural and engineering service companies, where workers earned an average of $60,000 a year. The top-paying states in 2003 were Michigan, Oregon, Indiana, Washington, and Minnesota. The highest concentration of workers were in Michigan, Indiana, Ohio, Wisconsin, and Connecticut.

Apprenticeships

Apprenticeships in this area usually take about four to five years. New competency-based programs rely more on apprentice knowledge than years of study, giving an advantage to more experienced workers, but this apprenticeship requires a great deal of skill and precision, and those without experience in the field should expect to spend at least four years training, probably more. In addition to the on-the-job training, expect to spend at least 144 hours a year in related classroom training. As with machinists (see above), new standards developed by the National Institute of Metalworking are incorporated into the curriculum of many of the vocational schools and community colleges that offer related course work for tool and die makers. As you go through the related studies for the apprenticeship program, you can begin to work on a college degree at the same time.

Typical courses for this apprenticeship might include related mathematics, including practical measurements, safety, manufacturing theory, blueprint reading, tools instruction, machining skills, metal processing, machine skills, metallurgy of materials, and computer-assisted design.

Related Skills

Precision, precision, precision. If you are a stickler for detail, this could be the job for you. You will need excellent math skills as well. Good eye-hand coordination and excellent eyesight are essential. Take as much math as you can while you are in high school. Algebra, geometry, trigonometry, and statistics will help improve your chances of excelling in this area. Chemistry and computer skills are helpful as well.

Resources

Your local apprenticeship organization can direct you to programs in the field, and the following resources will also be helpful.

International Association of Machinists
   & Aerospace Workers
9000 Machinists Place
Upper Marlboro, MD 20772-2687
Phone: (301) 967-4500
Email: websteward@goiam.org
Internet: www.iamaw.org/

The National Institute for Metalworking Skills
3251 Old Lee Highway, Suite 205
Fairfax, VA 22030
Phone: (703) 352-4971
Internet: http://www.nims-skills.org/

National Tooling and Machining Association
9300 Livingston Rd.
Ft. Washington, MD 20744
Internet: http://www.ntma.org

Precision Machine Products Association
6700 West Snowville Rd.
Becksville, OH 441-3292
Phone: (440) 526-0300
Internet: http://www.pmpa.org

Precision Metalforming Association Educational Foundation
6363 Oak Tree Blvd.
Independence, OH 44131-2500
Internet: http://www.pmaef.org
Tool and Die Division
Internet: http://www.metalforming.com

Protective and Investigative Services

People who choose careers in the protective and investigative services are usually those who have a strong desire to be of service to their town, their city, their state, or their country. Although workers in this field are not among the best paid in the nation, most workers don't do it for the money. They are especially committed to service and public safety. On the plus side, many of these jobs come with strong benefit programs that allow workers to retire early and have a second career while they are still young.

With the exception of private investigators, workers in this field work for cities, towns, states, or the federal government. In addition to the 50 state governments, there are about 87,500 local governments in the United States. Workers in the protective services can work for any of these. They may be employed by small towns, protecting small populations, or they could work for a state and protect both suburban neighborhoods and cities. Some work fighting forest fires, protecting people, property, and the environment. Obviously the work environment for police officers and firefighters varies widely.

There are close to one million police officers and firefighters in the United States today, and another 400,000 work as correctional officers keeping local jails and state penitentiaries safe and secure. These jobs are among the most dangerous occupations in the country and require a serious commitment to service.

Also included in this chapter are private investigators who may work protecting individuals, but most often work gathering information for individuals, businesses, and the government. As you will see, this is a career that is very different from what we have seen in the movies and on television.

Correctional Officers

Correctional Officers	O*NET/SOC	33-3012
	DOT	372-667-018
	RAID	0851

Most correctional officers staff the nation's jails, state and federal prisons, and juvenile detention facilities overseeing the prisoners who have been convicted of crimes. Their job is to maintain security and to prevent disturbances, assaults, or escapes. As part of their job, they monitor the prisoners' activities, supervise work assignments, settle disputes, and enforce discipline. They may also have to search inmates and their quarters. They escort inmates to and from cells and other areas, and escort visitors, including lawyers, doctors, parole officers, and family members.

Part of their job is to see that the prison quarters are secure by checking locks, window bars, grilles, doors, and gates for signs of tampering. Correctional officers must also provide oral and written reports of disturbances, rule violations, and any unusual occurrences.

Because correctional officers are working with people who have broken the law, their job can range from difficult to dangerous. Prison guards are injured each year in confrontations with inmates. Depending on the prison, the working environment may be comfortable or, in older facilities, officers may work in hot, crowded, noisy environments. Because their services are necessary 24 hours a day, correctional officers may work in shifts that can include days, nights, weekends, and holidays.

The job calls for a special individual who is eager to serve and to make a difference in the community. Those who work helping rehabilitate prisoners make positive changes in people's lives.

Job Outlook and Wages

With new mandatory sentencing laws, more prisoners are going to jail and staying there. The expansion and construction of new correction facilities will also create new jobs for correctional officers. This means an excellent outlook for those looking for jobs in this field. Jobs are expected to grow faster than average—up 23.7 percent through 2012.

The average salary for correctional officers in 2003 was $35,090. The highest-paid workers were in New Jersey, Massachusetts, California, New York, and Nevada. The best-paid correctional officers in the country worked in San Francisco, where they averaged more than $55,000 a year. The highest concentrations of workers were in Louisiana, Texas, Mississippi, New York, and Georgia.

Apprenticeships

Apprenticeship programs lasting one to two years are available. Most often, apprentices start out by attending a basic training facility for several months before beginning the on-the-job part of their training. Beginning workers, supervised by experienced officers, may have little actual contact with prisoners. As they gain more experience, they may be assigned to specialized tasks within certain cell blocks, work areas, or recreation areas.

Federal correctional officers must undergo 2,000 hours of formal training within their first year and then complete 120 hours of specialized training at the U.S. Federal Bureau of Prisons. All officers receive annual inservice training.

Correctional officers must be at least 18, and some communities require them to be 21. In order to be hired as an apprentice, applicants must have a high school diploma or equivalent, and must have no felony convictions. Applicants must take written and physical tests to meet formal standards of fitness, eyesight, and hearing. Other tests to determine an applicant's suitability to work in a correctional environment may also be required.

Related Skills

People in this job must be emotionally stable and physically fit. If you want to work as a correctional office, it is important that you work well with people and that you can work under stressful conditions. Self-defense skills are important.

Applicants with a stable job history will have an advantage as will those who have some postsecondary courses in law enforcement, social science, or a related field. To advance in this career, postsecondary work will be necessary and inservice training will help as well.

Resources

To find out about opportunities in your area, contact your local apprenticeship organization or local or regional prison system. For more information about work in corrections, contact:

The American Jail Association
1135 Professional Court
Hagerstown, MD 21740-5853
Internet: http://www.corrections.com/aja/

Corrections.com
Internet: www.corrections.com

Federal Bureau of Prisons
320 First St., NW
Washington, DC 20534
Telephone: (202) 307-3198
Internet: http://www.bop.gov

Firefighters

Firefighters	O*NET/SOC	33-2011.01
	DOT	373-364.010
	RAIS	0195

Firefighters are trained to respond to fires and other emergencies. At the scene of a fire, firefighters perform specific duties including connecting hose lines to hydrants, operating pumps to send water to the hoses, and positioning ladders for fire fighting and for rescue. In addition to fighting the fire, firefighters rescue victims, provide emergency medical attention, and try to salvage the contents of buildings. In some fire departments, firefighters are trained as emergency medical technicians as well.

Most firefighters work for cities and towns protecting urban and suburban areas, but some firefighters work at airports, chemical plants, and other industrial sites as well. Some firefighters specialize in forest fires (see wildland firefighters, below). When they are not out on emergency calls, firefighters clean and maintain the equipment and conduct training sessions and practice drills. Some firefighters work as fire inspectors, examining buildings to prevent fires. Others work directly with developers and planners to check and approve plans for new buildings.

Firefighters work unusual hours, often more than 50 hours a week. They may work rotating schedules that require them to be on the job for 24 hours and then off for 48, or work day shifts of 10 hours for three or four days and then night shifts for several days, followed by a few days off. Fire departments in individual cities and towns set their own schedules.

Job Outlook and Wages

Competition for jobs in the fire department is fierce. Many people are called to public service and some like the fact that a pension is guaranteed after 20 years of work. The number of applicants for jobs usually exceeds the number of job openings and that is expected to continue. There will be job growth in the area resulting from the need to replace firefighters who retire or stop working for other reasons. Most growth will come in communities where a volunteer fire force is converted to a paid force.

Wages for firefighters averaged $38,280 in 2003, with the most experienced firefighters averaging close to $60,000 a year.

Firefighters often qualify for overtime pay while working to maintain minimum staffing levels or during emergency situations. As firefighters advance in rank, salaries increase. Fire chiefs can earn as much as $80,000 a year. In 2003, workers in New Jersey, California, Connecticut, Washington, and the District of Columbia were among the best paid. The highest concentration of firefighters was in Alaska, Massachusetts, Rhode Island, Wyoming, and Ohio.

Apprenticeships

Many fire departments test prospective employees and then hire those with the highest scores. Once hired, they send the employee to an intensive period of training before he or she begins work at the fire station. If you are interested in this field, it is best to have something to do between the time you take the exam and the time you start training. The hiring of recruits can sometimes take years.

Some fire departments have accredited apprenticeship programs that last between three and five years. Applicants must be at least 18 years old (in some areas they must be 19) and have a high school diploma or GED. The apprentices learn their skills on the job under the supervision of several experienced firefighters. In some programs they spend the first two to four months in recruit training school and then go on to learn more about firefighting on the job. In addition to the on-the-job training, they must study an additional 144 hours each year. Related course work might include the fundamentals of fire suppression, arson detection, elementary chemistry, physics, related mathematics, fundamentals of building construction, building codes, and other fire-related materials.

Diversity is an issue in firefighting, according to Eric Lamar of the National Firefighter's Association. Although some towns and cities have done an excellent job of recruiting minorities and women, he says they are still woefully underrepresented. Lamar says several things contribute to the problem. In some areas, recruits are required to have EMT or paramedic training before they can even apply. That makes it difficult for those who have limited financial resources to enter the field.

APPRENTICE OR PROBATIONARY FIREFIGHTERS

According to Captain Mahoney of the Worcester Fire Department in Massachusetts, his recruit firefighters are sometimes called probationary firefighters during their apprenticeship training. Firefighter recruits are selected after taking a civil service exam and a practical exam (strength and agility), having an interview, and after background checks are complete.

Once hired, the new recruits go to firefighter school. In Worcester, they have their own training facility, but in other communities, firefighters may be sent to a regional training program. During the 16 weeks of training, they work on firefighter skills, emergency medical services, hazardous materials, and confined space and collapsed rescue. Once they have completed the school portion of the training program, they begin their on-the-job training. Each firehouse has an officer assigned to supervise an apprentice. If that firefighter is out for any reason, another officer is assigned to supervise. Apprentice firefighters can never work without a supervisor. The probationary period lasts one year from the time they begin school.

Apprentice firefighters are paid as recruits, and they receive a raise upon completion of firefighter school. Step raises continue for the next four years.

What should you expect at firefighter school?

"We knew nothing when we started, absolutely nothing," says probationary firefighter Michael Papagni of the recruits in his firefighter school class. Although many in the class had some college experience before entering the program, they had no experience with fighting fires or with the academics that were required to help make them informed probationary firefighters.

At the end of the 16 weeks, Papagni says the hardest parts of the firefighter training program were the academic requirements. "The days were pretty intensive, and the academic work was extensive. We covered all kinds of topics. We were trained as EMTs, studied fire behavior, fire prevention, everything down to the basics of rope and hose construction. We dealt with weapons of mass destruction, hazardous materials, firefighter safety and rescue—all in the classroom. Then, after working all day, we would go home and study for another five or six hours."

On the practical days, he and the other recruits worked with live fires in the department's "burn" building. They practiced using self-contained breathing apparatus (SCBA), had rope and ladder drills, and learned about hose evolutions (the best size hose for treating certain types of fires).

Having completed fire school, Papagni is now a probationary firefighter, just beginning the eight-month on-the-job training part of his apprenticeship. Working under the supervision of an officer, he says the new firefighters wear a special green shield on their helmets, so everyone will know they are still in training and "don't know what experienced firefighters know." The probationary/apprentice on-the-job training will help him gain that experience and knowledge.

Because there are so few minorities and women working, there are few role models for young people to see. This can limit applicants. "In the past, it just didn't seem possible to them," he says. But things are getting better. As the women in firefighting rise through the ranks, they become more visible. "Instead of looking at these women and saying, 'I want to be a firefighter,' the young girls will start saying, 'I want to be a fire captain.'" Lamar says California has one of the best apprenticeship programs for firefighters and they actively recruit minority applicants.

Related Skills

Firefighters must be physically fit and often have to pass tests of strength, stamina, coordination, and agility as part of the application process. Get yourself in shape if you plan to work in this field. You may want to take some courses in fire science at a local community college to help improve your chances of being hired. In recent years, more and more applicants have some postsecondary education.

Resources

For information about apprenticeships in your area, contact your local fire department on your local apprenticeship organization. For more information about firefighting, contact:

International Association of Firefighters
1750 New York Ave., NW
Washington, DC 20006
Internet: http://www.iaff.org

U.S. Fire Administration
16825 South Seton Ave.
Emmitsburg, MD 21727
Internet: http://www.usfa.fema.gov

National Fire Academy
16825 South Seton Ave.
Emmitsburg, MD 21727
Internet: http://www.usfa.fema.gov/nfa/index.htm
For a list of accredited schools offering fire prevention programs, enter "accredited colleges and universities" in the search window.

Wildland firefighters like this young man and woman are responsible for protecting natural resources, wildlife, timber, recreation areas, historic sites, and archaeological artifacts. Photo © Karen Wattenmaker/NIFC—National Interagency Fire Center.

Wildland Firefighter Specialist

Wildland Firefighter	O*NET/SOC	33-2011.02
Specialist	DOT	452-687.640
	RAIS	0544

You've seen them on the national news—those brave men and women fighting forest fires. One day they are in California. A week later, they are in Nevada. Their faces are black with soot, cutting a fireline, hoping to slow a fire's progress. It looks like one of the most exciting jobs in the world, and it is. It is also one of the most exhausting. Want to see if you are fit enough? Fill a backpack with 40–50 pounds of material, strap it on your back, and run for about 10 miles. If you are still standing, you may have what it takes for this type of work.

Most firefighters are temporary or seasonal workers who return year after year to fight fires, helping protect natural resources, wildlife, timber, recreation areas, historic sites, and archaeological artifacts. They may work on handcrews, constructing firelines around wildfires to help control them, on hotshot crews using chainsaws and backpack water pumps to fight fires, on engine crews fighting fires with water and flame-retardant chemicals, or as specialized airborne firefighters who may dump water and chemicals on the fire or may parachute into remote areas to help fight fires. In 2003 alone, there were 85,953 wildland fires, affecting 4,918,088 acres.

Job Outlook and Wages

This is one of those jobs that workers don't do for the money. It is dangerous work, and wildland firefighters seem to be a special breed of people who are drawn to the job. For every seasonal job, there are at least 25 applicants, making the competition for jobs very stiff. Taking a seasonal job or enrolling in an apprenticeship program is the best way to gain access to full-time work in the field. In 2003, workers received hourly wages of between $9 and $15 an hour. Those who advance to careers as specialists could earn up to $40,000 a year.

Apprenticeship

Many states hire workers for their forestry services on a state-by-state basis, but the Wildland Firefighter Apprenticeship Program hires workers from all over the United States. The program operates under an agreement with the Department of Labor, the USDA Forest Service, USDI Bureau of Land Management, and the National Park Service. According to recruitment materials, this program is designed to take a career-entry firefighter and provide education, training, and work experience that will help an individual reach journey-level status as a wildland firefighter. (For more information, see the resources below.)

Apprentices must sign a mobility agreement stating that they can be relocated for training and for work. They must also sign a service agreement promising to complete the program and stay in federal service for a period of three times the length of the training period.

Apprentices must complete a residential four-week basic academy, a related technical training program, a supplemental training program, and supervised on-the-job training, followed by an additional four-week advanced training academy. The formal training academy is held at the Wildland Fire Training and Conference Center in Sacramento, California. The apprenticeships run from two to four years.

Academy work includes programs in physical fitness, basic fire prevention, fire behavior, tactical decision making, leadership, forest responder medical training, and wildland fire skills. The advanced academy work includes ignition specialist training, basic air operations, advanced fire behavior, fireline leadership, fuels management, fire fatality case studies, and physical fitness.

Related Skills

Obviously, this job requires a high degree of physical fitness. Applicants are expected to pass what they call a work capacity test (pack test), a three-mile hike in 45 minutes, carrying a 45-pound pack. They must also be able to run between one and five miles each day. Course work in fire management offered at local community colleges can help you prepare for apprenticeship as well. Basic first aid and CPR certification are essential.

Resources

For more information about apprenticeships in your area, contact your local apprenticeship organization or visit your local forestry service for more information. You can find more information about the apprenticeship program and jobs in wildland firefighting from the following:

Wildland Firefighter Apprenticeship Program
Internet: http://www.wfap.net/

National Park Service—Fire and Aviation Management
Internet: http://www.nps.gov/fire

For information about the work capacity test:
Internet: http://www.nps.gov/fire/developmental/
    dev_workcapacity.html

National Interagency Fire Center
3833 S. Development Ave.
Boise, ID 83705-5354
Phone: (208) 387-5512
Internet: http://www.nifc.gov/index.html

For seasonal firefighting information:

U.S. Department of the Interior
Quickhire (FIRES)
Internet: http://www.firejobs.doi.gov/index.php?action=home

Police Officers and Detectives

Police Officers	O*NET/SOC	33-3051.01
and Detectives	DOT	375-263-014
	RIAS	0437

Uniformed police officers who work for cities and towns across the nation protect their communities by enforcing the laws. Their individual jobs and methods vary widely from community to community. In small towns, uniformed officers take on all of the duties of a police officer from directing traffic to arresting felons. In urban police departments, officers may specialize in a particular type of duty. They may work on horseback, on bicycle, in police cars, or on foot monitoring specific areas of the city.

State police officers enforce motor vehicle laws and make arrests statewide. They may act as support officers to other police departments, especially small-town forces.

Detectives, or plainclothes investigators, gather facts and information for criminal cases. In small towns they may do all types of work, and in larger cities they may specialize in specific areas such as homicide or fraud.

Job Outlook and Wages

Concern about security and the continued battle against illegal drug activities will keep police departments busy and growing. Employment is expected to grow faster than average—up 24.7 percent through 2012. Because state police officers are better paid and have excellent benefits packages, jobs will be more difficult to find in those areas. There will continue to be more applicants than jobs and hiring standards will become tougher as a result. For jobs in municipal police departments, the outlook is better.

The average annual salary for municipal police and sheriff's patrol officers was $44,880 in 2003. Those working for state police departments earned more, averaging $47,830. The average salary for the highest wage earners in police departments was $67,470.

In 2003, California, New Jersey, Alaska, Washington, and New York paid their police officers the highest salaries, on average, and workers in the Nassau-Suffolk areas of New York topped the nation at an average annual salary of $72,740. The states with the highest concentration of workers were New Mexico, Mississippi, New York, Louisiana, and Arizona.

Apprenticeships

Many police officers began their careers as apprentices. Most police departments must comply with civil service regulations, and candidates must be U.S. citizens, be at least 20 years old, and in excellent physical condition. Candidates must take civil service exams as well as exams testing vision, hearing, strength, and agility. Candidates may have to be interviewed by a psychiatrist or psychologist or take a personality test. Candidates are selected based on their test scores, educational background, and experience.

Training usually talks place at a local police academy or a state training facility in a program than runs from 12 to 14 weeks. Apprentices study laws and ordinances, civil rights, and accident investigation. They also receive training in the use of firearms, self defense, first aid, and emergency response. Once they have completed the academy studies, they serve as officers for a probationary period of six months to three years. Apprenticeship programs last two to three years.

Related Skills

In addition to looking for candidates who are physically and emotionally fit, police departments are increasingly looking for some postsecondary education as well. It is not uncommon for apprentices to have completed associate's degrees. Police departments are looking for people with excellent communications skills. High school courses in public speaking and writing can be helpful.

Resources

For more information about apprenticeships in your area, contact your local municipal or state police department. For more information about police work, contact:

National Association of Police Organizations
750 First St., NE, Suite 920
Washington, DC 20002
Phone: (202) 842-4420
E-mail: info@napo.org

Links to law enforcement organizations across the country
Internet: http://www.napo.org/links/

National Center for Women and Policing
Internet: http://www.womenandpolicing.org/
E-mail: womencops@feminist.org

Private Detectives and Investigators

Private Detectives	*O*NET/SOC*	*33-9021*
and Investigators	*DOT*	*376-267-018*
	RAIS	*0579*

If you imagine car chases, phone taps, and gunfights when you think about private investigators and private detectives, you have been watching too much television. In real life, private

John M. Lajoie, CLI, CCDI, CII, President, Lajoie Investigations, Inc. Photo courtesy of John M. Lajoie.

WORKING AS A PRIVATE INVESTIGATOR

So you want to be a private investigator (PI)? Go get a degree in liberal arts, says John Lajoie, a licensed private investigator who specializes in criminal investigations. As the 2002 PI of the Year, Lajoie has lots of experience on the job and knows that many people think a background in criminal justice is ideal for the profession.

Not so, he says. "It is more important that you know how to read and analyze what you are reading. Reading, writing, and speaking are the most important aspects in any job, but especially in the field of private investigation. The heart and soul of an investigation is interviewing people and taking statements. . . . Along with liberal arts, take some acting classes. I think the ability to act a part, if you are part of a sting operation, is very important in maintaining the viability of that operation," says Lajoie. Photography and videography experience can be very useful as well.

Author of the soon-to-be-released *How to Become a Professional Private Investigator*, Lajoie says you should sit down and talk to a private investigator. Many people think private investigators are like those characters they see on television. Ask an experienced investigator to tell you what the job is really like. Ask about the work, the hours, and the skills necessary to be a professional private investigator and then evaluate your own strengths and weaknesses to determine if the job is really right for you.

Entry-level jobs aren't glamorous and they aren't easy to come by. Workers interested in the field can get some background training working in a law office or insurance company where they train new employees to investigate insurance claims and legal matters. Many professional organizations sponsor seminars and continuing-education workshops that can be beneficial.

In any case, don't expect to put up a shingle and open your own practice right away. You have to start at the bottom and work your way up, says Lajoie. If this is really what you want to do, be ready to work long and irregular hours. Be ready to deal with all kinds of people, often people you would rather not spend time with. You will work in situations that are uncomfortable and in situations that are high-risk, and you will have to do it alone, with a meager budget, for a client who doesn't appreciate the difficulty of the job. Knowing all that, if you still think the job is right for you, check with your local private investigator professional organization or your local apprenticeship agency for information about opportunities in your area.

investigators use many methods to gather information, but they gather their information in legal ways that meet with state licensing requirements.

Instead of speeding through traffic chasing armed criminals, much of their time is spent talking to people, poring over documents, scrolling through computer databases, or sitting for very long periods of time observing a subject. To get a look at the actual work of private investigators, visit the "current news" link on the National Association of Legal Investigators website (address below). You can read about the current activities of today's PIs.

Private investigators are licensed in all but six states—Alabama, Alaska, Colorado, Idaho, Mississippi, and South Dakota. Licensing requirements vary widely among the 44 other states. In some states, investigators can be as young as 18 and in others, they must be a minimum of 25 years old to be licensed. Most require experience in the field and that can come in a variety of ways and in combinations of experiences. Previous experience in law enforcement, college courses in criminal justice, apprenticeship experiences, and other experience may count toward licensing requirements, depending on the state. For information about requirements in your state, see the resources section below.

Licensed private investigators and detectives may perform investigations in many areas, and some specialize.

Occupational Specialties and Job Descriptions

General   Many private investigators perform different types of investigations working for a variety of clients, from individuals to corporations.

Legal Investigators   Most often, legal investigators help prepare the defense, assisting lawyers in criminal cases. They may be responsible for locating witnesses, serving legal papers, interviewing the police and witnesses, and/or gathering and reviewing evidence. They may collect information relating to individuals involved in the case, take photographs, testify in court, and prepare reports for the trial. They may also work for the public defender's office.

Corporate Investigators   Corporate investigators may be involved in investigating criminal behavior in the workplace, including theft and drug use and abuse. They may review accounting procedures to ensure that accounts are accurate. They may be involved in investigations that prevent criminal schemes, such as the theft of company assets through fraudulent billing by suppliers.

Surveillance Specialists   These private investigators spend their time watching people and their activities. The investigator may be working for an individual client, looking for information about the fidelity of a spouse, or watching the physical activities of someone who has claimed an injury. This specialist may take photographs or videotapes of the activities.

Financial Investigators for Forensic Accountants   These investigators gather financial information, developing financial profiles of individuals or companies involved in large financial transactions. They are often certified public accounts working closely with investment bankers and accountants. They may also search for individual and corporate assets in order to recover damages in fraud or theft cases.

Background Investigators   As the name indicates, these investigators perform background checks for businesses and for individuals. Whether an individual is checking out a prospective spouse or a school wants a criminal background check on a prospective employee, background investigators pore over public records and perform interviews to gather relevant information.

Insurance Investigators   Working directly for insurance companies or for private investigative firms, insurance investigators examine insurance claims, policy fraud, and insurance coverage and liability investigations.

Environmental Investigators   Specializing in investigations that involve landfills, underground storage tanks, groundwater contamination, waste management practices, and other environmental issues, environmental investigators may assist prosecutors, defense attorneys, or civil litigants in gathering information for their cases.

Store and Hotel Detectives   These specialists work for retail stores apprehending anyone attempting to steal merchandise or destroy store property. They protect stores not only from shoplifters, but from vendor representatives, delivery personnel, and store employees who might be involved in theft as well. Hotel detectives protect the hotel and its guests from theft and may help with security in hotel restaurants and bars.

Protective Services   In some cases, detectives may serve as armed bodyguards, protecting celebrity or corporate clients. Investigators who carry weapons must have a license to carry a gun.

Job Outlook and Wages

Many people come into the private investigation business after careers in the military or law enforcement. Because retirement age in these areas can be quite young, and because they have experience that often transfers well into the field, retirees looking at beginning their own private investigation firms or going to work for an established agency take many of the job openings for investigators. For those looking to break into the business, entry-level jobs are available in detective agencies and large retail establishments.

Employment is expected to grow faster than average—up 25.3 percent through 2012. Job growth will also come as a result of increased litigation and the need to protect confidential information and property. Growth in investigative positions should also result from all of the recent corporate scandals.

Determining averages for salaries in this field is difficult. Incomes vary widely from specialty to specialty and from private practices to large investigative companies. The Department of Labor reported the average annual income for a private detective or investigator was $35,080 in 2003, with the top 10 percent of workers averaging just over $58,000. According to a study by Abbot, Langer and Associates, security and loss prevention directors and vice presidents had a median income of $77,500 a year in 2002. Investigators averaged $39,800, and store detectives earned an average of $25,000.

Department of Labor statistics showed that the highest-paid investigators worked for management and technical consulting services, with incomes averaging $65,580 in 2003. The top-paying states for investigators were Washington, New Jersey, Connecticut, Michigan, and New York.

Apprenticeships

Many states have apprenticeship programs for those interested in becoming private investigators. On-the-job training under the supervision of a licensed professional is typical and can range from one to three years. Additional training materials or course work may be required as well.

Because there are few apprenticeships available in this field and many experienced applicants, entry-level applicants usually have some background in investigative work. There are no formal educational requirements for most jobs, but many apprentices have associate's or bachelor's degrees in a related field, such as criminal justice. Some have related experience, having worked for an insurance company or a collection agency. In some specialties, experience in accounting or law is beneficial.

Apprentices must be drug free and have no felony convictions.

Related Skills

As mentioned previously, backgrounds in finance, accounting, law enforcement, and law are beneficial. Most often, you will need some college experience. Related college experience can often be applied to the experience requirement for some state licensing requirements. Good communication skills are essential. Attention to detail is also essential, as much information is gathered from public records, and patience is necessary because investigators can sit for hours at a time in surveillance activity.

Resources

For more information about apprenticeships in your state, contact your local apprenticeship agency. For more information about the work of private investigators:

Lajoie, John M. *How to Become a Professional Private Investigator*
Available online: http://www.privateinvestigator.com

National Association of Legal Investigators
908 21st St.
Sacramento, CA 95814-3118
Internet: http://www.nalionline.org

Social Service Careers

Whether working with children or adults, workers in the social services field provide for the well being of their clients. Apprenticeships in this area range from jobs in day care centers, helping develop the potential of preschoolers, to working with the elderly, helping them with the basic activities of daily living. Work in this field is traditionally low in pay and high in both work and rewards. New efforts on the part of the Department of Labor to provide structured training opportunities in some of these areas are helping provide more standardized competency requirements for workers in the field. Sponsored by local social service providers, the DOL registers apprenticeship opportunities in five areas. The hope is that apprenticeships in these areas will provide the growing number of workers who will be needed in this field.

Child Care Development Specialist

Child Care Development Specialist	O*NET/SOC	39-9011.00
	DOT	359.342-540
	RAIS	0840

Young people interested in working with young children often take entry-level jobs in the child care services industry. Here you can work directly with young children to help them reach their developmental potential. If you like young children and enjoy watching them change and develop, this might be a career option for you.

Unfortunately, entry-level positions in child care are low paying and can offer little in the way of advancement. In an effort to address those issues, the Department of Labor recently funded apprenticeship programs designed to address the skill level, wages, and retention of child care workers. You can read more about those efforts in the apprenticeship section below. Workers who start out in this field can advance to teaching positions, with further education. Here, both salary and benefits are significantly improved.

Supporting teachers and supervisors and child care workers provide basic care and help children develop language, social, and math skills. They encourage artistic endeavors as well. In addition to helping children learn, they take care of their basic needs as well, assisting them with meals, dressing, bathroom activities, and napping. In addition to working directly with the children, they keep child care centers clean, sterilize bottles and toys, prepare food, do laundry, and wash dishes. They may also be responsible for record keeping.

Child care workers may work in day care centers, nursery schools, specialty schools, or private businesses. Many child care centers are open up to 12 hours each day, and many full-time child care workers work more than 40 hours a week.

Job Outlook and Wages

In 2003, wages for child care workers were below the average for workers in the United States, averaging $17,400 a year. This is a little misleading because it includes workers who take care of children in their home or in the child's home, including nannies, as well as workers who help children in institutional settings. Experience and educational background can improve wages. The upper 10 percent of workers in this field earned $24,000 a year. Benefits varied as well, but most employers provided only minimal benefits for workers. One benefit many provided, however, was free or reduced-fee child care for the worker's children. Some employers provided educational incentives and tuition assistance for their workers as well.

In 2003, the top-paying states for child care workers were Massachusetts, New York, Connecticut, California, and

Maryland. The states with the highest concentrations of workers were Vermont, South Dakota, Wyoming, New Jersey, and Arkansas.

Jobs in this area are expected to grow about as fast as average—up 11.7 percent through 2012. Because of the low salaries and poor benefits, employment opportunities are often created as workers leave the field.

Apprenticeships

Recognizing the importance of early childhood education, the Department of Labor set about trying to improve the quality of day care programs with an apprenticeship program that addresses the low skill levels of many child care workers, the poor wages for workers in the field, and the poor retention rates for child care workers. In 2000, the DOL established the Child Care Worker Apprenticeship Program, providing 18-month grants to 32 states to set up the programs. The apprenticeships tackle training by providing a 3,000- to 4,000-hour on-the-job training program coupled with a related skills program of 150 hours each year.

In most programs, the related training takes place at a local community college, where apprentices can apply their related skills training to associate's degree programs at the school. In some cases, the programs are affiliated with a university, where the associate's degree classes can then be applied to bachelor's degree programs. Some programs provide the related training through distance learning programs. Although not all program sponsors pay for the related training, funding through grants or scholarships is usually available.

The classroom training provides the theoretical learning in programs like child development, child psychology, language development, child care systems, and curriculum planning.

Program sponsors are recruiting young people into these apprenticeship programs from within their own staff and they are recruiting new workers to the field as well. Although low pay continues to be an issue, all programs require that workers receive at least minimum wage and that wages increase with competency. On the plus side, related training is generally subsidized and you will be working toward a college degree while you work.

Related Skills

People who choose to work with children must be patient and caring. Although it is important to have a high school diploma or a GED, it is even more important that you like children and enjoy working with them. Because you will be helping little people learn and practice language and reading preparation skills, you should enjoy reading yourself, especially reading aloud. Many child care centers include music as part of the child's day. If you enjoy singing and dancing or you can play a musical instrument, you will be able to transfer that joy to children. The same goes for art. Young children love to draw and to paint, and if you do to, you will help validate their love of the arts.

Diaper changing comes with the territory. If you are squeamish about diaper duty, you might want to consider another career.

Babysitting jobs can help prepare you for an apprenticeship in child care. Because you will need to communicate with children, their parents, and the teachers in the child care setting, good communication skills are essential. Many day care programs include written reports for parents to take home at the end of the day, so writing skills will come in handy.

Language skills can be a real plus. Many child care centers have children and parents who do not speak English. If you can communicate in more than one language, you will have an enormous advantage.

High school classes in communication, the arts, nutrition, foreign language, and first aid will all help prepare you for this career.

Resources

For information about child care apprenticeships in your area, contact your local apprenticeship organization. In addition to the certification provided through a registered apprenticeship program, the following organizations provide certifications of qualifications for child care workers:

Council for Professional Recognition
2460 16th St., NW
Washington, DC 20009-3575
Internet: http://www.cdacouncil.org

National Childcare Association
1016 Rosser St.
Conyers, GA 30012
Internet: http://www.nccanet.org

The following groups provide information on child care jobs and child care issues:

Center for the Childcare Workforce
555 New Jersey Ave., NW
Washington, DC 20001
Phone: (202) 662-8005
E-mail: ccw@aft.org
Internet: http://www.ccw.org

National Child Care Information Center
10530 Rosehaven St., Suite 400
Fairfax, VA 22030
Internet: http://www.nccic.org

Career Development Technician

Career Development Technician	O*NET/SOC	13-1071.00
	DOT	166-267.901
	RIAS	1057

Brand new in 2004, this apprenticeship program is being implemented by HoustonWorks, a job placement, continuing education, and vocational training center in Houston. To date, it is the only sponsor offering this program, but according to Franchella Kendall at the Department of Labor's Bureau of Apprenticeship Training, other sponsors have expressed interest in the program. By the time this book is published, similar programs may be available in your area.

This apprenticeship falls in the Department of Labor's "employment, recruitment, and placement specialist" category.

Workers in this field help job seekers find work. They may interview the job seeker and evaluate job skills, experience, education, and training; conduct or arrange for aptitude or skill testing; and match the applicant's qualifications with employers' needs. They may help job applicants with resume writing skills, personal appearance, and interview techniques. Career development technicians monitor the worker's on-the-job performance. They establish agreements with businesses for job placements and with nonprofits and postsecondary institutions for life skills training. They maintain case records, program data, and other statistical records. They may also be responsible for performing reference or background checks for potential employers. Workers in this field may work for private or public employment services.

The qualifications required of employment interviewers depend partly on the occupations that the employment placement agency specializes in placing. For example, agencies that place professionals, such as accountants or nurses, usually employ interviewers with college degrees in similar fields. Agencies specializing in placing administrative support workers, such as secretaries or word processors, are more likely to hire interviewers with less education, but who have experience in those occupations. Although administrative support occupations, such as receptionists, usually do not require formal education beyond high school, related work experience may be needed. Sometimes, staff experienced in administrative support occupations advance to employment interviewer positions.

Job Outlook and Wages

Jobs in this area are expected to grow faster than average—up 27.3 percent through 2012. There will be 75,000 job openings in this area during that time, so the job outlook is excellent.

Wages for workers in this field averaged $47,730 in 2003, with those with the most experience and the most education earning higher wages. Those working in the placement and interviewing of professional job applicants, like those working for management and technical consulting services, averaged $74,000 a year! Workers in this area usually have bachelor's degrees in human resources.

In contrast, workers in this field working for state and local governments averaged $39,550 and $43,200, respectively. States with the highest wages for employment, recruitment, and placement specialists were California, New Jersey, Rhode Island, New York, and Connecticut. The highest concentrations of workers were in the District of Columbia, South Dakota, New York, Hawaii, and New Jersey.

Apprenticeships

Apprenticeship in this field was just recently established, and to date, no workers have completed the program. According to Franchella Kendall, the program will be a 4,000-hour, or two-year, program, with related training of at least 144 hours each year. The HoustonWorks program is doing related training in-house, but future programs may have that training take place in other ways, including classes at local community colleges, through distance online programs, or in other educational settings.

Related Skills

Obviously, people in this field need to be able to speak effectively. In order to interview job seekers, you will need to feel comfortable talking to people. Just as important, you will need excellent listening skills. Part of this job is finding out just what the job seeker has to offer and just what employers are looking for. Good writing and record-keeping skills are required as well. If you are still in high school, perhaps a public speaking program would be helpful. Work on your language arts classes strengthening your reading comprehension and writing skills. Many workforce offices have applicants who do not speak English, so once again, knowledge of a foreign language can be especially beneficial. General note-taking skills can be extremely useful as can general business courses including record keeping, word processing, and general office procedures.

Resources

To see if your state has established an apprenticeship in this field, contact your local apprenticeship agency. For more information about work in this field, contact:

American Staffing Association
277 South Washington St., Suite 200
Alexandria, VA 22314
Internet: http://www.staffingtoday.net

National Association of Personnel Services
The Village at Banner Elk, Suite 108
Banner Elk, NC 28604
Internet: http://www.napsweb.org
Click on "According to Danny" for some mentoring tips for those starting out in the profession and to get a sense of what this job entails.

Direct Support Specialist

Direct Support Specialist	*O*NET/SOC*	*21-1093.00*
	DOT	*195.367-900*
	RAIS	*1040*

One of the newest apprenticeship programs provides education and training for workers who assist those who need help to be self-sufficient. In 2002, the Department of Labor recognized the direct support specialist apprenticeship program providing a new training resource for those interested in entering this field.

Workers in this area support adults and children with physical, psychiatric, or cognitive problems as well as those with chronic illness, children and youth at risk, and families who need assistance in supporting family members. These workers are sometimes social or human service assistants.

This job is for young people who like to be personally involved, who want to help people directly, and who aren't intimidated by those with special needs.

Direct care workers help clients meet their daily needs as well as their goals and dreams. They may provide personal care,

A CRISIS IS COMING FOR THE MOST VULNERABLE

A serious shortage of workers available to deliver direct support services to those who need help with basic daily living tasks is on the way. As the baby boomer generation ages, more of them will want to stay at home and be supported by workers who can help them with meals preparation, basic hygiene, or getting around town. As workers in the field begin to support that population, there will be no one left to care for the neediest population, those with intellectual, mental, and physical disabilities.

There is already a shortage of direct support specialists in that field and low pay drives many caring workers out of the field. This is costly for the agencies and employers who provide for the disabled, as they must then retrain new workers to fill the void.

According to Bill Tapp of the College for Direct Support, it costs between $2,500 and $5,500 to train each new worker in the field. If employers spend that kind of money training them, they would like to keep them, and that isn't happening. The high cost of recruiting and retraining new workers prevents these organizations from paying decent wages, and the low wages create job shortages. It is a vicious circle.

Now, however, the Department of Labor and other sponsoring organizations hope to improve salaries for workers in the field by developing new training opportunities and career development ladders that will help keep workers in the field. The theory is that if companies can retain their workers, they will be able to improve salary levels.

Until recently, there was no set curriculum or uniform professional standards for workers in the field and little opportunity for career development or advancement. New apprenticeships for direct support services specialists hope to address those issues. Those currently working in apprenticeship programs will not only receive up-to-date skills instruction on the job, but programs like the one available at the College of Direct Support will offer structured related instruction that supports professional skills standards as well. Program developers expect the educational units completed there to be transferable to community colleges or four-year universities where workers can enter degree programs that will eventually lead to job advancement. With improved salary levels and career advancement opportunities, developers expect workers will stay in the field and help prevent a crisis in care in the future.

To view the new standards for workers in this field, visit http://www.collegeofdirectsupport.com/csss.htm.

instruction, transportation, health care assistance, and /or recreational or leisure assistance. They may access their client's needs, establish their eligibility for benefits and services such as food stamps, Medicaid, or welfare, and help them obtain them. Not only do they look after their client's financial needs, they help support their social lives as well. They help their clients find and use support services in the community that will strengthen social skills in order to help them develop and maintain relationships. These workers often act as advocates for their clients, helping them with a variety of issues including access, housing, employment, and financial management issues. They are also instrumental in helping their clients develop self-advocacy skills. In short, they do everything they can to help those they work with lead fulfilling and self-directed lives.

They may work with individuals, or they may work in group homes, adult day care centers, halfway houses or other supported-housing programs, psychiatric hospitals, rehabilitation programs, or other outpatient clinics.

Direct support specialists may also work as respite providers, helping family members by providing services when they need to be away or need a break.

Direct support services workers usually work under the direction or supervision of social and health services professionals including nurses, doctors, psychiatrists, psychologists, physical therapists, and social workers.

Job Outlook and Wages

Job opportunities for those who are interested in caring for others will be excellent. These are among the fastest-growing jobs in the country—expected to be up close to 49 percent through 2012. There will be more than 200,000 job openings for direct support specialists during that time.

More social service agencies are providing adult day care programs for those with special needs, and meal delivery programs are on the rise. The growth of the elderly population, who are more likely to need services, and the deinstitutionalization of many mentally and physically disabled people will create a demand for direct support services workers.

In addition, more community-based programs, supported independent-living sites, and group homes will assist the homeless and the intellectually and physically disabled and the mentally ill in the future. For those with the appropriate education and training, there will be many employment opportunities.

Wages for workers in this field averaged $25,450 in 2003. Those working in state government positions averaged $32,190. The District of Columbia topped the country in the highest wages for direct service specialists at an average wage of $37,380 annually. Connecticut, Alaska, Massachusetts, and California were also among the best-paying states. The highest concentrations of workers were in Vermont, Maine, Wyoming, Minnesota, and Rhode Island.

Apprenticeships

According to Wyoming Department of Workforce Services Director Kathy Emmons, the apprenticeship program "is an excellent way to build a targeted workforce to meet the needs of consumers and employers."

As would be expected, the training of apprentices is directly related to the sponsoring organization, with an emphasis placed on the needed services. This program is a 3,000- to 4,400-hour, or 1½- to 2½-year-program. Because it is competency based, those with previous experience will require less time to complete the program. Those with no experience will probably need the full 2½ years of on-the-job training. An additional 200+ hours of related instruction is also required. Among the courses included in this program may be an introduction to the special population, terminology, causes and issues, related safety and first aid, recognizing and reporting abuse, neglect, and exploitation, healthy lifestyles (including nutrition and exercise) medical abbreviations and terms, and confidentiality, as well as empowerment and citizenship programs, ethical and professional practices, and related financial management programs. The College of Direct Support, an Internet-based college, is one of the providers of related course work (see sidebar on page 259).

On-the-job apprentices will learn about the expectations and the needs of the individuals who will be receiving the support services. They may be trained in developmental disabilities, behavioral health, child development, the elderly, substance abuse, traumatic brain injury, or other specialized areas. Apprentices receive training in any health-related issues involved with their clients, including necessary safety precautions. They will learn to facilitate inclusion and will learn to promote appropriate social activities. They will be advocates for their client or clients and will promote self-advocacy in their clients.

Related Skills

Patience, understanding, and a strong desire to help others are essential qualifications for this work. Volunteer experience in the field can help prepare you for this career. Contact a disability organization in your area to find out about volunteer opportunities.

Because work in this area is as varied as the client's needs, a variety of high school programs can help you prepare. Any courses that improve communications skills, written and spoken, will be helpful. Because many direct support specialists have paperwork to complete, good writing skills are necessary. Classes in cooking and nutrition often come in handy. Social service, human service, and biology classes that cover mental retardation, physical disabilities, and mental illness provide background information for jobs in this field.

Resources

For information about apprenticeship opportunities in your area, contact your local apprenticeship organization. For more information about the work of direct support specialists, contact:

National Organization for Human Service Education
5601 Brodie Ln., Suite 620-215
Austin, TX 78745
Phone: (512) 692-9361
Internet: http://www.nohse.org
Click on "About Human Services" link at the top of the page.

Youth Development Practitioner

Youth Development	O*NET/SOC	13-1071.01
Practitioner	DOT	166-267.900
	RAIS	1039

Workers in this field help young people develop the skills necessary to be productive adults. They may work for social service organizations, youth development programs, after-school programs, programs for at-risk teenagers, or recreational programs for teens. Although the job classification for this job is the same as an employer interviewer or recruiter, workers in this field do much more than help teens find jobs (see sidebar on page 264). Youth workers usually deliver more comprehensive services to teens and young adults. In addition to helping young people find work, they may help them with prevocational skills, academic support, social and leadership skills, personal and family problems, and problems with drugs or alcohol. According to Brenda McGlaughlin, the education project coordinator for the YDPA program, today's young people come with more issues and life experiences than in the past and the people who work with them need more skills to serve them.

Job Outlook and Wages

Because workers in this category are placed in the same category as employment interviewers, but really function in a social service role as well, there is no specific Bureau of Labor wage information for this special job classification. Under the apprenticeship model, the classification is the same as the career development technician covered earlier in this chapter, and the basic employment outlook and wages would be the same. They are repeated here for your convenience. Most workers in this field, however, work for social service agencies, youth development programs, and other nonprofit youth services groups. Many of these groups rely on grants and public fundraising to support their programs. For this reason, salaries for those working in this specific area may be lower than those listed below.

YOUNG WORKER GOES FROM CLIENT TO SERVICE WORKER

Nidya Martinez knows what it is like to be an out-of-work, high school dropout. She knows from personal experience that young people can make wrong decisions that can lead to serious consequences. She also knows that with support, young people can turn their lives around and make a difference.

Nidya became involved in the YouthBuild USA program just three years ago. "I was seventeen. I had left school, met the wrong friends, did the wrong things. I had hit rock bottom when I heard about this program."

YouthBuild is a national nonprofit organization that supports 180 local YouthBuild programs servicing undereducated young people between 16 and 24. The organization helps young people gain their GEDs or high school diplomas while learning construction skills by building affordable housing for homeless and lower-income people. They place an emphasis on leadership development and community service in a positive mini-community of adults and youth committed to success. They actually pay young people to come in, study for their GEDs, and learn construction skills. Nidya says the program is a "second chance for young people." While in the program, she alternated weeks working on her high school diploma and working on the construction projects. Participants learn life skills as well.

"When I first came here, I didn't know how to keep a job or that it was important to get up at 5:30 in the morning to get here on time. . . . Never in my life did I think I would do community service just because it feels good. . . .

"I learned great work ethics. Attendance and attitude are very important. I learned that I can do things on my own, but I also learned that sometimes we can't do it all by ourselves. You can't lift a wall by yourself. It is okay to seek help. Help can only help."

Nidya got lots of help while she was completing her YouthBuild program. She got her high school diploma and developed excellent leadership skills. The administrators at YouthBuild were so impressed that they hired her as a staff member.

Now, Nidya is involved in a work-study program once again, but this time she is working toward certification in the Youth Development Practitioner Apprenticeship (YDPA). Working as a program assistant, she is now helping deliver the services she once needed. She says youth development workers need to be able to address a wide variety of issues, not just educational remediation. With supervision, she may assist young people in finding help dealing with domestic violence, conflicts at home, anger management, and sexual harassment. Some of the YouthBuild clients have been gang members and need help getting a new start. That may include the self-awareness and leadership skills necessary to leave a gang and the removal of gang tattoos as well.

She supervises the work of the young people in the program, making sure they get to their jobs on time. She tracks their attendance and their progress in school. She visits the job sites to ensure all is going well. Then she helps with leadership development programs that will give the participants the confidence they need to succeed. She also works with a group of young clients who evaluate the program and its success. "It's not about complaining," she says. They talk about what they think is wrong and what can be done about it.

(*continued*)

While not on the job, Nidya works on the 343 hours of related training that the program requires. She has worked on her related instruction through workshops and conferences and with community college courses. Combined with the on-the-job training, Nidya will complete her training in ten competency areas including knowledge and self awareness; youth development theory and practice; teaching, training, and education; counseling and cast management; life skills development; leadership development, community engagement; developing a satisfying worklife; organizational and program development; systems awareness and analysis; and health awareness and promotion. Increases in her training level will be met with increases in her salary. As an employee of YouthBuild, she receives health benefits including dental and vision coverage. At the end of the program, she will be certified by the Department of Labor as a youth developer.

Although she is only 20 years old, she says she has the direct experience that can help her help others. That direct experience has proved to be a challenge as well. Because Nidya went from training in theYouthBuild program to a staff position with the program, her relationship with some of her friends had to change. "I had to learn very fast and at a young age the line that separates me from friend and supervisor. My responsibilities were very different. It was very hard at first, because I have to do disciplinary work as well—it could be my best friend. I had a big title, and it came with a big responsibility."

Still, Nidya says she is doing what she always knew she was capable of doing. "Since I was a little girl I wanted to be a teacher. I knew that the job that I would do would consider people. I didn't know if it would be young people, the elderly, or babies, but I knew I would be involved with people. I have gone through a lot of the problems that these young people are going through. I know what works and I can show them how to succeed."

To learn more about the YouthBuild USA program, visit their website, http://www.youthbuild.org.

Jobs in the employment field are expected to grow faster than average—up 27.3 percent through 2012. There will be 75,000 job openings in this area during that time, so the job outlook is excellent.

Wages for workers in this field averaged $47,730 in 2003, with those with the most experience and the most education earned higher wages. Workers in this field working for state and local governments averaged $39,550 and $43,200, respectively. States with the highest wages for employment, recruitment, and placement specialists were California, New Jersey, Rhode Island, New York, and Connecticut. The highest concentrations of workers were in the District of Columbia, South Dakota, New York, Hawaii, and New Jersey.

Apprenticeships

YDPA apprenticeships are relatively new, but there are workers in this field who have completed the programs and gone on to work as youth development workers in a variety of agencies. Apprentices are required to complete one and a half to two years of on-the-job training, with an additional related instruction totaling 343 hours. Related training may come through conferences, workshops, credit courses at community colleges and universities, or online college programs. Related instruction may include youth and adolescent development, working with youth with special needs, preparing youth for the job market, counseling and case management, leadership development, drug and alcohol training, job counseling, general sociology, adolescent psychology, youth and family, multiculturalism and diversity, conflict resolution, violence prevention, and basic writing skills. In addition to learning the skills necessary to work directly with young people, apprentices also learn how to organize, develop, and run programs. In most cases, apprentices can earn credit toward a degree in social services, and the sponsoring group will pay for the related training. In some cases, they provide health benefits as well. As with most apprenticeship programs, apprentices usually start at about 50 percent of the salary of an experienced worker in the field. As they develop their skills and complete the related instruction, the salary increases. Young people who start out in this apprenticeship program can go on to complete degrees in the field and advance to professional positions.

Related Skills

According to specialists in the field of youth work, some of the best youth development workers have been clients—young people who have faced many of the same issues and problems they now help solve. They understand the problems young people must deal with and can act as role models for struggling youth. If you think you are too young to help other young people, read the story of one successful apprentice in the sidebar on pages 264 and 265.

According to McGlaughlin, "the main thing is that you have the desire to help others. You have to want to help other young people become successful. We need good people with good communication. Everything else can be learned."

Volunteers who help out in local organizations can gain experience as well. Currently, the National 4-H Council, Goodwill Industries, YMCA of the USA, Opportunities Industrialization Centers of America (OICA), YouthBuild USA, Service, Employment, and Redevelopment (SER) Jobs for Progress National, and the Academy for Educational Development's National Training Institute (NTI) are among the sponsoring organizations. Many local, community-based organizations also sponsor YDPA programs.

Resources

For more information about apprenticeship opportunities in your area, contact your local apprenticeship organization or one of the national sponsoring organizations listed above. For more information about youth development training, contact:

Academy for Educational Development
AED Headquarters
1825 Connecticut Ave., NW
Washington, DC 20009-5721
Phone: (202) 884-8000
Internet: http://www.aed.org

For information about work in the field and resources for more information, contact:

Massachusetts Partnership for Healthy Community's
    Youth Development Links
Internet: http://www.youthworkcentral.org/
    best_training_institute.html

Youthleadership.com
5593 Golf Course Dr.
Morrison, CO 80465
Phone: (303) 358-1563
Internet: http://www.youthleadership.com

For a list of resources for youth workers, visit:

Ohio Learning Work Connection
Resources for Youth Database
http://www.ohiolearningwork.org/statedatabase.asp

11 Military Opportunities

One of the most comprehensive providers of paid on-the-job training is the United States military. When we think of the military, especially during times of war, we imagine soldiers with rifles, tanks rolling through the streets, and armed conflict. We are all aware of the combat soldier, but many don't realize that the military also needs people to do almost all of the jobs that take place in the civilian world as well. In fact, more than 80 percent of military jobs have civilian counterparts. The armed forces needs people trained as carpenters and plumbers, electricians and line installers, nurses and nursing assistants, food service workers and cooks, protective service workers, automobile and truck mechanics, brochure writers and public relations personnel, and almost any field that is needed elsewhere. They need these workers and they are willing to train them, house them, feed them, and compensate them during training.

Of course, they expect something in return. Enlistment contracts call for up to eight years of service. Depending on the branch of the military and on the terms of the contract, you will spend two to six years on active duty and the rest of the time in the reserves. After enlisting, recruits spend 6 to 11 weeks in basic training and then begin formal training for their military specialty. Today's wartime army puts more emphasis on combat training for all personnel, whether direct combat forces or support personnel. Although in past military operations support personnel were often far from the front, that is often not the case today. Missions in Afghanistan and Iraq blurred the distinction between serving on the front lines and serving in support positions. Today, all soldiers need combat skills. In today's military, all soldiers are considered warriors and will receive the same combat training. Those who are assigned to combat jobs may go directly into the field. Those who specialize in support positions may receive additional training that can last from ten weeks up to one year. This training may take place in classroom situations in the United States or may take place at the first duty assignment.

Not sure what specialty is for you? The military has a test to help determine where you will find success. The Armed Service Vocational Aptitude Battery (ASVAB) test does not measure intelligence or IQ but rather evaluates skills in ten areas: general science, arithmetic reasoning, word knowledge, paragraph comprehension, numerical operations, coding speed, auto and shop information, mathematics knowledge, mechanical comprehension, and electronics. It measures readiness to become proficient in a particular type of activity or your capacity to learn a particular type of work. ASVAB tests are now given either online or in the more traditional pen-and-pencil way. Tests are offered in most high schools across the country. You can use the results of the test with *Exploring Careers: ASVAB Workbook* that contains an interest inventory and an exercise to help you learn about civilian and military occupations and how you match up to them. Recruitment officers can arrange for you to take the test, but you will have a distinct advantage if you take the test before talking to recruitment personnel. You will know whether you have a good chance of being accepted for training in a particular specialty before you even talk to the recruiter.

Each branch of the military has its own recruitment package and eligibility requirements. You can find out more about careers in the U.S. Army, Navy, Marines, Coast Guard, Air Force, and the Air and Army National Guard from your high school guidance counselor, at a local recruitment office, or from the websites listed at the end of this chapter.

If you plan to remain in the same job category once you complete military service, you may want to spend some time researching civilian opportunities in that field. Job prospects can vary greatly from career sector to career sector, with some job opportunities growing much faster than others. You can find information about career exploration in the last chapter of this book.

Some jobs in the military are open to enlisted personnel, some to commissioned soldiers, and others to warrant officers. In order to qualify as commissioned officers, recruits must have at least a bachelor's degree. They may complete ROTC training while in college, go to Officer's Candidate School after college graduation, graduate from a military academy, or be a civilian degreed professional (doctor, lawyer, chaplain, etc.).

Many jobs in the military, however, do not require college course work. High school graduates may qualify for warrant officer training and appointments. Warrant officers are the military's technical experts. They manage and maintain the army's combat systems, vehicles and networks. To qualify to be a warrant officer, you must meet qualification levels on the ASVAB test as well as the Flight Aptitude Selection Test and meet certain fitness, age, and weight standards. Once the basic qualifications are met, you must attend Warrant Officer's Candidate School. Warrant officer positions are highly competitive—the Warrant Officer Corps represents less than 5 percent of the total army. This is not an entry-level position and is restricted to those with the rank of E-5 or higher. Your local recruiter can provide more information about warrant officer qualifications.

Qualifications for enlisted personnel may vary slightly among branches of the armed forces, but all require recruits to be U.S. citizens or permanent resident aliens, at least 17 years old, healthy and in good physical condition, and in good moral standing. Some branches have age restrictions ending at 28; others allow enlistment up to age 35. Some branches of the military require a high school diploma; others will accept those with a GED. Specific job titles for enlisted soldiers vary among the different branches of service, but related jobs are included in all branches in categories much like those in civilian job sectors. Openings in specific fields are not always available, however.

The following are job opportunities for enlisted personnel. Enlisted personnel, who make up about 85 percent of the armed forces, carry out the fundamental operations of the military in areas such as combat, administration, construction, engineering, health care, and human services.

Administrative Support

Do you like office work? Does the idea of keeping everything running smoothly by keeping records in order appeal to you? Maybe you prefer working with videos and video production. There is something here for you as well.

Many of the jobs you would find in the human resources department of a business are available in this sector. All businesses need administrative assistants to type, answer the phone, schedule meetings, and order office supplies. In the military, these jobs are done by administrative specialists.

In addition to basic clerical and information-organizational work, some jobs in this area document activities and operations on film and video. In addition to keeping clerical records, the military also records and documents activities on film and video. Combat documentation/production specialists are primarily responsible for supervising, planning, and operating electronic and film-based still, video, and audio equipment in order to document combat and noncombat operations.

Arts and Media

In addition to documenting military activities, there are also more creative opportunities for those interested in the film business. Although we seldom think about it, someone must design and produce the recruitment films we see on television, the posters we see around town, and the materials that recruitment officers hand out.

The military needs workers to set up, operate, and maintain cameras, video equipment, audio recording devices, and telecommunications equipment. They need people to design and build scenery, graphics, and special effects, and they need people to work with writers and producers interpreting scripts.

The visual information equipment operator/maintainer is responsible for jobs in this area.

Broadcast journalists and newswriters write and present news programs, music, programs, and radio shows for the military. The military also produces recruitment materials, posters, training manuals, newspapers, and reports. They need people to help design and create the graphics that go along with these materials. These multimedia illustrators might also design cartoons for filmstrips or animation displays and design backdrops or other props for film sets.

Most of us don't think of music when we think of the military, but they need musicians, too. Parades, ceremonies, special events, and festivals require skilled musicians. Positions are available for all types of instrument players.

Combat

This is the category that represents the infantry, artillery specialists, special operations and tank crews, reconnaissance, security, and other offensive and defensive combat positions. There are 29 specific combat jobs in the army. All are closed to women.

Construction, Engineering, Mechanics

Like to build? Want to drive a truck? Do you enjoy tinkering? In addition to all of the jobs listed in the construction and maintenance chapters of this book, the military also offers specialty training in other construction-related work. They need surveyors to map and plan construction projects and combat engineers to take those maps and plans and combine them with their own road-building and other construction skills to build the roads, runways, and bridges necessary for troop movement. In addition to building roads and bridges, they are also responsible for preparing and installing firing systems for demolition and explosives.

Just as civilian crews need trained people to operate and maintain their equipment, the military needs personnel to drive and take care of their construction equipment. In addition, they have specialists assigned to store and ship the petroleum-based products that are needed to run the machines. Other workers obtain and test samples of the fuels to ensure they are of high quality. Machinists operate the machines and fabricate replacement parts needed to operate equipment and other machinery.

Mechanics may work operating and repairing radios. Some specialize in repair-construction equipment. Armament repair specialists take care of the tanks as well as smaller weapons, maintaining their launch and guidance systems. From jeeps to ships to helicopters and airplanes, the military needs specially trained workers to keep them operational.

The military also needs plumbers and electricians.

Computers, Technology, Intelligence

Are you computer savvy? Do you enjoy foreign languages? Do you like analyzing data? In the military, computers and technology are important in gathering and interpreting information. Most of the jobs in this category involve technology, but some are jobs that require the personal skills of an individual.

The army communications maintenance team is responsible for making sure that all communications equipment is in top working order. Jobs in this category include all of those associated with all types of communication systems. Those who work with computers and computer systems, whether installing them, maintaining them, or working with software applications, are information systems operators/analysts.

To further the communications performance in the military, they need specialists who can locate and then translate foreign language information. In the military, people who do this work are called cryptologic linguists. They may also be responsible for interrogating prisoners and informers in their native language.

Analysts, both imagery analysts and intelligence analysts, are responsible for interpreting information gathered through aerial photographs, electronic monitoring, and human observation.

Legal and Law Enforcement

Have you always wanted to be a police officer or a firefighter? Military bases at home and abroad need the same types of protective and legal services that civilian communities need. The military has its own law enforcement specialists to take care of issues on military bases. Military police protect the lives and property of those living on base. They respond to emergencies, control traffic, and work in crime prevention. In combat areas, they are responsible for security, prisoner of war, and law and order operations.

Just as military bases have their own police department, they have their own firefighters as well. They perform the same functions as firefighters at home and take care of preventing and controlling fires on board ships and aircraft as well.

The military has its own lawyers, too, and they need the support services of paralegals who do much of the research and paperwork for the professionals in the field.

Health, Medical, Emergency

If a job exists in the civilian field, there is a comparable job in the military. They need doctors, nurses, nurse's assistants, mental health specialists, medical technicians, dental workers, pharmacy specialists, lab technicians, radiology specialists, optical lab specialists, and mortuary affairs specialists. Workers in this area also inspect the military food supply. The military also conducts medical research.

In addition to helping the humans in the military, they also need workers to support patrol dogs, ceremonial horses, sled dogs, and marine mammals.

Support Personnel

Maybe you like to cook. Maybe you like to sew. Or maybe you're more interested in religion and the spiritual side of life.

Military personnel need food and clothing. Food service workers, from prep cooks to chefs, prepare and serve all meals and clean up afterward. The military also needs people to take care of clothing and supplies. The shower/laundry and clothing repair specialist does just what the title implies. These workers keep uniforms clean and repaired and make sure they get back to the right individual or group. In addition to managing clothing, people are needed to manage supplies. In the army, these workers are called unit supply specialists. They make sure the right supplies get to the right place at the right time and keep the appropriate records

Support personnel in the military not only take care of the body, but the spirit as well. Offering a different type of support are those that offer spiritual guidance. Chaplain's assistants help in this area. In addition to helping with administrative duties, they also learn how to respond to soldiers during times of crisis.

This is just an overview of jobs in the military. For more information, visit the Military Careers website listed in the resources section below.

Job Outlook and Wages

The military, as they say, is always looking for "a few good men," and that phrase now includes a "few good women" as well. Today, there are shortages in the military and that presents wide opportunities for those interested in military service. Most young people who enlist in the military are eager to be of service to their country. They are also looking for the job training and educational opportunities the military provides. To make reentry into civilian life a little easier, many companies now help enlistees with jobs once they leave the service. The Partnership for Youth Success (PaYS) Program is a partnership between the military and employers. After a successful tour of duty, the army helps its soldiers get jobs. The program gives veterans priority consideration for jobs at select companies all over the country as qualified individuals are employed by the preselected PaYS employer. The agreement is established prior to enlisting in the army.

Each branch of the military provides food, housing, and clothing for its enlistees. This needs to be considered when comparing salaries between the military and civilian jobs. In addition, cost of living allowances are provided for those living on bases in high-cost areas of the United States.

Salary classifications are the same across all branches of the military. See the sample below:

2004 Annual Pay for Active Duty Enlisted Soldiers

Rank	<2 Years
Private—E-1 (after 4 months)	$14,321
Private—E-2	$16,052
Private First Class	$16,884
Specialist or Corporal	$18,698
Sergeant	$20,401

As with apprenticeship jobs in civilian sectors, those in the military receive increases with experience. Every job in the military has a career path leading to increased pay and responsibility with well-defined promotion criteria. In the army, for example, after six months of service, new soldiers advance to private (E-2). The next step in the promotion ladder is private first class (E-3), which occurs after the 12th month. Promotion to corporal or specialist (E-4) occurs after established time-in-grade and time-in-service requirements are met. These times vary, but every soldier can ordinarily expect to become a corporal within his or her first three years of service. Starting with grade E-5, promotions to sergeant through sergeant major are accomplished on a competitive basis. At each grade, there are minimum periods of time in service and time in grade that must be met before a soldier can be considered for promotion. In some cases, there also are educational requirements that must be met for promotion.

Resources

For more information about jobs in the military, contact your local recruiter. Each branch of the military has its own website with excellent job descriptions and enlistment information.

Military Careers Homepage
Internet: http://www.careersinthemilitary.com/

United States Air Force
Internet: http://www.airforce.com

United States Army
Internet: http://www.goarmy.com

United States Army Reserve
Internet: http://www.4.army.mil/USAR

United States Coast Guard
(Now part of Homeland Security)
Internet: http://www.gocoastguard.com

United States Marines
Internet: http://www.marines.com

United States Navy
Internet: http://www.navy.com

For more information about the ASVAB program, including sample tests:

Internet: http://www.asvabprogram.com

United States Military Apprenticeship Program (USMAP)

In addition to the traditional training available in the military, those already on active duty can choose to participate in registered apprenticeship programs (see sidebar for a list of apprenticeship options) while still on duty through the United States Military Apprenticeship Program (USMAP). Here the program parallels those available in the civilian sector. Apprenticeships last between 2,000 and 10,000 hours, and related instructional hours average 144 each year. Apprentices are required to document their hours of on-the-job and related training in military-specific logbooks provided by the program.

USMAP allows those in the military to begin preparing for their civilian jobs while still serving their country. In fact, the USMAP work is performed in unison with the individual's military job and is not a program to be worked after hours.

APPRENTICEABLE JOBS IN THE MILITARY

The United Services Military Apprenticeship Program offers career training through apprenticeship in the following jobs. Currently, the U.S. Navy, the U.S. Coast Guard, and the U.S. Marines offer apprenticeship programs registered with the Department of Labor. Other branches of the military may offer programs in the near future.

Apprenticeship Opportunities in the Military

Occupational Title	O*NET/SOC Code	DOT Code	RAIS Code	OJT Hours	Related Training Hours
Aircraft Mechanic, Plumbing and Hydraulics	51-2011.02	806.381-066	0866	8000	576
Airframe Mechanic	49-3011.01	621.281.900	1044	3100	223
Airframe and Power-Plant Mechanic	49-3011.01	621.281-014	0005	5000	360
Audio-Video Repairer	49-2097.00	729.281-010	0880	6000	432
Automobile Mechanic	49-3023.01	620.261-010	0023	8000	576
Aviation Safety Equipment Technician	49-9099.99	621.261-520	0605	8000	576
Aviation Support Equipment Repairer	49-9041.00	639.281-010	0599	8000	576
Baker	51-3011.02	526.381-010	0028	6000	432
Barber	39.5011.00	330.371-010	0030	2000	144
Boilerhouse Mechanic	47-2011.00	805.361-010	0038	8000	576
Bulk Fuel Specialist Pumper-Gauger	53-7121.00	914.382.014	0933	6000	432
Calibration Laboratory Technician	17-3023.02	019.281-010	0895	8000	576
Camera Operator	27-4031.00	143.062-022	0955	6000	432
Camera Repairer	49-9061.00	714.281-014	0062	4000	288
Canvas Worker	51.9199.99	739.381-010	0641	4000	288
Carpenter (Construction)	47-2031.01	860.381-022	0067	8000	576
Cement Mason (Construction)	47-2051.00	844.364-010	0075	6000	432
Central Office Repairer	49-2022.01	822.281.014	0076-77	8000	576
Computer Programmer	15-1021.00	030.162-010	0811	4000	288
Computer-Peripheral-Equipment Operator	43-9011.00	213.382-010	0817	2000	144
Cook (Any Industry)	35-2012.00	315.361-010	0090	6000	432
Correction Officer	33-3012.00	372.667-018	0851	2000	144
Counselor	21-1012.00	045.107-010	0569	4000	288

(*continued*)

Occupational Title	O*NET/SOC Code	DOT Code	RAIS Code	OJT Hours	Related Training Hours
Dental Assistant (Medical Service)	31-9091.00	079.361-018	0101	2000	144
Dental-Equipment Installer and Servicer	49-9062.00	829.261-014	0650	6000	432
Dental-Laboratory Technician	51-9081.00	712.381-018	0103	6000	432
Diesel Mechanic	49-3031.00	625.281-010	0124	8000	576
Drafter, Architectural (Professional and Kindred)	17-3011.01	001.261-010	0126	8000	576
Drafter, Civil	17-3011.02	005.281-010	0128	6000	432
Electrician (Construction)	47-2111.00	824.261-010	0159	8000	576
Electrician (Ship and Boat)	47-2111.00	825.381-030	0771	8000	576
Electrician, Aircraft	49-2091.00	825.261-018	0160	8000	576
Electrician, Maintenance (Any Industry)	47-2111.00	829.261-018	0643	8000	576
Electric-Motor Repairer (Any Industry)	49-2092.02	721.281-018	0149	8000	576
Electromedical Equipment Repairer	49-9062.00	729.281-030	0168	8000	576
Electronics Mechanic	49-2011.02	828.261-022	0170	8000	576
Electronics Technician	17-3023.01	003.161-014	0169	8000	576
Electronics Tester	51-9061.04	726.261-018	0570	8000	432
Emergency Medical Technician	29-2041.00	079.374-010	0730	6000	432
Engieering Equipment Mechanic	49-3042.00	620.261-022	0336	8000	576
Firefighter (Any Industry)	33-2011.01	373.364-010	0195	2000	144
Firefighter, Crash, Fire and Rescue	33-2011.01	373.663-010	0192	2000	144
Fuel System Maintenance Worker	49-9041.00	638.381-010	0610	4000	288
Graphic Designer	27-1-24.00	141.061-018	0010	3000	216
Heavy Vehicle Operator (Truck Driver)	53-3032.01	905.663-014	0980	3500	252
Household Manager	37-1011.01	301.137-010	n/a	4000	288
Housekeeper (Commercial, Residential, Industrial)	37-2012.00	381.684-560	0943	2000	144
Hydroelectric-Machinery Mechanic	49-9041.00	631.261-010	0237	4000	288
Illustrator	27-1013.01	141.061-022	0240	8000	576
Internetworking Technician	15-1081.00	823.261-900	1038	5000	360

(continued)

Occupational Title	O*NET/SOC Code	DOT Code	RAIS Code	OJT Hours	Related Training Hours
Legal Secretary	43-6012.00	201.362-010	0800	2000	144
Lithographer (Offset Press Operator)	51-5023.04	651.482-010	0683	8000	576
Locksmith (Any Industry)	49-9094.00	709.281-010	0289	8000	576
Machinist	51-4041.00	600.280-022	0296	8000	576
Machinist, Outside (Ship)	51.4041.00	623.281-030	0300	10000	720
Maintenance Mechanic (Any Industry)	49-9041.00	638.281-014	0308	8000	576
Maintenance Mechanic, Telephone	49-2022.05	822.281-018	0309	8000	576
Manager, Food Service	11-9051.00	187.167-106	0593	6000	432
Manager, Retail Store	41.1011.00	185.167-046	0578	6000	432
Marine-Services Technician	49-9042.00	806.261-026	0946	6000	432
Medical Laboratory Technician	29-2012.00	078.381-014	0323	4000	288
Medical Secretary	43-6031.00	201.362-014	0751	2000	144
Meteorologist	19-2021.00	025.062-010	0940	6000	432
Molder (Aircraft Mfg.; Concrete Prod.)	51-4071.00	518.361-010	0349	8000	576
Nondestructive Tester	17-3029.99	011.261-018	1010	2000	144
Nurse Assistant	31-1012.00	355.674-014	0824	2000	144
Office Manager/Administrative Services	11-3011.00	169.167.034	1033	8000	288
Office-Machine Servicer (Any Industry)	49-2011.03	633.281-018	0359	6000	432
Offset-Press Operator I	51-5023.02	651.382-042	0361	8000	576
Operating Engineer (Construction)	47-2073.02	859.683-010	0365	8000	576
Optical-Instrument Assembler	51-9083.02	711.381-010	1250	4000	288
Ordnance Artificer (Gov't. Service)	55-3014.00	632.261-018	0372	4000	288
Paralegal	23-2011.00	119.267-026	1003	6000	432
Paramedic (Medical Service)	29-2041.00	079.364-026	0543	4000	288
Patternmaker, Wood (Foundry)	51-7032.00	661.281-022	0398	2000	576
Pharmacist Assistant (Mil Serv)	29-2052.00	074.381-010	0844	2000	144
Photographer, Motion Picture	27-4031.00	143.062-022	0955	6000	432
Photographer, Still	27-4021.01	143.062-030	0403	6000	432
Pipe Coverer and Insulator	47-2132.00	863.381-014	0411	8000	576

(continued)

Occupational Title	O*NET/SOC Code	DOT Code	RAIS Code	OJT Hours	Related Training Hours
Pipe Fitter (Construction)	47-2152.01	862.281-022	0414	8000	576
Pipe Fitter (Ship and Boat Mfg.)	47-2152.01	862.261-010	0412	8000	576
Police Officer I	33-3051.01	375.263-014	0437	4000	288
Post-Office Clerk	43-5051.00	243.367-014	0596	4000	288
Powerplant Mechanic	49-3011.02	621.281-901	1045	3000	216
Power-Plant Operator (Utilities)	51-8013.01	952.382-018	0440	6000	432
Program Assistant (Radio-TV Broad.)	27-2012.01	962.167-014	0913	6000	432
Pump Repairer (Any Industry)	49-9041.00	630.281-018	0933	6000	432
Pumper-Gauger	53-7121.00	914.382-014	0950	2000	144
Purchasing Agent	13-1023.00	162.157-038	0948	8000	576
Radio Station Operator	27-4013.00	193.262-026	0952	8000	576
Recording Engineer	27-4014.00	194.362-010	0926	4000	288
Refrigeration Mechanic (Any Industry)	49-9021.02	637.261-026	0666	8000	576
Rigger (Any Industry)	49-9096.00	921.260-010	0474	8000	576
Rigger (Ship and Boat Bldg.)	49-9096.00	806.261-014	0473	4000	288
Sheet Metal Worker (Any Industry)	47-2211.00	804.281-010	0510	8000	576
Shipfitter (Ship and Boat)	51-4192.00	806.381-046	0513	8000	576
Silk-Screen Cutter (Any Industry)	51-9031.00	979.681-022	0519	6000	432
Station Installer and Repairer	49-2022.05	822.261-022	0647	8000	576
Surveyor Assistant	17-3031.01	018.167-034	0551	4000	288
Television and Radio Repairer	49-2097.00	720.281-018	0565	8000	576
Upholsterer, Inside	51-6093.00	780.381-038	0606	6000	432
Watch Repairer (Clock and Watch)	49-9064.00	715.281-010	0616	6000	432
Water-Treatment-Plant Operator	51-8031.00	954.382-014	0619	6000	432
Weather Observer	19-4099.99	025.267-014	0001	4000	288
Welder, Combination	51-4121.02	819.384-010	0622	6000	432
X-ray Equipment Tester (Any Industry)	51-9061.03	078.381-014	0919	4000	288

Source: USMAP, http://www.cnet.navy.mil/usmap/usn_trades.html

Although all enlistees receive training while in the military, this program recognizes, documents, and certifies the service member's training and the skills learned in the process of performing regular military jobs. With an apprenticeship option, those in the military can receive civilian certification for skills and training attained while on active duty. This translates into better job opportunities in the civilian world.

The program, first established in the U.S. Navy in 1976, has been expanded and now includes the U.S. Marines and the U.S. Coast Guard as well. The USMAP develops highly skilled journey workers who will use their skills while in military service and then transfer those skills to the civilian sector once their enlistment is over or they are ready for retirement. In addition to the excellent training for postmilitary jobs, the apprenticeship training often leads to advancement within the military system as well. As with apprenticeships in civilian life, military apprenticeships require a signed apprenticeship agreement. In most cases, apprenticeships take place in the career sector, what the military calls "rate," to which the trainee has been assigned. Sometimes, however, it is possible to change career paths, and with the permission of supervising officers, enlistees may apply for other apprenticeships. Those involved in military apprenticeships complete their on-the-job training requirements while doing their military jobs, whether in the United States or while deployed in other parts of the world. The military provides the related training or classroom program as well. Most of this training comes in what the military calls "A" school, that period of instructional time that follows basic training. In appenticeships with on-the-job (OJT) requirements above 8,000 hours, apprentices may receive college credit toward an associate's degree.

According to Mary Beth Ramos, who helps administer the USMAP, civilian employers are thrilled to hire those who have completed military apprenticeships. They come with detailed resumes that include well-documented job experiences and they come with a level of regimentation that accompanies military training. The employees know how to work and they know how to get things done.

For the enlistee, it is an easy way to develop a resume. "They are doing the job anyway. All they need to do is register for an apprenticeship, do their regular job, complete the paperwork, and get the necessary signatures documenting the work."

One of the advantages of the USMAP documentation standards is that it gives civilian employers a good understanding of the specifics of military training. Civilian employers might not always be familiar with military job descriptions and titles. The documentation allows them to see what specific skills a job applicant has and how they relate to the employer's job categories.

At the end of the apprenticeship, the DOL issues a certificate of completion that attests to the fact that the individual has completed all the work. Upon completion of a military apprenticeship, trained veterans may begin civilian jobs at the higher-paid journeyman rate. Others may receive advanced standing in civilian job categories.

For those in the military, the USMAP is an excellent professional development tool that allows enlistees to do the job they signed up for, get free apprenticeship training, and leave the military with a documented and certified resume.

If you are considering a military career, ask your recruiter about jobs that include apprenticeship as an option.

For more information, visit USMAP at https://www.cnet .navy.mil/usmap/.

National Guard

Those serving as traditional National Guard soldiers (one weekend per month and two weeks of annual training each summer), who have enlisted for six years of military service, have a high school diploma or GED, and have completed their initial specialty training may apply for employment in *any* apprenticeship program registered in their state. Once accepted into a program, those in the army or Air National Guard can collect monthly Montgomery GI Bill benefits in addition to their regular full-time apprentice wages during their training period. These educational benefits provide $211.50 a month

DEVELOPING PROGRAMS IN THE NATIONAL GUARD

PILOT PROGRAM OFFERS ADDITIONAL OPTIONS FOR NATIONAL GUARD

MASSACHUSETTS ARMY NATIONAL GUARD APPRENTICESHIP PROGRAM

In addition to the apprenticeship programs available to the traditional National Guard soldier, there is a new pilot apprenticeship program for those who would like to become full-time military technicians for the Massachusetts Army or Air National Guard. According to Major Troy M. Gipps, Director of Apprenticeship Programs for the Massachusetts National Guard, there are currently 28 registered apprenticeable jobs: air transport pilot, aircraft electrician, airframe and powerplant mechanic, airframe mechanic, auto repair service estimator, auto truck mechanic, automotive mechanic, blacksmith (gunsmith), canvas worker, diesel mechanic, electronics mechanic, hoisting and portable (heavy duty mechanic), hoisting and portable engineer, human resources assistant, industrial maintenance repairer, inspector quality assurance, machinist, manager trainee, materials handler, mobile equipment worker, optical instrument repairer, painter, purchasing agent, small arms repairer, supply technician, teacher assistant, turbine operator, and welder. Major Gipps expects additional jobs to be added in the future.

In this pilot program, the Massachusetts National Guard is the sponsoring employee. Applicants for these full-time apprentice positions must be members of the Army or Air National Guard. Those who enlist for six years of service, have at least a high school diploma or GED, and have completed their specialty training are eligible to collect monthly GI Bill benefits in addition to their full-time apprentice pay.

A similar program to the one piloted by the Massachusetts National Guard may become available in your state in the future.

for the first six months of an apprenticeship, $155.10 a month for the second six months, and $98.70 a month for the remainder of the apprenticeship program. This is in addition to the incomes Guard members receive for their weekend drill and annual training pay and their wages as full-time apprentices, giving them an additional income boost as they complete their on-the-job training and related instruction. For a four-year apprenticeship program, this would mean an additional $5,752.80 over four years! For National Guard members who have served three or more years on active duty prior to their enlistment in the Guard, the GI Bill benefits are more than three times higher!

There is also a pilot program currently under way in Massachusetts (see sidebar) that provides apprenticeship opportunities for those who want to become full-time military technicians in the army or Air National Guard.

Helmets to Hardhats

For those who don't complete apprenticeships while in the military and for those who do not qualify for the USMAP program, apprenticeships are available upon leaving the military through the Helmets to Hardhats program. The program is open to all (including the National Guard) who are making the transition from military service to the civilian job sector and to those who are currently serving in the Reserves. The congressionally funded program is administered by a non-profit trust working in conjunction with the 15 building trades unions. The program gives qualified veterans admissions preference in union apprenticeship programs. Those with experience may receive credit toward the apprenticeship OJT hours and may enter at a higher wage level than first-year apprentices. What makes this program special is that although apprentices are usually paid at a percentage of the journeymen's pay rate, these apprentices may use their Montgomery GI Bill benefits as well. The Montgomery GI Bill stipend during the first six months of qualified apprenticeship is $600 a month. Rates will vary depending on type of service and length of training and are published at http://www.gibill.va.gov/. Apprentices are able to use these benefits because the Building and Construction Trades Development (BCTD) program provides an educational certification.

So, in addition to the on-the-job training, the related classroom training, and the union wage, the apprentice's salary is supplemented for six months while he or she works toward journeyman wages. As with many apprenticeship programs, related classroom training may be applied toward college credit.

Interested apprenticeship applicants should register on the Helmets to Hardhats website and complete the profile and assessment section. You can then search through the online career list. Applicants select a trade and submit an interest notification for a local trade apprenticeship. They may also choose to get the help of an online mentor. The Helmets to Hardhats staff contacts the applicant and a related trade organization in an effort to make a match. The local unions make selections from interested applicants.

To find out more about the Helmets to Hardhats program, visit http://www.HelmetstoHardhats.org.

Making Choices— Finding Opportunities

Deciding on a career path while still in high school can be daunting. Apprenticeships require a commitment to a training program and to an employer or union. They require an enormous amount of work, both on the job and during the related training components that are a part of apprenticeship. Before making a decision, explore your options. Although many high school students have a sense of the general field they would like to enter, a specific job may not be as clear a choice. How can you know if you are really cut out for that job? And even if you have made a specific job choice and feel confident about your abilities, how can you be sure jobs will be available that field?

This section is designed to help you. It provides an overview of interest and aptitude evaluations, sources for more specific information about jobs, and a guide to programs that can provide experiences that can help you when you begin applying for apprenticeships or other jobs.

WHAT KIND OF JOB IS RIGHT FOR ME?

Most of us have little trouble detailing our weaknesses. "I'm no good in math!" "Oh, I can't draw!" "I could never be a writer!" These and other negative comments are common among high school students. I guess most of us are more ready to declare our shortcomings than to highlight the things we are good at. Sometimes, we don't even realize we are good at certain things.

Aptitude and interest evaluations can help identify areas where we might excel. High school guidance counselors and workforce development agencies all have interest and aptitude tests than can help identify strengths and help you focus your career goals in those areas. The military's ASVAB is given at most high schools and can help identify areas of strength. It can help you evaluate whether you have an aptitude for a specific field of work. (You can read more about this particular test in Chapter 11).

The Differential Aptitude Test (DAT) comes in two parts; one measures your ability to learn in specific areas such as verbal reasoning and spatial relations. The Career Interest Inventory assesses your interests in work-related activities. The results can point out jobs that may be of interest to you.

The Career Decision-Making Revised (CDM-R) assesses your interest in work tasks and points out which of 18 career clusters may be interesting to you. It measures interests, not abilities, but there are few people who can excel at work they aren't interested in! The Career Occupational Preference System (COPS) test also measures interests. These are just a few of the tests than can help you examine your interests and your strengths.

Many online services provide interest and aptitude tests. Sometimes a quick quiz is introduced and then you have the option to take an entire test for a fee. Most aren't terribly expensive, but why pay for them when you can find tests elsewhere for free? Check out the vocational guidance section of your school library or your local public library. There are many books that help identify interests and strengths and many contain tests that can help you evaluate your own. Books like *Discover What You're Best At* by Linda Gale, *What Color is Your Parachute?* by Richard N. Bolles, and *Putting Your Talent to Work* by Lucia Capacchione and Peggy Van Pelt are just a few. I took a test from one of these choices recently and was surprised to learn that a career in the business world might be a good choice for me. Your school or public librarian can direct you to the vocational guidance section of the library.

You can also take an interest inventory online for free. Many state websites provide interest and ability tests online. You can link to State Career Information Delivery Systems by clicking on the "Career Resource Library" link of America's CareerInfoNet (see below).

Keep in mind, the results of these tests are only indicators. They shouldn't keep you from exploring an area you think you are really good in or are really interested in.

CAREER INFORMATION RESOURCES

Once you have evaluated your areas of interest and strength, you can begin doing a little career exploration. There are many resources in print and online that can help you explore possibilities. Most libraries have copies of Occupational Outlook, or you can access it quite easily online at http://www.bls.gov/oco/home.htm. This resource is great for browsing. You can search jobs by broad category or by specific job title.

If you want specific information about a particular job, including a general outlook, a specific outlook for your state, a detailed wage report (including wages in your state), industry trends, job qualifications, and job lists, check out America's CareerInfoNet at http://www.acinet.org. They also provide almost 450 career videos from accountants to zoologists, giving you a look at real people doing real work.

O*NET OnLine, at http://online.onetcenter.org/, is the Occupational Information Network, a comprehensive database of worker attributes and job characteristics. On this site you can explore jobs by occupational title or by using any of the job classification codes included with the list of apprenticeable jobs listed in Appendix D. You can also do a skills evaluation here, using the results to match your strengths with matching occupations.

Not all jobs can be trained for through apprenticeships, but many can. Once you have determined the kind of work you would like to do, you can explore apprenticeship options at the U.S. Department of Labor Employment and Training

Administration's Program Sponsor Database, http://bat.doleta
.gov/bat.cfm. This site lists apprenticeship opportunities in your
area. Although this is a good resource, it is not always current.
Your best bet is to check with your local apprenticeship
organization. Find your state information in Appendix A at the
back of the book.

GETTING EXPERIENCE

As with most jobs, employers may be looking for apprentices
with some experience. Of course, the most obvious way to get
work experience is by working. Those who have been able to
juggle schoolwork with part-time work during the school year
have developed good life skills. Summer work can provide
work experience as well. If possible, find work in an
occupational area you are interested in. If you want to work in
construction, find a construction-related job. Be an assistant
bricklayer, or a plumber's helper, or a carpenter's assistant. Even
though you may not end up in that specific job, the experience
on a job site will be a plus.

Although most apprenticeships don't require more than a
high school diploma, you may not be able to find an
apprenticeship in an area of interest right away. Now what? See
if you can get your foot in the door of the career field by taking
an entry-level job. Sometimes businesses only open up
apprenticeships to those already on staff. Sometimes just the
experience you gain on the job will be enough to secure an
apprenticeship.

Take advantage of any volunteer opportunity in a career
sector of interest. As with entry-level jobs, those who have a
volunteer position have a foot in the door when apprenticeship
opportunities arise. If a paycheck is not essential while you are
in high school, volunteer experiences in related work fields can
help when seeking apprenticeship opportunities.

If you can't find a specific job opportunity in your
community, look at some of the national programs that provide
experience for volunteers:

Americorps, http://www.cns.gov

Each year, more than 40,000 members serve with programs in every state in the nation. You can tutor kids in your own community or build new homes for families far away from your home or restore coastlines or help families traumatized by domestic violence. You might do the work yourself, or help others serve by organizing projects and recruiting volunteers.

City Year, http://www.cityyear.org

City Year corps members engage in a variety of activities to meet critical needs in their communities.

Habitat for Humanity, http://www.habitat.org

Although many states require that Habitat for Humanity construction workers be at least 18, they sometimes schedule special workdays for those over 14.

OTHER OPPORTUNITIES

Educational Enrichment

Maybe you will have difficulty finding just the right apprenticeship after high school. Perhaps the job you are interested in requires programs you weren't able to take in high school. Maybe you need to brush up on some of your academic skills to prepare for the tests required by many apprenticeship programs.

Many community colleges offer courses that can strengthen skills and programs that can provide introductory-level educational opportunities in vocational fields. Contact your local community college for more information.

There are thousands of vocational schools that offer career training. Some provide the kinds of skills apprenticeship sponsors are looking for. For more information about vocational schools, talk to your high school guidance counselor and look at one of the Peterson's guides to vocational and technical schools for your part of the country. (See the resources section at the end of this chapter.)

Pre-Apprenticeship Programs

Many unions, trade organizations, and women's support organizations offer preparatory programs designed to help young people prepare for apprenticeships. Often these programs are directed to women, minorities, and those who come from low-income households. The programs may help prepare individuals for the aptitude tests required of apprenticeship applicants, offer remedial classes in math or reading, and offer specific instruction in blueprint reading and other trade-related skills. Training directors may provide information on application requirements and the fees and dates for aptitude testing. These programs help develop interview skills as well. To find out more about these programs, contact your local union or trade organization or your local apprenticeship agency.

Registered School-to-Apprenticeship Programs

Registered school-to-apprenticeship programs, sometimes called youth apprenticeship programs, help students in the 11th and 12th grades who plan to enter the workforce directly after high school. These programs provide flexibility for the high school apprentice, allowing him or her the opportunity to continue with related school-based instruction while receiving paid on-the-job training at a work site. The student graduates from high school and receives a certification of mastery of work skills. Those who successfully complete the program may receive credentials from both the participating school and the apprenticeship sponsor. In most cases, the youth apprentice can apply his OJT time to a registered apprenticeship program, giving him or her a head start that allows for a shortened apprenticeship term. For information about school-to-apprenticeship programs, contact the Department of Education in your state or your local apprenticeship organization.

Job Corps

Job Corps is a voluntary program for young people who are motivated to learn the skills and work ethic they need to start and sustain their careers. It is an academic, vocational, and social skills training program for low-income young people between 16 and 24. Job Corps students are trained in three specific areas: trade skills, education, and employability skills. Students are trained in one of over 100 vocations. The industries include health care, foodservice, business administration, technology, construction facilities maintenance and many more.

The program provides education, job training, room and board, health care, and an allowance for daily living expenses. There are 118 primarily residential Job Corps centers nationwide. For more information, visit the website, http://www.jobcorps.doleta.gov, or call 1-800-733-JOBS.

FURTHER RESOURCES

The Capstone Press Careers without College series explores promising career paths that do not require a four-year degree. Each book covers one of 28 specific jobs that require on-the-job training.

Ferguson's Guide to Apprenticeship Programs
Edited by Elizabeth Oakes
Chicago, IL, Ferguson Publishing Company, 1998
Last published in 1998 and now a little dated, it still gives an excellent overview of apprenticeship opportunities.

The Teenager's Guide to the Real World Online
A guide to part-time work for teenagers
Internet: http://www.bygpub.com/books/tg2rw/
part-time.htm

Improving your Job Skills as a Teenager
Internet: http://www.bygpub.com/books/tg2rw/jobskills.htm

Career Education Search
Internet: http://www.collegesurfing.com/ce/search/
Helps you find a career/vocational school in your area.

Vocational and Technical Schools Guide, East
Princeton, NJ, Peterson's Guides, 2003

Vocational and Technical Schools Guide, West
Princeton, NJ, Peterson's Guides, 2003

These books allows students to explore thousands of fully accredited programs that provide training for many of today's hottest jobs—computer technician, car maintenance and repair specialist, fashion designer, and more. This regional directory helps you choose from thousands of training programs in fast-growing career fields at more than 2,500 colleges, schools, and technical training centers.

Appendix A: Office of Apprenticeship Training, Employer and Labor Services/ Bureau of Apprenticeship and Training State Offices

ALABAMA

USDOL/ETA/OATELS-BAT
Medical Forum Bldg., Room 648
950 22nd St. North
Birmingham, AL 35203
Phone: (205) 731-1308

ALASKA

USDOL/ETA/OATELS-BAT
605 W. 4th Ave., Room G-30
Anchorage, AK 99501
Phone: (907) 271-5035

ARIZONA

USDOL/ETA/OATELS-BAT
230 N. 1st Ave., Suite 510
Phoenix, AZ 85025
Phone: (602) 514-7007

ARKANSAS

USDOL/ETA/OATELS-BAT
Federal Building, Room 3507
700 West Capitol St.
Little Rock, AR 72201
Phone: (501) 324-5415

CALIFORNIA

USDOL/ETA/OATELS-BAT
1301 Clay St., Suite 1090-N
Oakland, CA 94612-5217
Phone: (510) 637-2951

COLORADO

USDOL/ETA/OATELS-BAT
U.S. Custom House
721 19th St., Room 465
Denver, CO 80202
Phone: (303) 844-4794

CONNECTICUT

USDOL/ETA/OATELS-BAT
Federal Building
135 High St., Room 367
Hartford, CT 06103
Phone: (860) 240-4311

DELAWARE

Temporarily Closed
For more information call:
(215) 861-4830

FLORIDA

USDOL/ETA/OATELS-BAT
550 Water St., Room 1228
Federal Building
P.O. Box 14
Jacksonville, FL 32202
Phone: (904) 232-2596

GEORGIA

USDOL/ETA/OATELS-BAT
61 Forsyth St., SW, Room 6T80
Atlanta, GA 30303
Phone: (404) 562-2323

HAWAII

USDOL/ETA/OATELS-BAT
300 Ala Moana Blvd., Room 5-117
Honolulu, HI 96850
Phone: (808) 541-2519

IDAHO

USDOL/ETA/OATELS-BAT
1150 North Curtis Rd., Suite 204
Boise, ID 83706-1234
Phone: (208) 321-2973

ILLINOIS

USDOL/ETA/OATELS-BAT
230 South Dearborn St., Room 656
Chicago, IL 60604
Phone: (312) 596-5508

INDIANA

USDOL/ETA/OATELS-BAT
Federal Building and U.S. Courthouse
46 East Ohio St., Room 414
Indianapolis, IN 46204
Phone: (317) 226-7592

IOWA

USDOL/ETA/OATELS-BAT
210 Walnut St., Room 715
Des Moines, IA 50309
Phone: (208) 321-2972

KANSAS

USDOL/ETA/OATELS-BAT
444 SE Quincy St., Room 247
Topeka, KS 66683-3571
Phone: (785) 295-2624

KENTUCKY

USDOL/ETA/OATELS-BAT
Federal Building, Room 168
600 Martin Luther King Place
Louisville, KY 40202
Phone: (502) 582-5223

LOUISIANA

Temporarily Closed
For more information, call:
(214) 767-4993

MAINE

Office Temporarily Closed
For more information call:
(617) 788-0177

MARYLAND

USDOL/ETA/OATELS-BAT
Federal Building, Room 430-B
31 Hopkins Plaza
Baltimore, MD 21201
Phone: (410) 962-2676

MASSACHUSETTS

USDOL/ETA/OATELS-BAT
JFK Federal Building, Room E-370
Boston, MA 02203
Phone: (617) 788-0177

MICHIGAN

USDOL/ETA/OATELS-BAT
801 South Waverly, Room 304
Lansing, MI 48917
Phone: (517) 377-1746

MINNESOTA

USDOL/ETA/OATELS-BAT
316 N. Robert St., Room 144
St. Paul, MN 55101
Phone: (651) 290-3951

MISSISSIPPI

USDOL/ETA/OATELS-BAT
Federal Building, Suite 321
100 West Capitol St.
Jackson, MS 39269
Phone: (601) 965-4346

MISSOURI

USDOL/ETA/OATELS-BAT
1222 Spruce St., Room 9.102E
Robert A. Young Federal Building
St. Louis, MO 63103
Phone: (314) 539-2522

MONTANA

USDOL/ETA/OATELS-BAT
Federal Building
10 West 15th St., Suite 1300
Helena, MT 59626
Phone: (406) 441-1076

NEBRASKA

USDOL/ETA/OATELS-BAT
111 South 18th Plaza, Suite C-49
Omaha, NE 68102-1322
Phone: (402) 221-3281

NEVADA

USDOL/ETA/OATELS-BAT
600 S. Las Vegas Blvd., Suite 520
Las Vegas, NV 89101
Phone: (702) 388-6396

NEW HAMPSHIRE

USDOL/ETA/OATELS-BAT
143 North Main St., Room 205
Concord, NH 03301
Phone: (603) 225-1444

NEW JERSEY

USDOL/ETA/OATELS-BAT
485 Route 1 South
Building E, 3rd Floor
Iselin, NJ 08830
Phone: (732) 750-9191

NEW MEXICO

USDOL/ETA/OATELS-BAT
500 4th St. NW, Suite 401
Albuquerque, NM 87102
Phone: (505) 245-2155

NEW YORK

USDOL/ETA/OATELS-BAT
Leo O'Brien Federal Building, Room 809
North Pearl & Clinton Ave.
Albany, NY 12207
Phone: (518) 431-4008

NORTH CAROLINA

USDOL/ETA/OATELS-BAT
Terry Sanford Federal Building
310 New Bern Ave., Suite 260
Raleigh, NC 27601
Phone: (919) 856-4062

NORTH DAKOTA

USDOL/ETA/OATELS-BAT
304 East Broadway, Room 332
Bismarck, ND 58501
Phone: (701) 250-4700

OHIO

USDOL/ETA/OATELS-BAT
200 North High St., Room 605
Columbus, OH 43215
Phone: (614) 469-7375

OKLAHOMA

USDOL/ETA/OATELS-BAT
1500 South Midwest Blvd., Suite 202
Midwest City, OK 73110
Phone: (405) 732-4338

OREGON

USDOL/ETA/OATELS-BAT
256 Warner-Milne Rd., Room 3
Oregon City, OR 97045
Phone: (503) 557-8257

PENNSYLVANIA

USDOL/ETA/OATELS-BAT
Federal Building
228 Walnut St., Room 356
Harrisburg, PA 17108
Phone: (717) 221-3496

RHODE ISLAND

USDOL/ETA/OATELS-BAT
Federal Building
100 Hartford Ave.
Providence, RI 02909
Phone: (401) 528-5198

SOUTH CAROLINA

USDOL/ETA/OATELS-BAT
Strom Thurmond Federal Building
1835 Assembly St., Room 838
Columbia, SC 29201
Phone: (803) 765-5547

SOUTH DAKOTA

USDOL/ETA/OATELS-BAT
320 E. Capitol, Room 205
Pierre, SD 57501
Phone: (605) 224-6693

TENNESSEE

USDOL/ETA/OATELS-BAT
Airport Executive Plaza
1321 Murfreesboro Rd., Suite 541
Nashville, TN 37210
Phone: (615) 781-5318

TEXAS

USDOL/ETA/OATELS-BAT
300 East 8th St., Suite 914
Austin, TX 78701
Phone: (512) 916-5435

UTAH

USDOL/ETA/OATELS-BAT
1600 West 2200 South, Suite 101
Salt Lake City, UT 84119
Phone: (801) 975-3650

VIRGINIA

USDOL/ETA/OATELS-BAT
400 North 8th St.
Federal Building, Suite 404
Richmond, VA 23219-23240
Phone: (804) 771-2488

WASHINGTON

USDOL/ETA/OATELS-BAT
1111 Third Ave., Suite 815
Seattle, WA 98101-3212
Phone: (206) 553-0076

WEST VIRGINIA

USDOL/ETA/OATELS-BAT
One Bridge Place—2nd Floor
No. 10 Hale St.
Charleston, WV 25301
Phone: (304) 347-5794

WISCONSIN

USDOL/ETA/OATELS-BAT
740 Regent St., Suite 104
Madison, WI 53715-1233
Phone: (608) 441-5377

WYOMING

USDOL/ETA/OATELS-BAT
American National Bank Building
1912 Capitol Ave., Room 508
Cheyenne, WY 82001-3661
Phone: (307) 772-2448

Source: U.S. Department of Labor Employment and Training
Administration

Appendix B: State Apprenticeship Councils

ARIZONA

Workforce Development Apprenticeship
  Office
Arizona Department of Commerce
1700 W. Washington St., Suite 200
Phoenix, AZ 85007
Phone: (602) 771-1181

CALIFORNIA

Division of Apprenticeship Standards
455 Golden Gate Ave., 8th Floor
San Francisco, CA 94102
Phone: (415) 703-5477

CONNECTICUT

Apprenticeship Program Manager
Connecticut Department of Labor
  Apprenticeship Training Division
200 Folly Brook Blvd.
Wethersfield, CT 06109-1114

DELAWARE

State Administrator
Apprenticeship and Training Section
Division of Employment and Training

Delaware Department of Labor
4425 North Market St., Station 313
P.O. Box 9828
Wilmington, DE 19809
Phone: (302) 761-8118

DISTRICT OF COLUMBIA

DC Apprenticeship Council
609 H St., SE
Washington, DC 20002-4347
Phone: (202) 698-5099

FLORIDA

Director of Apprenticeship
Florida Department of Education
325 W. Gaines St., #754
Tallahassee, FL 32399-0400
Phone: (850) 245-0454

HAWAII

Workforce Development Division
Department of Labor and Industrial
  Relations
830 Punchbowl St., Room 329
Honolulu, HI 96813
Phone: (808) 586-8837

KANSAS

Kansas Department of Commerce
Apprenticeship Program
100 S.W. Jackson St., Suite 100
Topeka, KS 66612-1354
Phone: (785) 296-4161

KENTUCKY

Kentucky Labor Cabinet
Division of Employment Standards and
    Mediation
1047 U.S. 127 South, Suite 4
Frankfort, KY 40601
Phone: (502) 564-3070

LOUISIANA

Louisiana Department of Labor,
    Apprenticeship Division
P.O. Box 94094
Baton Rouge, LA 70804-9094
Phone: (225) 342-7820

MAINE

Director of Apprenticeship Standards
Department of Labor
Employment and Training Administration
    Programs
55 State House Station
Augusta, ME 04333-0055
Phone: (207) 624-6431

MARYLAND

Maryland Apprenticeship and Training
    Program

Department of Labor
Licensing and Regulation
1100 Eutaw St., Room 606
Baltimore, MD 21201

MASSACHUSETTS

Department of Workforce Development
Division of Apprentice Training
P.O. Box 146759
19 Staniford St., 1st Floor
Boston, MA 02114
Phone: (617) 626-5407

MINNESOTA

Division of Apprenticeship
Department of Labor and Industry
443 Lafayette Rd.
St. Paul, MN 55155-4303

MONTANA

Apprenticeship and Training Program
Montana Department of Labor and
    Industries
P.O. Box 1728
Helena, MT 59624-1728
Phone: (406) 444-3556

NEVADA

State Apprenticeship Council
c/o Office of the Nevada Labor
    Commissioner
555 E. Washington Ave., Suite 4100
Las Vegas, NV 89101
Phone: (702) 486-2738

NEW HAMPSHIRE

New Hampshire Apprenticeship Consultant
Department of Education
21 S. Fruit St., Suite 20
Concord, NH 03301
Phone: (603) 271-3893

NEW MEXICO

State Director of Apprenticeship
Labor and Industrial Division
New Mexico Department of Labor
Mountain Road, NE
Albuquerque, NM 87102
Phone: (505) 841-8989

NEW YORK

Office of Employability Development
Apprentice Training
New York State Department of Labor
State Campus Building 12, Room 436
Albany, NY 12240
Phone: (518) 547-6820

NORTH CAROLINA

Apprenticeship Division
North Carolina Department of Labor
4 West Edenton St.
Raleigh, NC 27601
Phone: (919) 733-0327

OHIO

Director of Apprenticeship
Ohio State Apprenticeship Council
Ohio Department of Job and Family Services
145 South Front St.
Columbus, OH 43215
Phone: (614) 644-2242

OREGON

Apprenticeship and Training Division
Oregon State Bureau of Labor and
    Industries
800 N.E. Oregon St., #32
Portland, OR 97232

PENNSYLVANIA

Bureau of Labor
Law Compliance
Pennsylvania Department of Labor and
    Industry
1301 Labor and Industry Building
7th and Forster St.
Harrisburg, PA 17120
Phone: (717) 787-0746

PUERTO RICO

Services to Participants Area
Right to Employment Administration
P.O. Box 364452
San Juan, PR 00936-4452
Phone: (787) 754-5151

RHODE ISLAND

Apprenticeship Training Programs
Rhode Island Department of Labor and
    Training
Division of Professional Regulations,
    Bldg. #70
1511 Pontiac Ave.
P.O. Box 20247
Cranston, RI 02920-0943

VERMONT

Apprenticeship and Training
Department of Employment and Training
5 Green Mountain Dr.
Montpelier, VT 05601-0488
Phone: (802) 828-5082

VIRGIN ISLANDS

Director, Training Division
Virgin Islands Department of Labor
2162 King Cross St.
Christiansted, St. Croix, VI 00820-4660
Phone: (340) 773-1449, ext. 244

VIRGINIA

Apprenticeship Program
Virginia Department of Labor and Industry

13 South 13th St.
Richmond, VA 23219
Phone: (804) 786-8009

WASHINGTON

Apprenticeship Program Manager
Department of Labor and Industries
P.O. Box 44530
Olympia, WA 98504-4530
Phone: (360) 902-5320

WISCONSIN

Bureau Director
State of Wisconsin Department of
    Workforce Development
Bureau of Apprenticeship Standards
P.O. Box 7972
Madison, WI 53707
Phone: (608) 266-3133

Source: U.S. Department of Labor Employment and Training
Administration

Appendix C:
Arts Organizations
and Programs

Funding for individual programs may change from year. Contact your local arts organization for further details.

ALABAMA

Alabama State Council on the Arts & the Alabama Artists Gallery
201 Monroe St.
Montgomery, AL 36130-1800
Phone: (334) 242-4076
Internet: http://www.arts.state.al.us/
Artist Fellowships (crafts, dance, design, media/photography, music, literature, theater and visual arts)

Alabama Center for Traditional Culture
410 N. Hull St.
Montgomery, AL 36104
Phone: (334) 242-3601
Internet: http://www.arts.state.al.us/actc/index-folkarts-actc.html
Folk Art Apprenticeships

ALASKA

Alaska State Council on the Arts
411 W 4th Ave., Suite 1E
Anchorage, AK 99501-2343
Phone: (907) 269-6610

Internet: http://www.educ.state.ak.us/aksca/
Master Artist and Apprenticeship Grants— traditional arts of Alaska natives

ARIZONA

Arizona Commission on the Arts
417 W. Roosevelt
Phoenix, AZ 85003
Phone: (602) 255-5882
Internet: http://www.arizonaarts.org/
No specific awards program. Site contains excellent *Arts Opportunities/Resources* link, including in-state and out-of-state resource opportunities.

ARKANSAS

Arkansas Arts Council
1500 Tower Building
323 Center St.
Little Rock, AR 72201
Phone: (501) 324-9766
Internet: http://www.arkansasarts.com/
Individual artist's fellowships

CALIFORNIA

California Arts Council
1300 I St., Suite 930
Sacramento, CA 95814

Phone: (916) 322-6555
Internet: http://www.cac.ca.gov/
Individual artist's fellowships

COLORADO

Colorado Council on the Arts
1380 Lawrence St., Suite 1200
Denver, CO 80204
Phone: (303) 866-2723
Internet: http://www.coloarts.state.co.us
Grants and fellowships in fine, folk, and
    performing arts

CONNECTICUT

The Institute for Community Research
Two Hartford Square West, Suite 100
Hartford, CT 06106-5128
Phone: (860) 278-2044
Email: info@icrweb.org
Internet: http://www.incommunityresearch.org
Southern New England Folk and Traditional
    Arts and Apprenticeship Program
    (Connecticut, Rhode Island,
    Massachusetts)

DELAWARE

Delaware Division of the Arts
Delaware State Arts Council
Carvel State Office Bldg.
820 N. French St., 4th Floor
Wilmington, DE 19801
Internet: http://www.artsdel.org
Phone: (302) 577-8280
Individual artist's fellowships (visual,
    performing, media, folk, and literary)

DISTRICT OF COLUMBIA

District of Columbia Commission on the Arts
    and
410 8th Street, NW, 5th Floor
Washington, DC 20004
Phone: (202) 724-5613
Internet: http://dcarts.dc.gov/
Individual artist's fellowships (media, visual
    arts, crafts, dance,
    interdisciplinary/performance art,
    literature, music, theater)
Minigrants for folk and traditional artists

FLORIDA

Division of Cultural Affairs
1001 DeSoto Park Dr.
Tallahassee, FL 32301
Phone: (850) 245.6470
Internet: http://www.florida-arts.org
Individual artist's fellowships (dance, music,
    folk/traditional arts, literature, theater,
    interdisciplinary

GEORGIA

Georgia Council for the Arts
260 14th St., Suite 40
Atlanta, GA 30318
Phone: (404) 685-2787
Internet: http://www.web-
    dept.com/gca/home.asp
GCA Folklife Program—apprenticeships
Individual artist's fellowships for teaching
    artists

HAWAII

State Foundation on Culture and Arts
250 South Hotel St., 2nd Floor
Honolulu, HI 96813
Phone: (808) 586-0300
Internet: http://www.state.hi.us/sfca/
Folk Art Apprenticeship Program
Individual artist's fellowships

IDAHO

Idaho Commission on the Arts
2410 North Old Penitentiary Rd.
Boise, ID 83712
Phone: (208) 334-2119
Internet: http://www2.state.id.us/
    arts/index.html
Traditional Arts Apprenticeship Program
Individual artist's fellowships

ILLINOIS

Illinois Arts Council
James R. Thompson Center
100 West Randolph, Suite 10-500
Chicago, IL 60601
Phone: (312) 814-6750
Internet: http://www.state.il.us/agency/iac
Ethnic and Folk Arts Master/Apprenticeship
    Program
Individual artist's fellowships
    (interdisciplinary/computer art, music
    composition, photography, poetry, visual
    arts, choreography, crafts, ethnic and folk
    arts, media arts, new performance forms,
    prose, and scriptworks)

INDIANA

Indiana Arts Commission
402 West Washington St., W072
Indianapolis, IN 48204
Internet: http://www.in.gov/arts/
Individual artist's fellowships

IOWA

Iowa Arts Council
600 East Locust
Capital Complex
Des Moines, IA 50319
Phone: (515) 281-6412
Internet: http://www.iowaartscouncil.org/
Traditional Arts Apprenticeship Grant

KANSAS

Kansas Arts Commission
Jay Hawk Tower
700 SW Jackson, Suite 1004
Topeka, KS 66603
Phone: (913) 296-3335
Internet: http://arts.state.ks.us/
Individual artist's fellowships

KENTUCKY

Kentucky Arts Council
Old Capitol Annex
300 West Broadway
Frankfort, KY 40601-1980
Phone: (502) 564-3757
Internet: http://www.kyarts.org/
Folk and Traditional Arts Apprenticeship
    Program
Individual artist's fellowships

LOUISIANA

Louisiana Division of the Arts
P.O. Box 44247
Baton Rouge, LA 70804
Phone: (504) 342-8180
Internet: http://www.crt.state.la.us/arts/
Folklife Apprenticeship Program
Individual artist's fellowships

MAINE

Maine Arts Commission
193 State St.
25 State House Station
Augusta, ME 04333
Phone: (207) 287-2724
Internet: http://www.mainearts.com/
Traditional Arts Apprenticeship Program

MARYLAND

Maryland State Arts Council
175 West Ostend St., Suite E
Baltimore, MD 21230
Phone: (410) 767-6555
Email: msac@msac.org
Internet: www.MSAC.org and
    www.MarylandStateArtsCouncil.org
Maryland Traditions Apprenticeship Program
Individual artist's fellowships (choreography,
    music composition, playwriting, poetry,
    crafts, photography, visual arts,
    installation, sculpture)

MASSACHUSETTS

Massachusetts Cultural Council
10 St. James Ave.
Boston, MA 02116
Phone: (617) 727-3668

Internet: http://www.massculturalcouncil.org/
Folk Arts Heritage—Traditional Arts
    Apprenticeships
Individual artist's fellowships (crafts, film and
    video, music composition, photography,
    playwriting, sculpture, installation,
    choreography, drawing, printmaking,
    artist books, fiction/creative nonfiction,
    painting, poetry, traditional arts)
Southern New England Apprenticeship
    Program

MICHIGAN

Michigan Council for Arts and Cultural
    Affairs
702 West Kalamazoo
P.O. Box 30705
Lansing, MI 48909-8205
Phone: (517) 241-4011
E-mail: artsinfo@michigan.gov
Internet: http://www.michigan.gov/hal/
    0,1607,7-160-17445_19272---,00.html
Traditional Arts Apprenticeship

MINNESOTA

Minnesota State Arts Board
Park Square Court
400 Sibley St., #200
St. Paul, MN 55101
Phone: (612) 215-1600
Internet: http://www.arts.state.mn.us
Artist's initiative grants

MISSISSIPPI

Mississippi Arts Commission
239 North Lamar St.
Jackson, MS 39201

Phone: (601) 359-6030
Internet: http://www.arts.state.ms.us/
Folk Arts Apprenticeship Program
Folks Arts Fellowships
Individual artist's fellowships (visual, crafts,
    media, performing)

MISSOURI

Missouri Arts Council
Wainwright State Office Complex
111 North 7th St., Suite 105
St. Louis, MO 63101
Phone: (314) 340-6845
Internet: http://www.missouriartscouncil.org
Missouri Folk Arts Program—Traditional
    Arts Apprenticeship Program

MONTANA

Montana Arts Council
City County Bldg.
316 North Park Ave., Room 252
Helene, MT 59620
Phone: (406) 444-6430
Internet: http://www.art.state.mt.us/
Folk and Traditional Arts Apprenticeships

NEBRASKA

Nebraska Arts Council
Plaza Level—Burlington Bldg.
1004 Farnam St.
Omaha, NE 68102
Phone: (402) 595-2122
Internet: http://www.nebraskaartscouncil.org/
Mentoring Program for Artists of Color and
    Traditional Artists
Individual artist's fellowships (literature,
    visual, performing)

NEVADA

Nevada Department of Cultural Affairs
Nevada Arts Council
716 North Carson St., Suite A
Carson City, NV 89701
Phone: (775) 687-6680
Internet: http://dmla.clan.lib.nv.us/docs/arts/
Folklife Apprenticeship Program
Individual artist's fellowships (literary, visual,
    performing)

NEW HAMPSHIRE

New Hampshire State
Council on the Arts
2½ Beacon St., 2nd Floor
Concord, NH 03301-4974
Phone: (603) 271-2789
Individual artist's grants

NEW JERSEY

New Jersey State Council on the Arts
225 West State St.
Trenton, NJ 08625
Phone (609) 292-6130
Internet: http://www.njartscouncil.org/
Individual artist's fellowships

NEW MEXICO

New Mexico Arts Division
New Mexico Arts—A Division of the
    Department of Cultural Affairs
P.O. Box 1450
Santa Fe, NM 87504-1450
Phone: (505) 827-6490
Internet: http://www.nmarts.org/
Folk Arts Apprenticeship Program

NEW YORK

New York Foundation for the Arts
155 Avenue of the Americas
New York, NY 10013-1507
Phone: (212) 366-6900
Internet: www.nyfa.org
Re-grants NYSCA funds (see below) to
    artists
Includes an interactive link for a wide variety
    of arts apprenticeship programs across the
    country

New York State Council on the Arts
175 Varick St.
New York, NY 10014
Phone: (212) 627-4455
Internet: http://www.nysca.org

NORTH CAROLINA

North Carolina Arts Council
Department of Cultural Resources
Raleigh, NC 27699
Phone: (919) 733-2111
Internet: http://www.ncarts.org/
Folklife grants
Individual artist's fellowships (painters,
    sculptors, photographers, printmakers,
    craft artists, installation artists, visually
    based performance artists, filmmakers,
    videographers)

NORTH DAKOTA

North Dakota Council on the Arts
1600 East Century Ave., Suite Six
Bismark, ND 58503
Phone: (701) 328-7595
E-mail: comserve@state.nd.us

Individual artist's fellowships
Traditional Art Apprenticeship

OHIO

Ohio Arts Council
727 East Main St.
Columbus, OH 43205
Phone: (614) 466-2613
Internet: http://www.oac.state.oh.us/
Traditional Artists Apprenticeship Program
Individual artist's fellowships
    (choreography, music composition, visual
    arts, crafts, design arts, photography,
    media arts, criticism, playwriting, poetry,
    fiction/nonfiction, interdisciplinary/
    performance)

OKLAHOMA

Oklahoma Arts Council
P.O. Box 52001-2001
Oklahoma City, OK 73152
Phone: (405) 521-2931
Internet: http://www.state.ok.us/%7earts/
    index.html
Traditional Arts Master/Apprenticeship
    Program

OREGON

Oregon Arts Commission
775 Summer St., NE
Salem, OR 97310
Phone: (503) 986-0082
Internet: http://www.oregonartscommission
    .org/main.php
Individual artist's fellowships

PENNSYLVANIA

Pennsylvania Council on the Arts
Finance Bldg., Room 216
Harrisburg, PA 17120
Phone: (717) 787-6883
Internet: http://www.pacouncilonthearts.org/
Individual artist's fellowship

RHODE ISLAND

Rhode Island State Council on the Arts
One Capitol Hill
Providence, RI 02908
Phone: (401) 222-3880
Internet: http://www.arts.ri.gov/
Folk Art Apprenticeship Program
Individual artist's fellowships
Southern New England Apprenticeship
    Program

SOUTH CAROLINA

South Carolina Arts Commission
1800 Gervais St.
Columbia, SC 29201
Phone: (803) 734-8696
Internet: http://www.state.sc.us/arts/
Folklife and Traditional Arts Apprenticeship
    Initiative
Individual artist's fellowships

SOUTH DAKOTA

South Dakota Arts Council
South Dakota State Library Building
800 Governors Dr.
Pierre, SD 57501
Phone (605) 773-3131
Internet: http://www.artscouncil.sd.gov

Traditional Arts Apprenticeship Grants
Individual artist's grants

TENNESSEE

Tennessee Arts Commission
401 Charlotte Ave.
Nashville, TN 373243
Phone: (615) 741-1701
Internet: http://www.arts.state.tn.us/
Individual artist's fellowships

TEXAS

Texas Commission on the Arts
E. O. Thompson Office Building
920 Colorado, Suite 501
Austin, TX 78701
Phone: (512) 463-5535
Internet: http://www.arts.state.tx.us/
Nonprofit arts organizations can apply for
    programs on behalf of individual artists.

UTAH

The Utah Arts Council
617 East South Temple
Salt Lake City, UT 84102-1177
Phone: (801) 236-7555
Internet: http://arts.utah.gov/
Folk arts apprenticeship grants
Individual artist's fellowships (visual)
Individual artist's grants

VERMONT

Vermont Arts Council
136 State St., Drawer 33
Montpelier, VT 05633
Phone: (802) 828-3291

Internet: http://www.vermontartscouncil.org/
Individual artist's fellowships

VIRGINIA

Virginia Commission for the Arts
Lewis House—Second Floor
223 Governor St.
Richmond, VA 23219
Phone: (804) 225-3132
Internet: http://www.arts.state.va.us/
Individual artist's fellowships

WASHINGTON

Washington State Arts Commission
711 Capitol Way S., Suite 600
P.O. Box 42675
Olympia, WA 98504-2675
Phone: (360) 753-3860
Internet: http://www.arts.wa.gov/
Folk Arts Apprenticeship Program
Folk arts fellowships

WEST VIRGINIA

West Virginia Commission on the Arts
The Cultural Center

1900 Kanawha Blvd. East
Charleston, WV 25305-0300
Phone: (304) 558-0220
Internet: http://www.wvculture.org/arts/
artsindex.aspx
Folk Arts Apprenticeship Program
Individual artist's fellowships

WISCONSIN

Wisconsin Arts Board
101 East Wilson St., 1st Floor
Madison, WI 53702
Phone: (608) 266-0190
Internet: http://arts.state.wi.us/static/
Traditional Native Arts Apprenticeship
Individual artist's fellowships (literary, music
composition, choreography, performance
arts, visual arts)

WYOMING

Wyoming Arts Council
2320 Capital Ave.
Cheyenne, WY 82002
Phone: (307) 777-7742
Internet: http://wyoarts.state.wy.us/index.html
Individual artist's fellowships

Appendix D: OATELS Officially Recognized List of Apprenticeable Occupations

OCCUPATIONAL TITLE	O*NET/SOC	HOURS	RAIS	DOT CODE
MANAGEMENT OCCUPATIONS				
BEEKEEPER	11-9012.00	8000	0886	413161010
DIRECTOR, FUNERAL	11-9061.00	4000	0820	187167030
FARMER, GENERAL (agriculture)	11-9012.00	8000	0177	421161010
MANAGER, FOOD SERVICE	11-9051.00	6000	0593	187167106
OFFICE MANAGER/				
ADMIN SERVICES	11-3011.00	4000	1033	169167034
WINE MAKER (vinous liquor)	11-3051.00	4000	0034	183161014
BUSINESS AND FINANCIAL OPERATIONS				
INSPECTOR, QUALITY				
ASSURANCE	13-1041.04	6000	0992	168287014
PURCHASING AGENT	13-1023.00	8000	0948	162157038
YOUTH DEVELOPMENT				
PRACTITIONER	13-1071.01	4000	1039	166267900
COMPUTER AND MATHEMATICAL				
COMPUTER PROGRAMMER	15-1021.00	4000	0811	030162010
INTERNETWORKING				
TECHNICIAN	15-1081.00	5000	1038	823261900
PROGRAMMER, ENGR &				
SCIENTIFIC	15-1021.00	8000	0949	030162018
ARCHITECTURE AND ENGINEERING				
ASSEMBLER,				
ELECTROMECHANICAL	17-3024.00	8000	0875	828381018

(continued)

OCCUPATIONAL TITLE	O*NET/SOC	HOURS	RAIS	DOT CODE
ARCHITECTURE AND ENGINEERING (Continued)				
CALIBRATION LABORATORY TECH	17-3023.02	8000	0895	019281010
CHIEF OF PARTY (professional & kindred)	17-3031.01	8000	0053	018167010
DESIGN DRAFTER, ELECTROMEC	17-3012.01	8000	0106	017261014
DETAILER	17-3013.00	8000	0108	017261018
DIE DESIGNER	17-3013.00	8000	0113	007161010
DRAFTER, ARCHITECTURAL	17-3011.01	8000	0126	001261010
DRAFTER, AUTO DESIGN LAYOUT	17-3013.00	8000	0019	017281026
DRAFTER, AUTOMOTIVE DESIGN	17-3013.00	8000	0018	017261042
DRAFTER, CARTOGRAPHIC	17-1021.00	8000	0109	018261010
DRAFTER, CIVIL	17-3011.02	8000	0128	005281010
DRAFTER, COMMERCIAL	17-3011.01	8000	0129	017261026
DRAFTER, DETAIL	17-3013.00	8000	0130	017261030
DRAFTER, ELECTRICAL	17-3012.02	8000	0131	003281010
DRAFTER, ELECTRONIC	17-3012.01	8000	0995	003281014
DRAFTER, HEATING & VENTILA	17-3011.01	8000	0133	017261034
DRAFTER, LANDSCAPE	17-3011.01	8000	0134	001261014
DRAFTER, MARINE	17-3011.01	8000	0135	014281010
DRAFTER, MECHANICAL	17-3013.00	8000	0136	007281010
DRAFTER, PLUMBING	17-3011.01	8000	0111	017261038
DRAFTER, STRUCTURAL	17-3011.01	6000	0139	005281014
DRAFTER, TOOL DESIGN	17-3013.00	8000	0140	007261022
ELECTRICAL INSTRUMENT REPR	17-3023.02	6000	0157	729281026
ELECTRICAL TECHNICIAN	17-3023.03	8000	0155	003161010
ELECTROMECHANICAL TECH	17-3024.00	6000	0167	710281018
ELECTRONICS TECHNICIAN	17-3023.01	8000	0169	003161014
ENGINEERING ASST, MECH EQU	17-3013.00	8000	0764	007161018
ESTIMATOR AND DRAFTER	17-3012.02	8000	0965	019261014
FOUNDRY METALLURGIST	17-2131.00	8000	0207	011061010
GEODETIC COMPUTATOR	17-3031.02	4000	0217	018167014
HEAT TRANSFER TECHNICIAN	17-3027.00	8000	0257	007181010
INDUSTRIAL ENGINEERING TECH	17-3026.00	8000	0259	012267010
INSTRUMENT MECH, WEAPONS SYS	17-3023.02	8000	0996	711281014
INSTRUMENT MECHANIC (any industry)	17-3023.02	8000	0644	710281026

(continued)

OCCUPATIONAL TITLE	O*NET/SOC	HOURS	RAIS	DOT CODE
ARCHITECTURE AND ENGINEERING (Continued)				
INSTRUMENT REPAIRER				
(any industry)	17-3023.02	8000	0775	710261010
INSTRUMENT TECHNICIAN				
(utilities)	17-3023.02	8000	0252	710281030
INSTRUMENTATION TECHNICIAN	17-3023.02	8000	0252	003261010
LABORATORY ASST,				
METALLURGICAL	17-3029.99	4000	0621	011261022
LOGISTICS ENGINEER	17-2112.00	8000	0632	019167010
MATERIALS ENGINEER	17-2131.00	10000	0328	019061014
MECH ENGINEERING				
TECHNICIAN	17-3027.00	8000	0777	007161026
MINE INSPECT. (government)				
metal-nonmetal	17-2151.00	8000	1028	168267074
MINE INSPECTOR (government) coal	17-2151.00	8000	1029	168267074
MOLD DESIGNER (plastics)	17-3013.00	4000	1030	007261560
NONDESTRUCTIVE TESTER	17-3029.99	2000	1010	011261018
OPTOMECHANICAL TECHNICIAN	17-3027.00	8000	0368	007161030
PHOTOGRAMMETRIC				
TECHNICIAN	17-3031.02	6000	0546	18260580
QUALITY CONTROL TECHNICIAN	17-3026.00	4000	0462	012261014
RESEARCH MECH (aircraft)	17-3021.00	8000	0788	002261014
SURVEYOR ASSISTANT, INSTRU	17-3031.01	4000	0551	018167034
TEST EQUIPMENT MECHANIC	17-3021.00	10000	0190	710361014
TOOL DESIGN CHECKER	17-3027.00	8000	0587	007267014
TOOL DESIGNER	17-2141.00	8000	0580	007061026
WELDING TECHNICIAN	17-3029.99	8000	0498	011261014
WIND TUNNEL MECHANIC	17-3021.00	8000	0499	869261026
LIFE, PHYSICAL, AND SOCIAL SCIENCE				
CHEMICAL ENGINEERING TECH	19-4031.00	8000	0969	008261010
CHEMICAL LABORATORY TECH	19-4031.00	8000	0050	022261010
DAIRY TECHNOLOGIST	19-4021.00	8000	0630	040061022
ENVIRONMENTAL ANALYST	19-2041.00	7000	0648	029081010
HORTICULTURIST	19-1013.01	6000	0236	040061038
LABORATORY ASSISTANT	19-4091.00	6000	0267	029361018
LABORATORY TECHNICIAN	19-4031.00	2000	0268	019261030

(continued)

OCCUPATIONAL TITLE	O*NET/SOC	HOURS	RAIS	DOT CODE
LIFE, PHYSICAL, AND SOCIAL SCIENCE (Continued)				
LABORATORY TESTER	19-4031.00	4000	0269	029261010
METEOROLOGIST	19-2021.00	6000	0940	025062010
RADIATION MONITOR	19-4051.02	8000	1007	199167010
SOIL CONSERVATION TECHNICIA	19-1031.01	6000	0450	040261010
TEST ENGINE OPERATOR	19-4041.02	4000	0482	029261018
TESTER (petroleum refining)	19-4041.02	6000	0956	029261022
WEATHER OBSERVER	19-4099.99	4000	0001	025267014
COUNSELING				
COUNSELOR	21-1012.00	4000	0569	045107010
DIRECT SUPPORT SPECIALIST	21-1093.00	3000	1040	195367900
LEGAL				
PARALEGAL	23-2011.00	6000	1003	119267026
TEACHING AND COUNSELING				
TEACHER AIDE I	25-9041.00	4000	0657	099327010
ARTS, DESIGN, ENTERTAINMENT, SPORTS				
ACTOR	27-2011.00	4000	0862	150047010
AUDIO OPERATOR	27-4012.00	4000	0879	194262010
BANK-NOTE DESIGNER	27-1021.00	10000	0640	142061010
CAMERA OPERATOR	27-4031.00	6000	0955	143062022
CARTOONIST, MOTION PICTURE	27-1013.03	6000	0037	141081010
CLOTH DESIGNER	27-1021.00	8000	0081	142061014
COMMERCIAL DESIGNER	27-1021.00	8000	0013	141061038
DECORATOR (any industry)	27-1026.00	8000	0082	298381010
DIRECTOR, TELEVISION	27-2012.02	4000	0970	159067014
DISPLAY DESIGNER				
(professional & kindred)	27-1027.02	8000	0098	142051010
DISPLAYER, MERCHANDISE	27-1026.00	2000	0324	298081010
FIELD ENGINEER (radio & tv)	27-4012.00	8000	0960	193262018
FILM OR VIDEOTAPE EDITOR	27-4032.00	8000	0127	962262010
FLORAL DESIGNER	27-1023.00	2000	0202	142081010
FUR DESIGNER	27-1022.00	8000	0224	142081014
FURNITURE DESIGNER	27-1021.00	8000	0225	142061022
GRAPHIC DESIGNER	27-1024.00	3000	0010	141061018
ILLUSTRATOR (professional & kindred)	27-1013.01	8000	0240	141061022

(continued)

OCCUPATIONAL TITLE	O*NET/SOC	HOURS	RAIS	DOT CODE
ARTS, DESIGN, ENTERTAINMENT, SPORTS (Continued)				
INDUSTRIAL DESIGNER	27-1021.00	8000	0016	142061026
INTERIOR DESIGNER	27-1025.00	4000	0265	142051014
LIGHT TECHNICIAN	27-4011.00	8000	0276	962362014
PAINTER (professional & kindred)	27-1013.01	2000	0626	144061010
PHOTOGRAPHER, STILL	27-4021.01	6000	0403	143062030
PROGRAM ASSISTANT	27-2012.01	6000	0913	962167014
RADIO STATION OPERATOR	27-4013.00	8000	0952	193262026
RECORDING ENGINEER	27-4014.00	4000	0926	194362010
SOUND MIXER	27-4014.00	8000	0527	194262018
STAGE TECHNICIAN	27-4011.00	6000	0521	962261014
STAINED GLASS ARTIST	27-1021.00	8000	0382	142061054
TAXIDERMIST (professional & kindred)	27-1012.00	6000	0562	199261010
HEALTHCARE PRATITIONER AND TECH				
EMERGENCY MEDICAL TECH	29-2041.00	6000	0730	079374010
HEALTH CARE SANITARY TECH	29-2099.99	2000	0602	079364641
MEDICAL-LABORATORY TECH	29-2012.00	4000	0323	078381014
NURSE, LICENSED PRACTICAL	29-2061.00	2000	0837	079374014
OPTICIAN DISPENSING	29-2081.00	4000	0089	299361010
ORTHOTIST	29-2091.00	8000	0458	078261018
PARAMEDIC	29-2041.00	4000	0543	079364026
PHARMACIST ASSISTANT	29-2052.00	2000	0844	074381010
PROSTHETIST (medical service)	29-2091.00	8000	0418	078261022
SAFETY INSPECTOR/TECHNICIAN	29-9011.00	6000	0707	168264014
TUMOR REGISTRAR	29-2071.00	4000	1004	079362018
HEALTHCARE SUPPORT				
DENTAL ASSISTANT	31-9091.00	2000	0101	079361018
NURSE ASSISTANT	31-1012.00	2000	0824	355674014
PODIATRIC ASSISTANT	31-9092.00	4000	0406	079374018
PROTECTIVE SERVICE				
ARSON AND BOMB INVESTIGATOR	33-2021.02	4000	0531	373267640
CORRECTION OFFICER	33-3012.00	2000	0851	372667018
FIRE APPARATUS ENGINEER	33-2011.01	6000	0535	373364640
FIRE CAPTAIN	33-1021.01	6000	0576	373134010
FIRE ENGINEER	33-2011.01	2000	0541	373364641
FIREFIGHTER	33-2011.01	6000	0195	373364010

(continued)

OCCUPATIONAL TITLE	O*NET/SOC	HOURS	RAIS	DOT CODE
PROTECTIVE SERVICE (Continued)				
FIREFIGHTER, CRASH, FIRE	33-2011.01	2000	0192	373663010
FIRE INSPECTOR	33-2021.01	8000	0516	373267010
FIRE MEDIC	33-2011.01	6000	0754	379374580
FISH & GAME WARDEN				
(government service)	33-3031.00	4000	0902	379167010
GUARD, SECURITY	33-9032.00	3000	0695	372667034
INVESTIGATOR, PRIVATE	33-9021.00	2000	0579	376267018
POLICE OFFICER I	33-3051.01	4000	0437	375263014
WILDLAND FIREFIGHTER				
SPECIALIST	33-2011.02	2000	0544	452687640
FOOD PREPARATION AND SERVICE				
BAKER, PIZZA (hotel & restaurant)	35-2011.00	2000	0883	313381014
BARTENDER	35-3011.00	2000	0608	312474010
COOK (any industry)	35-2012.00	4000	0090	315361010
COOK (hotel & restaurant)	35-2014.00	6000	0663	313361014
BUILDING AND GROUNDS MAINTENANCE				
AGRICULTURAL SERVICE WORKER	37-3012.00	4000	0703	408381560
EXTERMINATOR, TERMITE	37-2021.00	4000	1000	383364010
GREENSKEEPER II	37-3011.00	4000	0934	406683010
HOUSEKEEPER (commercial,				
residential, industrial)	37-2012.00	2000	0943	381684560
LANDSCAPE GARDENER	37-3011.00	8000	0271	408161010
LANDSCAPE MANAGEMENT TECH	37-3011.00	2000	0574	408684640
LANDSCAPE TECHNICIAN	37-3011.00	4000	0571	408364640
MULTI-STORY WINDOW/BUILD	37-2011.00	6000	0688	389684560
RUG CLEANER, HAND	37-2019.99	2000	0433	369384014
SWIMMING-POOL SERVICER	37-2011.00	4000	0838	891684018
TREE SURGEON	37-3013.00	6000	0595	408181010
TREE TRIMMER(LINE CLEAR)	37-3013.00	4000	0607	408664010
PERSONAL CARE AND SERVICE				
ANIMAL TRAINER	39-2011.00	4000	0871	159224010
BARBER	39-5011.00	2000	0030	330371010
CHILD CARE DEV SPECIALIST	39-9011.00	4000	0840	359342540
COSMETOLOGIST	39-5012.00	2000	0096	332271010

(continued)

OCCUPATIONAL TITLE	O*NET/SOC	HOURS	RAIS	DOT CODE
BUILDING AND GROUNDS MAINTENANCE (Continued)				
EMBALMER (personal service)	39-4011.00	4000	0665	338371014
HORSE TRAINER	39-2011.00	2000	1001	419224010
HORSESHOER	39-2021.00	4000	0235	418381010
WARDROBE SUPERVISOR	39-3092.00	4000	0494	346361010
SALES				
MANAGER, RETAIL STORE	41-1011.00	6000	0578	185167046
SALESPERSON PARTS	41-2022.00	4000	0753	279357062
OFFICE AND ADMINISTRATIVE SUPPORT				
ALARM OPERATOR (government service)	43-5031.00	2000	0870	379162010
COMPUTER OPERATOR	43-9011.00	6000	0676	213362010
COMPUTER-PERIPHERAL-EQ-OP	43-9011.00	2000	0817	213382010
DISPATCHER, SERVICE	43-5032.00	4000	0681	959167010
ELECTRONIC PREPRESS SYSTEM OP	43-9031.00	10000	0617	979282010
HOTEL ASSOCIATE	43-4081.00	4000	1035	238162900
LEGAL SECRETARY	43-6012.00	2000	0800	201362010
MAILER	43-9051.02	8000	0304	222587030
MATERIAL COORDINATOR	43-5061.00	4000	0856	221167014
MEDICAL SECRETARY	43-6013.00	2000	0751	201362014
PHOTOCOMPOSING-PERFORAT-MA	43-9021.00	4000	0285	203582042
POST OFFICE CLERK	43-5051.00	4000	0596	243367014
SCRIPT SUPERVISOR	43-6014.00	2000	0445	201362026
SUPERCARGO (water transportation)	43-5061.00	4000	0366	248167010
TELECOMMUNICATOR	43-5031.00	8000	1002	379362018
TELEGRAPHIC-TYPEWRITER OPER	43-9022.00	6000	0951	203582050
TRANSPORTATION CLERK	43-5011.00	3000	0655	248362640
FARMING, FISHING, FORESTRY				
FARMWORKER, GENERAL I	45-2091.00	2000	0981	421683010
FISH HATCHERY WORKER	45-2093.00	2000	1024	446684010
LOGGER, ALLROUND	45-4021.00	4000	0900	454684018
CONSTRUCTION AND EXTRACTION				
ACOUSTICAL CARPENTER	47-2081.01	8000	0861	860381010
ARCHITECTURAL, COATINGS FINISHER	47-2141.00	6000	0105	840381640

(*continued*)

OCCUPATIONAL TITLE	O*NET/SOC	HOURS	RAIS	DOT CODE
CONSTRUCTION AND EXTRACTION (Continued)				
ASPHALT PAVING MACHINE OPER	47-2071.00	6000	0872	853663010
ASSEMBLER, METAL BUILDING	47-2221.00	4000	0877	801381010
BOATBUILDER, WOOD	47-2031.05	8000	0036	860361010
BOILERHOUSE MECHANIC	47-2011.00	6000	0038	805361010
BOILERMAKER FITTER	47-2011.00	8000	0039	805361014
BOILERMAKER I	47-2011.00	6000	0040	805261014
BOILERMAKER II	47-2011.00	6000	0041	805381010
BRICKLAYER (brick & tile)	47-2021.00	8000	0051	861381014
BRICKLAYER (construction)	47-2021.00	6000	0052	861381018
BRICKLAYER, FIREBRICK & REF	47-2021.00	8000	0706	861381026
CARPENTER	47-2031.01	8000	0067	860381022
CARPENTER, INTERIOR SYSTEMS	47-2031.01	8000	0653	869381583
CARPENTER, MAINTENANCE	47-2031.01	8000	0068	860281010
CARPENTER, MOLD	47-2031.01	2000	0762	860381034
CARPENTER, PILEDRIVER	47-2031.02	8000	1009	860381581
CARPENTER, ROUGH	47-2031.02	8000	0069	860381042
CARPENTER, SHIP	47-2031.04	8000	0070	860281014
CARPET LAYER	47-2041.00	6000	0071	864381010
CASKET ASSEMBLER	47-2031.03	6000	0073	739684190
CEMENT MASON	47-2051.00	4000	0075	844364010
CHIMNEY REPAIRER	47-2021.00	2000	0849	899364010
CONSTRUCTION CRAFT LABORER	47-2061.00	4000	0661	869463580
COPPERSMITH (ship & boat)	47-2152.01	8000	0091	862281010
CORK INSULATOR, REFRIG PLT	47-2131.00	8000	0095	863381010
DRILLING-MACHINE OPER	47-5042.00	6000	0125	930482010
DRY-WALL APPLICATOR	47-2081.02	4000	0145	842684014
ELECTRICIAN	47-2111.00	8000	0159	824261010
ELECTRICIAN (ship & boat)	47-2111.00	8000	0771	825381030
ELECTRICIAN (water transportation)	47-2111.00	8000	0158	825281014
ELECTRICIAN, MAINTENANCE	47-2111.00	8000	0643	829261018
ELEVATING-GRADER OPERATOR	47-2073.01	4000	0138	850663014
ELEVATOR CONSTRUCTOR	47-4021.00	8000	0173	825361010
ELEVATOR REPAIRER	47-4021.00	8000	0174	825281030
FENCE ERECTOR	47-4031.00	6000	0711	869684022
FLOOR COVER LAYER (railroad equipment)	47-2042.00	6000	0201	622381026

(continued)

OCCUPATIONAL TITLE	O*NET/SOC	HOURS	RAIS	DOT CODE
CONSTRUCTION AND EXTRACTION (Continued)				
FLOOR LAYER	47-2042.00	6000	0199	864481010
FORM BUILDER (construction)	47-2031.02	4000	0206	860381046
GAS-MAIN FITTER	47-2152.01	8000	0964	862361014
GLAZIER	47-2121.00	6000	0221	865381010
GLAZIER, STAINED GLASS	47-2121.00	8000	0222	779381010
HAZARDOUS-WASTE MATERIAL TECH	47-4099.99	4000	0591	168364640
INSPECTOR, BUILDING	47-4011.00	6000	0941	168167030
INSULATION WORKER	47-2131.00	8000	0909	863364014
JOINER (ship & boat building)	47-2031.04	8000	0264	860381050
LATHER	47-2031.01	6000	0272	842361010
MARBLE FINISHER	47-3011.00	4000	0973	861664010
MARBLE SETTER	47-2022.00	6000	0313	861381030
MINER I (mine & quarry)	47-5081.00	2000	0354	939281010
MONUMENT SETTER (construction)	47-2022.00	8000	0352	861361014
MOSAIC WORKER	47-2044.00	6000	0353	779381014
MOTOR-GRADER OPERATOR	47-2073.01	6000	0932	850663022
NEON-SIGN SERVICER	47-2111.00	8000	0692	824281018
OPERATING ENGINEER	47-2073.02	6000	0365	859683010
ORNAMENTAL IRON WORKER	47-4099.99	6000	0373	809381022
PAINTER (construction)	47-2141.00	6000	0379	840381010
PAINTER, SHIPYARD	47-2141.00	6000	0385	840381018
PAPERHANGER	47-2142.00	4000	0390	841381010
PAVEMENT STRIPER	47-2141.00	4000	1042	869664900
PIPE COVERER & INSULATOR	47-2132.00	8000	0411	863381014
PIPE FITTER (construction)	47-2152.01	8000	0414	862281022
PIPE FITTER (ship & boat)	47-2152.01	8000	0412	862261010
PLASTERER	47-2161.00	4000	0423	842361018
PLUMBER	47-2152.02	8000	0432	862381030
PROP MAKER (amusement & recreation)	47-2031.01	8000	0455	962281010
PROSPECTING DRILLER (petroleum)	47-5012.00	4000	0416	930382018
PROTECTIVE-SIGNAL INSTALLER	47-2111.00	8000	0459	822361018
PROTECTIVE-SIGNAL REPAIRER	47-2111.00	6000	0006	822361022
REINFORCING METAL WORKER	47-2171.00	6000	0471	801684026
RESIDENTIAL CARPENTER	47-2031.01	4000	0564	860381640

(continued)

OCCUPATIONAL TITLE	O*NET/SOC	HOURS	RAIS	DOT CODE
CONSTRUCTION AND EXTRACTION (Continued)				
RESIDENTIAL WIREMAN	47-2111.00	4800	1022	824261900
ROOFER	47-2181.00	4000	0480	866381010
SHEET METAL WORKER	47-2211.00	8000	0510	804281010
SHIPWRIGHT (ship & boat)	47-2031.05	8000	0979	860381058
SIGN ERECTOR I	47-4099.99	6000	0517	869381026
SOFT TILE SETTER (construction)	47-2042.00	6000	0449	861381034
STEAM SERVICE INSPECTOR	47-2152.01	8000	0460	862361022
STONEMASON	47-2022.00	6000	0540	861381038
STREET-LIGHT SERVICER	47-2111.00	8000	0545	824381010
STRUCTURAL-STEEL WORKER	47-2221.00	6000	0669	801361014
TANK SETTER (petroleum production)	47-2221.00	4000	0558	801361022
TAPER	47-2082.00	4000	0561	842664010
TERRAZZO FINISHER	47-2053.00	4000	0972	861664014
TERRAZZO WORKER	47-2053.00	6000	0568	861381046
TILE FINISHER	47-3011.00	4000	0971	861664018
TILE SETTER	47-2044.00	6000	0573	861381054
TUCKPOINTER, CLEANER, CAULKER	47-2061.00	6000	0680	869684540
WELL DRILL OPERATOR (construction)	47-5021.02	8000	0629	859362010
INSTALLATION, MAINTENANCE, AND REPAIR				
AIR & HYDRONIC BALANCING TECH	49-9021.01	6000	0990	637261034
AIR CONDITIONING MECH (auto service)	49-3023.02	2000	0686	620281010
AIRCOND INSTALLER WINDOW	49-2092.01	6000	0002	637261010
AIRCRAFT MECHANIC, ELECTRICAL	49-2091.00	8000	0003	825381010
AIRCRAFT PHOTOGRAPH EQUIP	49-9061.00	8000	0867	714281010
AIRFRAME & POWERPLANT MECHANIC	49-3011.01	8000	0005	621281014
ASSEMBLY TECHNICIAN	49-2011.03	4000	0878	633261010
AUDIO-VIDEO REPAIRER	49-2097.00	4000	0880	729281010
AUTO COOLING SYS DIAG TECH	49-3023.02	4000	0836	620261034
AUTO-MAINT-EQUIP SERVICER	49-9041.00	8000	0027	620281018
AUTOMATED EQUIP ENGR-TECH	49-9044.00	8000	0821	638261010

(*continued*)

OCCUPATIONAL TITLE	O*NET/SOC	HOURS	RAIS	DOT CODE
INSTALLATION, MAINTENANCE, AND REPAIR (Continued)				
AUTOMATIC-EQUIP TECHNICIAN	49-2022.03	8000	0021	822281010
AUTOMOBILE BODY REPAIRER	49-3021.00	8000	0024	807381010
AUTOMOBILE MECHANIC	49-3023.01	8000	0023	620261010
AUTOMOTIVE-GENERATOR-STARTER REP	49-2092.02	4000	0882	721281010
AUTO-RADIATOR MECHANIC	49-3023.02	4000	0784	620381010
AVIATION SAFETY EQUIP TECH	49-9099.99	8000	0605	621261520
AVIATION SUPPORT EQUIP REP	49-9041.00	8000	0599	639281010
AVIONICS TECHNICIAN	49-2094.00	8000	0464	823261026
BAKERY-MACHINE MECHANIC	49-9041.00	6000	0029	629281010
BATTERY REPAIRER	49-2092.03	4000	0885	727381014
BIOMEDICAL EQUIPMENT TECH	49-9062.00	8000	0888	019261010
BRAKE REPAIRER (auto service)	49-3023.02	4000	0892	620281026
CABLE INSTALLER-REPAIRER	49-9051.00	6000	0056	821361010
CABLE SPLICER	49-9051.00	8000	0058	829361010
CABLE TELEVISION INSTALLER	49-9052.00	2000	0566	821281010
CAMERA REPAIRER	49-9061.00	4000	0062	714281014
CANAL EQUIPMENT MECHANIC	49-9041.00	4000	0790	899281010
CAR REPAIRER (railroad equipment)	49-3043.00	8000	0642	622381014
CARBURETOR MECHANIC	49-3023.02	8000	0896	620281034
CASH-REGISTER SERVICER	49-2011.03	6000	0072	633281010
CENTRAL-OFFICE INSTALLER	49-2022.01	8000	0076	822361014
CENTRAL-OFFICE REPAIRER	49-2022.01	8000	0077	822281014
COIN-MACH-SERVICE REPAIRER	49-9091.00	6000	0609	639281014
COMPOSING-ROOM MACHINIST	49-9041.00	12000	0086	627261010
CONSTRUCTION EQUIP MECHANIC	49-3042.00	8000	0336	620261022
CONTROL EQUIP ELEC-TECH	49-2094.00	10000	0693	829261560
CONVEYOR MAINTENANCE MECH	49-9041.00	4000	0066	630381010
COOLING TOWER TECHNICIAN	49-9041.00	4000	0634	549381640
CORROSION-CONTROL FITTER	49-2095.00	8000	0920	820361010
CUSTOMER SERVICE REPRESENT	49-9031.02	6000	1008	959361010
DAIRY EQUIPMENT REPAIRER	49-3041.00	6000	0099	629281018
DENTAL-EQUIP INSTAL & SERV	49-9062.00	6000	0650	829261014
DICTATING-TRANS-MACH SERV	49-2011.03	6000	0085	633281014
DIESEL MECHANIC	49-3031.00	8000	0124	625281010

(continued)

OCCUPATIONAL TITLE	O*NET/SOC	HOURS	RAIS	DOT CODE
INSTALLATION, MAINTENANCE, AND REPAIR (Continued)				
DOOR-CLOSER MECHANIC	49-9011.00	6000	0104	630381014
ELECT-MOTOR ASSEM & TESTER	49-2092.02	8000	0829	721281014
ELECT-PROD-LINE-MAINT-MECH	49-9041.00	2000	0171	629261022
ELECTRIC METER INSTALLER I	49-9012.01	8000	0330	821361014
ELECTRIC METER REPAIRER	49-9012.01	8000	0151	729281014
ELECTRIC MOTOR REPAIRER	49-2092.02	8000	0149	721281018
ELECTRIC TOOL REPAIRER	49-2092.01	8000	0150	729281022
ELECTRICAL APPLIANCE REPR	49-2092.01	6000	0154	723381010
ELECTRICAL APPLIANCE SERV	49-2092.01	6000	0156	827261010
ELECTRICIAN, AIRCRAFT	49-2091.00	8000	0160	825261018
ELECTRICIAN, AUTOMOTIVE	49-2096.00	4000	0161	825281022
ELECTRICIAN, LOCOMOTIVE	49-2093.00	8000	0162	825281026
ELECTRICIAN, POWERHOUSE	49-2095.00	8000	0163	820261014
ELECTRICIAN, RADIO	49-2021.00	8000	0164	823281014
ELECTRICIAN, SUBSTATION	49-2095.00	6000	0166	820261018
ELECTRIC-TRACK-SWITCH MAIN	49-9097.00	8000	0132	825261010
ELECTROMEDICAL EQUIP REPAIRER	49-9062.00	4000	0168	729281030
ELECTRONIC SYSTEMS TECH	49-2022.03	8000	1041	823261901
ELECTRONIC-ORGAN TECHNICIAN	49-2097.00	4000	0137	828261010
ELECTRONICS MECHANIC	49-2011.02	8000	0170	828261022
ELECT-SALES & SERVICE TECH	49-2094.00	8000	0906	828251010
ENGINE REPAIRER, SERVICE	49-3053.00	8000	0176	625281018
EQUIPMENT INSTALLER (telephone & telegraph)	49-2022.03	8000	0165	822381010
FACILITIES LOCATOR	49-9098.00	4000	0672	959384640
FARM EQUIPMENT MECH I	49-3041.00	6000	0187	624281010
FARM EQUIPMENT MECH II	49-3041.00	8000	0789	624381014
FIELD SERVICE ENGINEER	49-2094.00	4000	0916	828261014
FORGE-SHOP-MACHINE REPAIRER	49-9041.00	6000	0203	626261010
FRETTED INSTRUMENT REPAIRER	49-9063.02	6000	0215	730281026
FRONT-END MECHANIC	49-3023.02	8000	0209	620281038
FUEL INJECTION SERVICER	49-3023.02	8000	0922	625281022
FUEL SYSTEM MAINT WORKER	49-9041.00	4000	0610	638381010
FURNACE INSTALLER	49-9021.01	6000	0794	862361010
FURNACE INSTALLER & REPAIRER	49-9021.01	8000	0678	869281010

(continued)

OCCUPATIONAL TITLE	O*NET/SOC	HOURS	RAIS	DOT CODE
INSTALLATION, MAINTENANCE, AND REPAIR (Continued)				
GAS APPLIANCE SERVICER	49-9031.02	6000	0917	637261018
GAS UTILITY WORKER	49-9012.02	4000	0594	953384640
GAS-ENGINE REPAIRER	49-3053.00	8000	0230	625281026
GAS-METER MECHANIC I	49-9012.03	6000	0331	710381022
GAS-REGULATOR REPAIRER	49-9012.02	6000	0232	710381026
GLASS INSTALLER (auto service)	49-3022.00	4000	0714	865684010
HEATING & AIR-COND INST-SERV	49-9021.01	6000	0637	637261014
HYDRAULIC REPAIRER	49-9041.00	8000	0651	638281034
HYDRAUL-PRESS SERVICR(ordinance)	49-9041.00	4000	0783	626381018
HYDROELECTRIC-MACHINERY ME	49-9041.00	6000	0237	631261010
INDUSTRIAL MACH SYS TECH	49-9041.00	4000	1037	638261900
LAUNDRY-MACHINE MECHANIC	49-9041.00	6000	0691	629261010
LINE ERECTOR	49-9051.00	6000	0281	821361018
LINE INSTALLER-REPAIRER	49-9052.00	8000	0282	822381014
LINE MAINTAINER	49-9051.00	8000	0283	821261014
LINE REPAIRER	49-9051.00	6000	0284	821361026
LOCKSMITH	49-9094.00	8000	0289	709281010
LOGGING-EQUIPMENT MECHANIC	49-3042.00	8000	0299	620281042
MACHINE ERECTOR	49-9044.00	8000	0293	638261014
MACHINE FIXER(carpet & rug)	49-9041.00	8000	0302	628281010
MACHINE REPAIRER, MAINTEN	49-9041.00	8000	0292	638261030
MACHINIST, LINOTYPE	49-9041.00	8000	0297	627261022
MACHINIST, MARINE ENGINE	49-3031.00	8000	0298	623281026
MACHINIST, MOTIONPIC EQUIP	49-9061.00	4000	0191	714281018
MAINT MECH (any industry)	49-9041.00	8000	0308	638281014
MAINT MECH (construction; petroleum)	49-3031.00	8000	0022	620281046
MAINT MECH (grain & feed)	49-9041.00	4000	0307	629281030
MAINT REPAIRER, INDUSTRIAL	49-9042.00	8000	0311	899261014
MAINTENANCE MECH, COMPGAS	49-9041.00	8000	0020	630261010
MAINTENANCE MECHANIC, TELE	49-2022.05	6000	0309	822281018
MAINTENANCE REPAIRER, BUILD	49-9042.00	4000	0310	899381010
MARINE SERVICES TECHNICIAN	49-9042.00	6000	0946	806261026
MECHANIC, ENDLESS TRACK VEH	49-3042.00	8000	0319	620381014
MECHANIC, INDUSTRIAL TRUCK	49-3031.00	8000	0153	620281050
MECHANICAL-UNIT REPAIRER	49-3043.00	8000	0337	620381018
METEOROLOGICAL EQUIP REPR	49-2094.00	8000	0329	823281018

(continued)

OCCUPATIONAL TITLE	O*NET/SOC	HOURS	RAIS	DOT CODE
INSTALLATION, MAINTENANCE, AND REPAIR (Continued)				
METER REPAIRER (any industry)	49-9012.03	6000	0332	710281034
MILLWRIGHT	49-9044.00	8000	0335	638281018
MINE-CAR REPAIRER	49-3043.00	4000	0350	622381030
MOTORBOAT MECHANIC	49-3051.00	6000	0355	623281038
MOTORCYCLE REPAIRER	49-3052.00	6000	0356	620281054
OFFICE-MACHINE SERVICER	49-2011.03	6000	0359	633281018
OIL BURNER-SERVICER & INST	49-9021.01	4000	0966	862281018
OIL FIELD EQUIP MECHANIC	49-3031.00	4000	0364	629381014
OUTBOARD-MOTOR MECHANIC	49-3051.00	4000	0378	623281042
OVERHAULER (textile)	49-9041.00	4000	0384	628261010
PHOTO-EQUIPMENT TECHNICIAN	49-9061.00	6000	0924	714281022
PHOTOGRAPHIC EQUIP MAINTEN	49-9061.00	6000	0563	714281026
PIANO TECHNICIAN	49-9063.01	8000	0408	730281038
PIANO TUNER	49-9063.01	6000	0793	730361010
PINSETTER ADJUSTER, AUTOMA	49-9041.00	6000	0387	829381010
PINSETTER MECH, AUTOMATIC	49-9043.00	4000	0985	638261022
PIPE ORGAN TUNER & REPAIR	49-9063.01	8000	0388	730361014
PNEUMATIC TOOL REPAIRER	49-9041.00	8000	0434	630281010
PNEUMATIC TUBE REPAIRER	49-9041.00	4000	0435	630281014
POWERHOUSE MECHANIC	49-9041.00	8000	0443	631261014
POWER-SAW MECHANIC	49-3053.00	6000	0441	625281030
POWER-TRANSFORMER REPAIRER	49-2092.04	8000	0442	821361034
PROPULSION MOTOR & GENERAT	49-2092.02	8000	0456	721281026
PRVTE-BRANCH EXCH INSTALLER	49-2022.01	8000	0646	822381018
PRVTE-BRANCH EXCH REPAIRER	49-2022.01	8000	1006	822281022
PUMP ERECTOR (construction)	49-9041.00	4000	0419	637281010
PUMP SERVICER	49-9041.00	6000	0933	630281018
RADIO MECHANIC (any industry)	49-2021.00	6000	0465	823261018
RADIO REPAIRER (any industry)	49-2097.00	8000	0466	720281010
REFRIGERATION MECH (any industry)	49-9021.02	6000	0666	637261026
REFRIGERATION UNIT REPAIRER	49-9021.02	6000	0918	637381014
RELAY TECHNICIAN	49-2095.00	4000	0975	821261018
REPAIRER I (chemical)	49-9041.00	8000	0674	630261018
REPAIRER, HANDTOOLS	49-2092.06	6000	0421	701381010
REPAIRER, HEAVY	49-3023.01	4000	0997	620381022

(continued)

OCCUPATIONAL TITLE	O*NET/SOC	HOURS	RAIS	DOT CODE
INSTALLATION, MAINTENANCE, AND REPAIR (Continued)				
REPAIRER, RECREATIONAL VEH	49-3092.00	8000	0807	869261022
REPAIRER, WELDING EQUIPMENT	49-9041.00	4000	0422	626384010
REPAIRER, WELDING SYS & EQ	49-9041.00	6000	1005	626261014
RIGGER	49-9096.00	6000	0474	921260010
RIGGER (ship & boat building)	49-9096.00	4000	0473	806261014
ROCKET-ENGINE-COMPONENT MEC	49-3011.02	8000	0425	621281030
RUBBERIZING MECHANIC	49-9041.00	8000	0485	630281030
SAFE & VAULT SERVICE MECH	49-9094.00	8000	0488	869381022
SCALE MECHANIC	49-9041.00	8000	0497	633281026
SERVICE MECHANIC				
(auto manufacturing)	49-3021.00	4000	0446	807381022
SERVICE PLANNER(light,heat)	49-9098.00	8000	0615	821564640
SEWING MACHINE REPAIRER	49-9041.00	6000	0508	639281018
SIGNAL MAINTAINER (railroad				
transportation)	49-9097.00	8000	0942	822281026
SMALL ENGINE MECHANIC	49-3053.00	4000	0525	625281034
SOUND TECHNICIAN	49-2022.03	6000	0528	829281022
SPRING REPAIRER, HAND	49-3023.02	8000	0533	619380018
STATION INSTALLER & REPAIRER	49-2022.05	8000	0647	822261022
STOKER ERECTOR & SERVICER	49-9041.00	8000	0467	637281014
TAPE-RECORDER REPAIRER	49-2097.00	8000	0560	720281014
TECHNICIAN, SUBMARINE CABLE	49-2022.03	4000	0552	822281034
TELECOMMUNICATIONS				
TECHNICIAN	49-2022.03	8000	0618	823281720
TELEVISION & RADIO REP	49-2097.00	8000	0565	720281018
TRACTOR MECHANIC	49-3031.00	8000	0589	620281058
TRANSFORMER REPAIRER	49-2092.04	8000	0590	724381018
TRANSMISSION MECHANIC	49-3023.01	4000	0592	620281062
TREATMENT PLANT MECHANIC	49-9041.00	6000	0847	630281038
TROUBLE SHOOTER II	49-9051.00	6000	0858	821261026
TRUCK BODY BUILDER	49-3021.00	8000	0598	807281010
TUNE-UP MECHANIC	49-3023.02	4000	0600	620281066
UNDERCAR SPECIALIST	49-3023.02	4000	1034	915384560
WATCH REPAIRER	49-9064.00	8000	0616	715281010
WIND INSTRUMENT REPAIRER	49-9063.03	8000	0357	730281054

(continued)

OCCUPATIONAL TITLE	O*NET/SOC	HOURS	RAIS	DOT CODE
PRODUCTION				
ACCORDION MAKER	51-7011.00	8000	0860	730281010
AIRCRAFT MECH, PLUMB & HYDRA	51-2011.02	8000	0866	806381066
AIRCRAFT MECHANIC, ARMAMENT	51-2011.02	8000	0865	806361030
AIRPLANE COVERER	51-9199.99	8000	0868	849381010
AIRPLANE INSPECTOR	51-9061.02	6000	0004	621261010
ALTERATION TAILOR	51-6052.01	4000	0007	785261010
ARTIFICIAL GLASS EYE MAKER	51-9195.04	10000	0011	713261010
ARTIFICIAL PLASTIC EYE MKR	51-9082.00	10000	0012	713261014
ASSEMBLER, AIRCRAFT POWERPLANT	51-2031.00	4000	0873	806381022
ASSEMBLER, AIRCRAFT STRUCTURES	51-2011.01	8000	0874	806381026
ASSEMBLER-INSTALLER,GENERAL	51-2011.01	4000	0876	806361014
ASSISTANT PRESS OPERATOR	51-5023.09	4000	0903	651585010
AUGER PRESS OPR, MAN CONTR	51-9041.02	4000	0779	575462010
AUTOMOBILE TESTER	51-9061.02	8000	0881	620261014
AUTOMOBILE UPHOLSTERER	51-6093.00	6000	0639	780381010
AUTOMOBILE-REPAIR-SERV EST	51-9061.02	8000	0638	620261018
BAKER (bakery production)	51-3011.02	6000	0028	526381010
BAKER (hotel & restaurant)	51-3011.01	6000	0776	313381010
BATCH-AND-FURNACE OPERATOR	51-9051.00	8000	0884	572382010
BENCH HAND (jewelry-silver)	51-9071.04	4000	0031	735381010
BEN-DAY ARTIST	51-5023.01	12000	0887	970681010
BINDERY WORKER	51-5011.02	8000	0033	653685010
BINDERY-MACHINE SETTER	51-5011.01	8000	0026	653360018
BLACKSMITH	51-4199.99	8000	0035	610381010
BLOCKER & CUTTER CONTACT LENS	51-9083.01	2000	0889	716681010
BOILER OPERATOR	51-8021.02	8000	0815	950382010
BOOKBINDER	51-5012.00	10000	0047	977381010
BOOTMAKER, HAND	51-6041.00	2000	0890	753381010
BRACELET & BROOCH MAKER	51-9071.04	8000	0891	735681010
BRILLIANDEER-LOPPER	51-9071.06	6000	0893	770261010
BUTCHER, ALLROUND	51-3023.00	6000	0662	525381014
BUTCHER, MEAT (hotel & restaurant)	51-3021.00	6000	0894	316681010

(*continued*)

OCCUPATIONAL TITLE	O*NET/SOC	HOURS	RAIS	DOT CODE
PRODUCTION (Continued)				
BUTTERMAKER	51-9012.00	4000	0054	529362010
CABINETMAKER	51-7011.00	8000	0055	660280010
CABLE TESTER (telephone & telegraph)	51-9061.04	8000	0059	822361010
CALIBRATOR (military)	51-9061.03	4000	1031	710381034
CANDY MAKER	51-3092.00	6000	0065	529361014
CANVAS WORKER	51-9199.99	6000	0641	739381010
CARD CUTTER, JACQUARD	51-6099.99	8000	0897	683582010
CARD GRINDER	51-4194.00	8000	0898	680380010
CARPET CUTTER (retail trade)	51-9031.00	2000	0899	929381010
CARVER, HAND	51-7011.00	8000	0042	761281010
CASING-IN-LINE SETTER	51-5011.01	8000	0043	653360010
CASTER (jewelry-silver)	51-9071.04	4000	0074	502381010
CASTER (nonferrous metal)	51-4072.04	4000	0044	502482010
CELL MAKER	51-9195.07	2000	0046	844681010
CHASER (jewelry-silver)	51-9071.02	8000	0049	704381010
CHEESEMAKER	51-3092.00	4000	0078	529361018
CHEMICAL OPERATOR III	51-9011.01	6000	0791	559382018
CHIEF OPERATOR (chemical)	51-8091.00	6000	0057	558260010
CLARIFYING-PLANT OPER (textile)	51-8031.00	2000	0060	955382010
COATING MACHINE OPERATOR I	51-9121.02	2000	1025	584382010
COLORIST, PHOTOGRAPHY	51-9131.01	4000	0084	970381010
COMPLAINT INSPECTOR	51-9061.04	8000	0061	829261010
COMPOSITOR	51-5022.01	8000	0087	973381010
CONTOUR WIRE SPEC DENTURE	51-9081.00	8000	0904	712381014
COOK, PASTRY (hotel & restaurant)	51-3011.01	6000	0722	313381026
COREMAKER	51-4071.00	8000	0094	518381014
CUPOLA TENDER	51-4051.00	6000	0991	512662010
CUSTOM TAILOR (garment)	51-6052.02	8000	0314	785261014
CUTTER, MACHINE 1	51-9031.00	6000	0613	781684014
CYLINDER GRINDER (print & publishing)	51-4194.00	10000	0080	500381010
CYLINDER PRESS OPERATOR	51-5023.03	8000	0677	651362010
DECORATOR (glass manufacturing)	51-9123.00	8000	0100	740381010
DENTAL CERAMIST	51-9081.00	4000	0102	712381042
DENTAL LABORATORY TECH	51-9081.00	6000	0103	712381018
DESIGN & PATTERNMAKER SHOE	51-6092.00	4000	0107	788281010

(continued)

OCCUPATIONAL TITLE	O*NET/SOC	HOURS	RAIS	DOT CODE
PRODUCTION (Continued)				
DIAMOND SELECTOR (jewelry)	51-9071.06	8000	0083	770281010
DIE FINISHER	51-4111.00	8000	0114	601381010
DIE MAKER (jewelry-silver)	51-4111.00	8000	0115	601381014
DIE MAKER (paper goods)	51-4111.00	8000	0654	739381018
DIE MAKER, BENCH, STAMPING	51-4111.00	8000	0668	601281010
DIE MAKER, STAMPING	51-4111.00	6000	0118	601280010
DIE MAKER, TRIM	51-4111.00	8000	0119	601280014
DIE MAKER, WIRE DRAWING	51-4111.00	6000	0939	601280018
DIE POLISHER (nonferrous metal)	51-4194.00	2000	0120	601381018
DIE SETTER (forging)	51-4022.00	4000	0121	612360010
DIE SINKER	51-4111.00	8000	0122	601280022
DIESEL ENGINE TESTER	51-9061.02	8000	0093	625261010
DOT ETCHER	51-5022.08	10000	0679	972281010
DRESSMAKER	51-6052.02	8000	0144	785361010
DRY CLEANER	51-6011.03	6000	0649	362382014
ELECT-MOTOR & GEN ASSEMBLER	51-2031.00	4000	0927	820361014
ELECTRIC METER TESTER	51-9061.03	8000	0792	821381010
ELECTRIC SIGN ASSEMBLER	51-2022.00	8000	0652	729684022
ELECTRIC-DISTRIBUTION CHECKER	51-9061.04	4000	0905	824281014
ELECTRONICS TESTER	51-9061.04	6000	0570	726261018
ELECTRONICS UTILITY WORKER	51-9199.99	8000	0967	726364018
ELECTROSTATIC POWDER COATING TECH	51-9121.01	8000	1036	599382900
ELECTROTYPER	51-5022.10	10000	0172	974381010
EMBOSSER	51-5023.07	4000	0704	659382010
EMBOSSING-PRESS OPERATOR	51-5023.07	8000	0684	659682014
ENGINE TURNER (jewelry)	51-9071.04	4000	0143	704381018
ENGINEERING MODEL MAKER (installation & application)	51-4061.00	8000	0249	693260018
ENGINE-LATHE SET-UP OP,TOOL	51-4034.00	4000	0782	604280010
ENGINE-LATHE SET-UP OPERATOR	51-4034.00	4000	0142	604380018
ENGRAVER (glass production)	51-9194.02	4000	0178	775381010
ENGRAVER I	51-9194.01	10000	0705	979381010
ENGRAVER, BLOCK (print & publishing)	51-9194.01	8000	0146	979281014

(continued)

OCCUPATIONAL TITLE	O*NET/SOC	HOURS	RAIS	DOT CODE
PRODUCTION (Continued)				
ENGRAVER, HAND, HARD METAL	51-9194.01	8000	0806	704381026
ENGRAVER, HAND, SOFT METAL	51-9194.01	8000	0147	704381030
ENGRAVER, MACHINE	51-5023.08	8000	0963	979382014
ENGRAVER, PANTOGRAPH I	51-9194.04	8000	0179	704382010
ENGRAVER, PICTURE				
(print & publishing)	51-9194.01	2000	0148	979281018
ENGRAVING PRESS OPERATOR	51-5023.08	6000	0915	651382010
ENVELOPE-FOLD-MACH ADJUSTER	51-9196.00	6000	0180	641380010
ETCHER, HAND (print & publishing)	51-5022.03	10000	0175	971261010
ETCHER, PHOTOENGRAVING	51-5022.03	8000	0182	971381014
EXPER MECH MOTOR & BIKES	51-4061.00	8000	0184	600260014
EXPERIMENTAL ASSEMBLER	51-9061.01	4000	0183	739381026
EXTRUDER OPERATOR (plastics)	51-4021.00	2000	0185	557382010
FABRICATOR-ASSEMBLER METAL				
PROD	51-2041.01	8000	0833	809381010
FASTENER TECHNOLOGIST	51-4022.00	6000	0808	612260010
FILM DEVELOPER	51-9132.00	6000	0921	976382018
FILM LAB TECHNICIAN	51-9132.00	6000	0907	976684014
FILM LAB TECHNICIAN I	51-9131.04	6000	0908	976381010
FINISHER, DENTURE	51-9081.00	2000	0181	712381050
FIRER, KILN (pottery & porcelain)	51-9051.00	6000	0188	573662010
FITTER (machine shop)	51-2041.02	4000	0197	801381014
FITTER I (any industry)	51-2041.02	6000	0189	801261014
FIXTURE MAKER (light fixtures)	51-4041.00	4000	0198	600380010
FOLDING MACHINE OPERATOR	51-5011.01	4000	0194	653382010
FORGING-PRESS OPERATOR I	51-4022.00	2000	0196	611482010
FORMER, HAND (any industry)	51-2041.01	4000	0200	619361010
FORMING-MACHINE OPERATOR	51-9041.01	8000	0048	575382014
FOURDRINIER-MACHINE OPER	51-9012.00	6000	0204	539362014
FOUR-SLIDE-MACHINE SETTER	51-4081.01	4000	0208	616380010
FREEZER OPERATOR (dairy)	51-9193.00	2000	0211	529482010
FUR CUTTER	51-9031.00	4000	0220	783381010
FUR FINISHER	51-6031.01	4000	0210	783381014
FURNACE OPERATOR	51-4051.00	8000	0944	512362014
FURNITURE FINISHER	51-7021.00	6000	0212	763381010
FURNITURE UPHOLSTERER	51-6093.00	8000	0213	780381018

(continued)

OCCUPATIONAL TITLE	O*NET/SOC	HOURS	RAIS	DOT CODE
PRODUCTION (Continued)				
FURRIER	51-6052.02	8000	0214	783261010
GANG SAWYER, STONE	51-9032.02	4000	0228	670362010
GAUGER (petroleum production)	51-8093.03	4000	0226	914384010
GEAR HOBBER SETUP OPERATOR	51-4081.01	8000	0241	602382010
GEARCUT-MACH SET-UP OP TOO	51-4081.01	6000	0664	602280010
GEAR-CUTTING-MACH SETUP OPER	51-4081.01	6000	0234	602380010
GEM CUTTER (jewelry)	51-9071.06	6000	0242	770281014
GLASS BENDER (fabrication)	51-9195.04	8000	0218	772381010
GLASS BLOWER	51-9195.04	6000	0219	772381022
GLASS BLOWER, LAB APPARATUS	51-9195.04	8000	0768	772281010
GLASS-BLOWING-LATHE OPERAT	51-9195.04	8000	0243	772482010
GRADER (woodworking)	51-9061.05	8000	0984	669687030
GRINDER I (clock & watch)	51-4033.01	8000	0244	603482030
GRINDER OP TOOL PRECISION	51-4194.00	8000	0671	603280018
GRINDER SET-UP OP, JIG	51-4033.01	8000	0635	603280026
GRINDER SET-UP OPERATOR, UNIVERSAL	51-4194.00	8000	0974	603280030
GUNSMITH	51-4081.01	8000	0229	632281010
HARNESS MAKER	51-6041.00	6000	0245	783381018
HARPSICHORD MAKER	51-7011.00	4000	0248	730281034
HAT-BLOCK MAKER (woodwork)	51-7011.00	6000	0253	661381010
HEAD SAWYER	51-7041.01	6000	0831	667662010
HEAT TREATER I	51-4191.02	8000	0233	504382014
HEAVY FORGER	51-4022.00	8000	0947	612361010
HYDROELECTRIC-STATION OPER	51-8013.01	6000	0238	952362018
HYDROMETER CALIBRATOR	51-9061.03	4000	0239	710381030
INJECTION-MOLDING-MACH OP	51-4072.01	2000	0246	556382014
INSPECTOR, ELECTROMECHANIC	51-9061.03	8000	0968	729361010
INSPECTOR, METAL FABRICATG	51-9061.01	8000	0697	619261010
INSPECTOR, OUTSIDE PRODUCT	51-9061.01	8000	0380	806261042
INSPECTOR, PRECISION	51-9061.03	4000	0424	716381010
INSPECTOR, SET-UP & LAY-OUT	51-9061.01	8000	0636	601261010
INSTRUMENT MAKER	51-4041.00	8000	0251	600280010
INSTRUMENT MAKER & REPAIRER	51-4041.00	10000	0254	600280014
JACQUARD-LOOM WEAVER	51-6063.00	8000	0270	683662010

(continued)

OCCUPATIONAL TITLE	O*NET/SOC	HOURS	RAIS	DOT CODE
PRODUCTION (Continued)				
JACQUARD-PLATE MAKER	51-6063.00	2000	0258	685381010
JEWELER	51-9071.01	4000	0260	700281010
JIG BUILDER (wood)	51-7031.00	4000	0261	761381014
JOB PRINTER	51-5021.00	8000	0262	973381018
KILN OPERATOR (woodworking)	51-9051.00	6000	0266	563382010
KNITTER MECHANIC	51-6063.00	8000	0273	685360010
KNITTING MACHINE FIXER	51-6063.00	8000	0850	689260026
LAST-MODEL MAKER	51-7011.00	8000	0275	761381018
LAY-OUT TECHNICIAN	51-9083.01	8000	0554	716381014
LAY-OUT WORKER I (any industry)	51-4192.00	8000	0825	809281010
LEAD BURNER	51-4121.03	8000	0274	819281010
LEATHER STAMPER	51-6041.00	2000	0935	781381018
LETTERER (professional & kindred)	51-5023.01	4000	0280	970661014
LINER (pottery & porcelain)	51-9123.00	6000	0279	740681010
LINOTYPE OPERATOR (print & publishing)	51-5022.12	10000	0286	650582010
LITHOGRAPHIC PLATEMAKER	51-5022.07	8000	0063	972381010
LITHOGRAPH-PRESS OPER, TIN	51-5023.04	8000	0683	651382014
LOFT WORKER (ship & boat)	51-7031.00	8000	0290	661281010
LOOM FIXER	51-6063.00	6000	0841	683260018
MACHINE ASSEMBLER	51-2031.00	4000	0301	638361010
MACHINE BUILDER	51-2031.00	4000	0291	600281022
MACHINE FIXER (textile)	51-6064.00	6000	0305	689260010
MACHINE OPERATOR I	51-4081.01	2000	0511	616380018
MACHINE SETTER (any industry)	51-4081.01	8000	0938	616360022
MACHINE SETTER (clock)	51-4081.01	8000	0317	600380022
MACHINE SETTER (machine shop)	51-4081.01	6000	0263	600360014
MACHINE SETTER (woodwork)	51-7042.01	8000	0321	669280010
MACHINE SET-UP OPER, PAPER	51-9196.00	8000	0327	649380010
MACHINE SET-UP OPERATOR	51-4081.01	4000	0958	600380018
MACHINE TRYOUT SETTER	51-4081.01	8000	0659	600360010
MACHINIST	51-4041.00	8000	0296	600280022
MACHINIST, AUTOMOTIVE	51-4041.00	8000	0294	600280034
MACHINIST, EXPERIMENTAL	51-4041.00	8000	0295	600260022
MACHINIST, OUTSIDE (ship)	51-4041.00	8000	0300	623281030
MACHINIST, WOOD	51-7011.00	8000	0303	669380014

(continued)

335

OCCUPATIONAL TITLE	O*NET/SOC	HOURS	RAIS	DOT CODE
PRODUCTION (Continued)				
MAINTENANCE MACHINIST	51-4041.00	8000	0306	600280042
MEAT CUTTER	51-3021.00	6000	0316	316684018
METAL FABRICATOR	51-2041.01	8000	0325	619361014
MILLER, WET PROCESS	51-9021.00	6000	0333	521662010
MILLING MACHINE SET-UP OP	51-4035.00	4000	0334	605280010
MOCKUP BUILDER (aircraft)	51-4061.00	8000	0358	693361014
MODEL & MOLD MAKER (brick)	51-9199.99	4000	0343	777381014
MODEL & MOLD MAKER, PLASTR	51-9199.99	8000	0344	777381018
MODEL BUILDER (furniture)	51-4061.00	4000	0339	709381014
MODEL MAKER (aircraft)	51-7031.00	8000	0341	693261018
MODEL MAKER (auto manufacturing)	51-4061.00	8000	0491	693380014
MODEL MAKER (clock & watch)	51-4061.00	8000	0363	693380010
MODEL MAKER (pottery & porcelain)	51-9195.05	4000	0340	777281014
MODEL MAKER II (jewelry)	51-9071.03	8000	0773	709381018
MODEL MAKER, FIREARMS	51-4061.00	8000	0780	600260018
MODEL MAKER, WOOD	51-7031.00	8000	0342	661380010
MOLD MAKER (pottery & porcelain)	51-9195.06	6000	0345	777684018
MOLD MAKER I (jewelry)	51-9071.03	8000	0346	700381034
MOLD MAKER II (jewelry)	51-9071.03	4000	0347	777381022
MOLD MAKER, DIE-CAST & PLAST	51-4111.00	8000	0116	601280030
MOLD SETTER	51-4072.01	2000	0348	556380010
MOLDER	51-4071.00	8000	0349	518361010
MOLDER, PATTERN (foundry)	51-9195.02	8000	0351	693381022
MONOTYPE-KEYBOARD OPERATOR	51-5022.12	6000	0367	650582014
MULTI-OPERATION-MACHINE OP	51-4022.00	6000	0371	612462010
MULTO-PER FORM MACH SETTER	51-4199.99	8000	0931	616260014
NUMERICAL CONTROL MACH OP	51-4011.01	8000	0845	609362010
OFFSET-PRESS OPERATOR I	51-5023.02	8000	0361	651382042
OPERATIONAL TEST MECHANIC	51-9061.01	6000	0959	806261050
OPTICAL INSTRUMENT ASSEMBL	51-9083.02	4000	0250	711381010
OPTICIAN (optical goods; retail trade)	51-9083.01	10000	0032	716280014
OPTICIAN (optical goods)	51-9083.02	8000	0377	716280018
ORNAMENTAL METAL WORKER	51-4081.01	8000	0374	619260014
ORTHO-BOOT-SHOE DESIGNER	51-6041.00	10000	0910	788261010
ORTHODONTIC TECHNICIAN	51-9081.00	4000	0375	712381030

(continued)

OCCUPATIONAL TITLE	O*NET/SOC	HOURS	RAIS	DOT CODE
PRODUCTION (Continued)				
ORTHOTICS TECHNICIAN	51-9082.00	2000	0911	712381034
PAINTER, HAND (any industry)	51-9123.00	6000	0383	970381022
PAINTER, SIGN	51-9199.99	8000	0386	970381026
PAINTER, TRANS EQUIPMENT	51-9122.00	6000	0381	845381014
PANTOGRAPH-MACHINE SET-UP OPER	51-4035.00	4000	0389	605382022
PASTE-UP ARTIST	51-5022.02	6000	0392	972381030
PATTERMAKER (textiles)	51-6092.00	6000	0710	781361014
PATTERNMAKER (metal production)	51-4062.00	8000	0394	693281014
PATTERNMAKER (stonework)	51-4062.00	8000	0796	703381010
PATTERNMAKER, ALL-AROUND	51-4062.00	10000	0857	693280014
PATTERNMAKER, METAL	51-4062.00	10000	0395	600280050
PATTERNMAKER, METAL, BENCH	51-4062.00	10000	0396	693281018
PATTERNMAKER, PLASTER	51-9199.99	6000	0397	777281018
PATTERNMAKER, PLASTICS	51-4062.00	6000	0923	754381014
PATTERNMAKER, WOOD	51-7032.00	10000	0398	661281022
PEWTER CASTER	51-9071.05	6000	0982	502384010
PEWTER FABRICATOR	51-9071.05	8000	0986	700381581
PEWTER FINISHER	51-9071.05	4000	0983	700281026
PEWTERER	51-9071.05	4000	0988	700261010
PHOTOENGRAVER	51-5022.03	10000	0399	971381022
PHOTOENGRAVING FINISHER	51-5022.03	10000	0400	971381030
PHOTOENGRAVING PRINTER	51-5022.03	10000	0401	971381034
PHOTOENGRAVING PROOFER	51-5022.03	10000	0402	971381038
PHOTOGRAPH RETOUCHER	51-9131.01	6000	0912	970281018
PHOTOGRAPHER, LITHOGRAPHIC	51-5022.04	10000	0685	972382014
PHOTOGRAPHER, PHOTOENGRAV	51-5022.03	12000	0405	971382014
PHOTOGRAPHIC-PLATE MAKER	51-5022.07	8000	0407	714381018
PIPE ORGAN BUILDER	51-7011.00	6000	0417	730281042
PLANT OPERATOR	51-9021.00	6000	0961	570682014
PLANT OPERATOR, FURNACE PRO	51-8091.00	8000	0393	559362026
PLASTER PATTERN CASTER	51-9195.01	10000	0404	777381038
PLASTIC FIXTURE BUILDER	51-4111.00	8000	0843	601381030
PLASTIC PROCESS TECHNICIAN	51-4072.01	8000	0660	556260540
PLASTIC TOOL MAKER	51-4111.00	8000	0426	601381026
PLASTICS FABRICATOR	51-9199.99	4000	0186	754381018

(*continued*)

OCCUPATIONAL TITLE	O*NET/SOC	HOURS	RAIS	DOT CODE
PRODUCTION (Continued)				
PLATE FINISHER (print & publishing)	51-5022.11	12000	0427	659360010
PLATEN-PRESS OPERATOR	51-5023.03	8000	0430	651362018
PLATER	51-4193.01	6000	0431	500380010
PONY EDGER (sawmill)	51-7041.02	4000	0901	667682050
POTTERY MACHINE OPERATOR	51-9195.05	6000	0439	774382010
POWER-PLANT OPERATOR	51-8013.01	8000	0440	952382018
PRECISION ASSEMBLER	51-2011.02	6000	0410	806381082
PRECISION ASSEMBLER, BENCH	51-2023.00	4000	0962	706381050
PRECISION-LENS GRINDER	51-9083.01	8000	0277	716382018
PRESS OPERATOR HEAVY DUTY	51-4031.03	8000	0928	617260010
PRINTER, PLASTIC	51-5023.04	8000	0452	651382026
PRINTER-SLOTTER OPERATOR	51-5023.09	8000	0451	659662010
PRODUCTION FINISHER	51-9121.01	4000	1023	741384900
PRODUCTION TECHNOLOGIST	51-2092.00	Competency	1027	726261560
PROJECTION PRINTER	51-9131.02	8000	0413	976381018
PROOF-PRESS OPERATOR	51-5023.09	10000	0288	651582010
PROOFSHEET CORRECTOR (print)	51-5022.01	8000	0415	973381030
PROSTHETICS TECHNICIAN	51-9082.00	8000	0376	712381038
PROTOTYPE MODEL MAKER	51-4061.00	8000	0846	693280540
PURIFICATION OPERATOR II	51-9012.00	8000	0461	551362010
QUALITY CONTROL INSPECTOR	51-9061.01	4000	0936	701261010
RADIOGRAPHER	51-9061.01	8000	0468	199361010
RECOVERY OPERATOR (paper)	51-9012.00	2000	0420	552362018
REFINERY OPERATOR	51-8093.02	6000	0852	549260010
RELAY TESTER	51-9061.04	8000	0687	729281038
REPRODUCTION TECHNICIAN	51-9131.02	2000	0092	976361010
RETOUCHER, PHOTOENGRAVING	51-5022.03	10000	0472	970381030
ROCKET MOTOR MECHANIC	51-4041.00	8000	0475	693261022
ROLL THREADER OPERATOR	51-4023.00	2000	0428	619462010
ROLLER ENGRAVER HAND	51-9194.06	4000	0795	979681018
ROTOGRAVURE-PRESS OPERATOR	51-5023.09	8000	0481	651362026
RUBBER TESTER	51-9061.01	8000	0429	559381014
RUBBER-STAMP MAKER	51-9195.07	8000	0484	733381014
SADDLE MAKER	51-6041.00	4000	0487	783381026
SAMPLE MAKER, APPLIANCES	51-4061.00	8000	0490	600280054
SAMPLE STITCHER (garment)	51-6052.01	8000	0436	785361018

(continued)

OCCUPATIONAL TITLE	O*NET/SOC	HOURS	RAIS	DOT CODE
PRODUCTION (Continued)				
SANDBLASTER, STONE	51-9195.03	6000	0493	673382010
SAW FILER (any industry)	51-4194.00	8000	0495	701381014
SAW MAKER (cutlery & tools)	51-4111.00	6000	0496	601381034
SCANNER OPERATOR	51-5022.05	4000	0855	972282010
SCREEN PRINTER	51-9123.00	4000	0520	979684034
SCREW-MACH SET-UP OP, SINGL	51-4034.00	6000	0506	604280018
SCREW-MACH SET-UP OPERATOR	51-4034.00	8000	0502	604380022
SCREW-MACHINE OP, MULTI SPIN	51-4034.00	8000	0500	604382010
SCREW-MACHINE OP, SINGLE SPI	51-4034.00	6000	0444	604382014
SHIP PROPELLER FINISHER	51-2041.01	6000	0611	623281720
SHIPFITTER (ship & boat)	51-4192.00	8000	0513	806381046
SHOE REPAIRER	51-6041.00	6000	0514	365361014
SHOEMAKER, CUSTOM	51-6041.00	6000	0812	788381014
SHOP OPTICIAN, BENCHROOM	51-9083.01	8000	0524	716280541
SHOP OPTICIAN, SURFACE ROOM	51-9083.01	8000	0526	716280540
SHOP TAILOR	51-6052.01	8000	0515	785361022
SIDEROGRAPHER (print & publishing)	51-9194.01	10000	0447	979381030
SIGN WRITER, HAND	51-9199.99	2000	0518	970281022
SILKSCREEN CUTTER	51-9031.00	6000	0519	979681022
SILVERSMITH II	51-9071.02	6000	0522	700281022
SKETCH MAKER I (print & publishing)	51-5023.01	10000	0448	979381034
SKETCH MAKER II (print & publishing)	51-9194.01	8000	0523	972381018
SOLDERER (jewelry)	51-9071.04	6000	0453	700381050
SPINNER, HAND	51-4034.00	6000	0530	619362018
SPRING COILING MACHINE SET	51-4031.03	8000	0457	616260018
SPRING MAKER	51-4081.01	8000	0532	616280010
SPRING-MANUFTRG SET-UP TECH	51-4081.01	8000	0534	619280018
STATIONARY ENGINEER	51-8021.02	8000	0536	950382026
STEEL-DIE PRINTER	51-5023.07	8000	0785	651382030
STENCIL CUTTER	51-9199.99	4000	0463	970381038
STEREOTYPER	51-5022.10	2000	0538	974382014
STONE CARVER	51-9195.03	6000	0539	771281014
STONE POLISHER	51-4033.02	6000	0017	673382018
STONE SETTER (jewelry)	51-9071.04	8000	0312	700381054
STONECUTTER, HAND	51-9195.03	6000	0542	771381014
STONE-LATHE OPERATOR	51-9032.04	6000	0470	674662010

(continued)

OCCUPATIONAL TITLE	O*NET/SOC	HOURS	RAIS	DOT CODE
PRODUCTION (Continued)				
STRIPPER (print & publishing)	51-5022.06	10000	0726	971381050
STRIPPER, LITHOGRAPHIC II	51-5022.06	8000	0064	972381022
SUBSTATION OPERATOR	51-8012.00	8000	0553	952362026
SURFACE-PLATE FINISHER	51-9021.00	4000	0478	775281010
SWITCHBOARD OPERATOR (utilities)	51-8012.00	6000	0801	952362034
TAP AND DIE MAKER TECHNICI	51-4111.00	8000	0559	601280034
TEMPLATE MAKER	51-4062.00	8000	0567	601381038
TEMPLATE MAKER, EXTRUSION DIE	51-4062.00	8000	0123	601280038
TEST TECH (professional & kindred)	51-4041.00	10000	0483	019161014
TESTING & REGULATING TECH	51-9061.04	8000	0572	822261026
THERMOMETER TESTER	51-9061.05	2000	0489	710384030
TINTER (paint & varnish)	51-9023.00	4000	0575	550381014
TOOL AND DIE MAKER	51-4111.00	8000	0586	601260010
TOOL BUILDER	51-4061.00	8000	0205	693281030
TOOL GRINDER I	51-4194.00	6000	0582	701381018
TOOL GRINDER OPERATOR	51-4194.00	8000	0765	603280038
TOOL MACHINE SET-UP OPERAT	51-4081.01	6000	0588	601280054
TOOL MAKER	51-4111.00	8000	0584	601280042
TOOL MAKER, BENCH	51-4111.00	8000	0585	601281026
TOOL PROGRAMMER, NUMERICAL	51-4012.00	6000	0690	007167018
TROUBLE LOCATOR TEST DESK	51-9061.04	4000	0805	822361030
TURBINE OPERATOR	51-8013.01	8000	0601	952362042
TURRET LATHE SET-UP OPERAT	51-4034.00	8000	1021	604280022
UPHOLSTERER	51-6093.00	4000	0097	780384014
UPHOLSTERER, INSIDE	51-6093.00	6000	0606	780381038
VIOLIN MAKER, HAND	51-7011.00	8000	0492	730281046
WALLPAPER PRINTER I	51-5023.04	8000	0612	652662014
WASTE TREATMENT OPERATOR	51-8031.00	4000	0614	955382014
WASTEWATER-TREATMT- PLT OPER	51-8031.00	4000	0507	955362010
WATER TREATMENT PLANT OPERATOR	51-8031.00	6000	0619	954382014
WEBPRESS OPERATOR	51-5023.03	8000	0667	651362030
WELDER, ARC	51-4121.02	8000	0620	810384014
WELDER, COMBINATION	51-4121.02	6000	0622	819384010
WELDERFITTER	51-4121.03	8000	0627	819361010

(continued)

OCCUPATIONAL TITLE	O*NET/SOC	HOURS	RAIS	DOT CODE
PRODUCTION (Continued)				
WELDING MACHINE OPER, ARC	51-4122.01	6000	0945	810382010
WIRE SAWYER (stonework)	51-9032.02	4000	0501	677462014
WIRE WEAVER, CLOTH	51-6063.00	8000	0504	616382014
WIRER (office machines)	51-2022.00	4000	0633	729281042
WOODTURNINGLATHE OPERATO	51-7042.02	2000	0505	664382014
X-RAY EQUIPMENT TESTER	51-9061.03	4000	0919	729281046
TRANSPORTATION AND MATERIAL MOVING				
ABLE SEAMAN	53-5011.01	2760	1043	911364010
AMBULANCE ATTENDANT (EMT)	53-3011.00	2000	0724	355374010
CONSTRUCTION DRIVER	53-3032.01	2400	1032	905363900
CONVEYOR SYSTEM OPERATOR	53-7011.00	8000	0557	921662018
DRAGLINE OPERATOR	53-7032.02	2000	0957	850683018
DREDGE OPERATOR	53-7031.00	2000	0117	850663010
INSPECTOR, MOTOR VEHICLES	53-6051.05	4000	0581	168267058
LOCOMOTIVE ENGINEER	53-4011.00	8000	0287	910363014
PILOT, SHIP	53-5021.03	3000	0623	197133026
PUMPER-GAUGER	53-7121.00	6000	0950	914382014
TRUCK CRANE OPERATOR	53-7021.00	6000	0014	921663062
TRUCK DRIVER, HEAVY	53-3032.01	2000	0980	905663014

Source: U.S. Department of Labor Employment and Training Administration

References

CHAPTER 1: THE HISTORY OF APPRENTICESHIP

Alder, David B. *Franklin the Printer*. New York: Holiday House, 2001.

"Apprenticeship Past and Present." Milwaukee Area Technical College. http://www.matc.edu/apprentice/past_and_present.htm (5 August 2004).

Colvin, Fred H. *Sixty Years with Men and Machines*. Bradlee, IL: Lindsay Publishing, 1947.

"First Apprenticeship Legislation." Michigan Regional Council of Carpenters, Michigan Carpenter and Millwright Apprenticeship Programs. http://www.realapprenticeship.com/mcat/mainweb/mcatweb.htm (25 September 2003).

Galway, Patricia. *Archers, Alchemists, and 98 Other Medieval Jobs You Might Have Loved or Loathed*. Toronto: Annick Press, 2003.

"History of Apprenticeship—1968." Washington State Department of Labor and Industries. http://www.lni.wa.gov/TradesLicensing/Apprenticeship/About/History/default.asp (30 January 2004).

Jacoby, Daniel, "Apprenticeship in the United States." Economic History Association. http://www.eh.net/encyclopedia/jacoby.apprenticeship.us.php (25 September 2003).

King, L.W. (trans.). "The Code of Hammurabi." Yale University, The Avalon Project, http://www.yale.edu/lawweb/avalon/medieval/hamframe.htm (22 January 2003).

Power, Eileen. *Medieval People*. New York: HarperPerennial, 1992.

"U.S. Department of Labor Bicentennial History of the American Worker." U.S. Department of Labor, Office of the Assistant Secretary for Policy. http://www.dol.gov/asp/programs/history/amworkerintro.htm (7 November 2003).

CHAPTER 2: APPRENTICESHIP TODAY

"29 CFR 29.5 Standards of Apprenticeship." U.S. Department of Labor. http://www.dol.gov/dol/allcfr/ETA/Title_29/Part_29/29CFR29.5.htm (6 July 2004).

"Apprenticeship." U.S. Department of Labor Employment and Training Administration, 1991.

"Apprenticeship in America: Apprenticeship May Be a Steady Ride in Unsteady Times." CareerOneStop Consumer Information: 2003. http://www.careertools.org/ci/apprentice_art.asp (13 March 2004).

"A Brighter Tomorrow: Apprenticeship for the 21st Century." Washington, D.C.: U.S. Department of Labor Office of Apprenticeship Training, Employment and Labor Services, July, 2003

Crosby, Olivia. "Apprenticeship: Career Training, Credentials—And a Paycheck in Your Pocketbook." *Occupational Outlook Quarterly*, Summer 2002.

"Department of Labor Announces Grants to Promote Women in Apprenticeship and Nontraditional Occupations" U.S. Department of Labor News Release, 1 October, 2002. http://www.dol.gov/opa/media/press/wb/WB2002566.htm (1 September 2004).

"Frequently Asked Questions and Discussions." National Association of State and Territorial Apprenticeship Directors. http://www.nastad.net/index.cfm?page=10 (9 September 2003).

"National Registered Apprenticeship System: Programs and Apprentices Fiscal Year 2003." U.S. Department of Labor Office of Apprenticeship Training, Employer and Labor Services, June, 2004.

"Top 25 Occupations for Active Apprentices." U.S. Department of Labor Employment and Training Administration. http://www.doleta.gov/atels_bat/top-25 occupations.cfm (5 August 2004).

"YDPA Weekly Competency Tracking Form for OJT and RI Hours." Somerville, MA: YouthBuild USA.

CHAPTER 3: THE CONSTRUCTION INDUSTRY

"Apprenticeship Training." Associated Builders and Contractors. http://www.abc.org (3 April 2004).

"Apprenticeship Training." National Joint Apprenticeship and
    Training Committee. http://www.njatc.org/apprentice.htm (28
    May 2004).

"Becoming an Ironworker." Ironworkers International.
    http://www.ironworkers,org/becoming/what_do_
    ironworkers_do.php (27 May 2004).

"BIGDIG.COM: Central Artery Tunnel Project." Massachusetts
    Turnpike Authority. http://www.bigdig.com (15 June 2004).

"Boilermakers National Apprenticeship Program, Classroom
    Training." http://www.bnap.com/process/class.htm
    (4 May 2004).

"Career Education Resources." Plumbing-Heating Contractors of
    America (PHCC), 2003. http://www.phccweb.org/
    foundation/career.cfm (3 March 2004).

"Certification: The CAT Curriculum" and "CET Program:
    The CAT Curriculum." National Association of Elevator
    Constructors. http://www.naec.org (5 August 2004).

"Construction. Career Guide to Industries, 2004–05 Edition." U.S.
    Department of Labor, Bureau of Labor Statistics.
    http://www.bls.gov/oco/cg/cgs003.htm (5 May 2004).

"Construction and Extraction Occupations." 2003 National
    Occupational Employment and Wage Estimates," U.S.
    Department of Labor, Bureau of Labor Statistics.
    http://www.bls.gov/oes/2003/may/oes_47Co.htm (8 May 2004).

"Construction Industry—Craft Laborers: Apprenticeship." National
    Skill Standards Board Institute. http://www.nssb
    .org/certapp_details.cfm?certapp_id=66 (29 March 2004).

"Construction Industry—Interior Systems Carpenters:
    Apprenticeship." National Skill Standards Board Institute.
    http://www.nssb.org/certapps/8ashipconstructionlaborers
    .1a1.htm (12 March 2004).

"Contren Learning Series Catalog, 2004." National Center for
    Construction Education and Research.

"Current Population Survey." U.S. Department of Labor, Bureau of
    Labor Statistics. http://www.bls.gov/cps/
    home.htm#overview, (15 June 2004).

Finishing Contractors Association.
    http://www.finishingcontractors.org (10 May 2004).

"Frequently Asked Questions." Portland Cement Association,
    http://www.cement.org/basics/concretebasics_faq.asp
    (11 May 2004).

References

"Heating, Ventilation, Air Conditioning, and Refrigeration (HVACR) Installation and Repair Industry: Air Conditioning Technicians." National Skill Standards Board Institute. http://www.nssb.org/certapps/5NATEairconditon.1a1.htm (10 April 2004).

"The History of Labor Day." U.S. Department of Labor. http://www.dol.gov/opa/aboutdol/laborday.htm (30 April 2004).

"HVAC Service Tech Training." International Training Institute for Sheet Metal and Air Conditioning Industry. http://www.sheetmetal-iti-org/ (6 May 2004).

International Brotherhood of Boilermakers Iron Ship Builders, Blacksmiths, Forgers, and Helpers. http://www.boilermakers.org/ (8 April 2004).

International Union of Bricklayers and Allied Craft Workers. http://www.bacweb.org (6 May 2004).

International Union of Painters and Allied Craft Workers. http://www.carpenters.org (8 May 2004).

Kent, Jim. "Mohawk Ironworkers to Be Honored at WTC Ceremony," *Canku Ota (Many Paths)*, An Online Newletter Celebrating Native America, 6 April, 2002, http://www.turtletrack.org/Issues02/Co04062002/CO_04062002_Ironworkers.htm (17 September 2004).

"Monthly Labor Review: February, 2004." U.S. Department of Labor, Occupational Employment Projections to 2012. http://www.bls.gov/opub/mlr/2004/02/art5full.pdf (8 May 2004).

Monthorn, David. "Mohawk Ironworkers Build New York: Booming Out High-Rise Feats of Ironworkers Celebrated at New York Exhibit." Associated Press. News from Indian Country, *The Independent Native Journal*, 2002. http://www.indiancountrynews.com/ironworkers.cfm (17 September 2004).

Norbert, Johnson. "Are We There Yet?" *Electrical Contractor*. http://www.ecmag.com/editorial_detail.aspx?id=1240 (11 June 2004).

"Organizations around the Country." Women Unlimited. http://www.womenunlimited.org (10 June 2004).

Plumbing-Heating-Cooling Contractors Association. http://www.phccweb.org (25 February 2004).

"Roto-Rooter History" Roto-Rooter http://www.rotorooter.com/comp_hist_1.html (14 February 2004).

"Secretary of Labor Elaine L. Chao Announces Skilled Trades Initiative." U.S. Department of Labor, 6 April 2004.

Sheet Metal and Air-Conditioning Contractors' National Association. http://www.smacna.org (15 May 2004).

Sheet Metal Workers International Association. http://www.smwia.org (4 December 2003).

Tradeswomen Now and Tomorrow (TNT). http://www.tradeswomennow.org (10 June 2004).

"Training Courses Available to Members." New England Regional Council of Carpenters. http://www.necarpetners.org/training.cfm?sct=cour (30 April 2004).

CHAPTER 4: ENTERTAINMENT AND THE ARTS

Actors, U.S. Department of Labor, Bureau of Labor Statistics, May 2003 National Occupational Employment and Wage Estimates, May 7, 2004 (27 July 2004).

"Actor's Apprenticeship." Williamstown Theatre Festival. http://www.wefestival.org/training/actors_apprentice.html (27 July 2004).

"Actors, Producers, and Directors." U.S. Department of Labor, Bureau of Labor Statistics. *Occupational Outlook Handbook, 2004–05 Edition*. 21 March 2004. http://www.gov/oco/ocos093.htm (27 July 2004).

"Arts, Entertainment, and Recreation." *The 2004–05 Career Guide to Industries*. U.S. Department of Labor, Bureau of Labor Statistics, 27 February 2004. http://www.bls/gov/oco/cg/cgs031.htm (22 July 2004).

"Audio and Video Equipment Technicians." United States Department of Labor, Bureau of Labor Statistics, May 2003 National Occupational Employment and Wage Estimates, 7 May 2004. http://bls.ogv/oes/2003/may/oes274011.htm (27 July 2004).

Auerbach, Susan. "In Good Hands: A Portrait of State Apprenticeship Program in Folk and Traditional Arts, 1983–1995." Washington, DC: National Endowment for the Arts, 1996.

Brumfield, Gary. "Craft Apprenticeship in Historic Site Museums." *The Abbey Newsletter*, Vol. 7, No. 2, Supplement, Education and Training, May 1983.

Crosby, Olivia. "You're a What? Historic Interpreter." U.S. Department of Labor, Bureau of Labor Statistics, Occupational Outlook Quarterly Online, Spring, 2003, http://www.bls.gov/opub/ooq/2003/spring/yawhat.htm (1 August 2004).

"Entertainment Industry—Stage Technicians: Apprenticeship."
National Skill Standards Board, 27 July 1999. http://www.nssb
.org/certapps/4ashipstagetech.1a1.htm (22 July 2004).

International Alliance of Theatrical Stage Employees, Moving Picture
Technicians, Artists and Allied Crafts of the United States, Its
Territories, and Canada. http://www.iatse-itl.org (23 July 2004).

Kent, Phoebe. "Patricia C. and Walter J. Arnell Endowment for
Historic Trades: Master/Mistress of Weaving, Tailoring, or
Millinery, Colonial Williamsburg." (development packet)
Colonial Williamsburg, November 2003.

"Molds, Shapers, and Casters, Except Metal and Plastic." United
States Department of Labor, Bureau of Labor Statistics, May
2003 National Occupational Employment and Wage Estimates,
7 May 2004. http://www.bls.gov/oes/may/oes519196.htm
(28 July 2004).

"Overview of Careers for Stage Technicians." Virginia Department
of Education, Office of Career and Technical Education
Services, Career Prospects in Virginia. http://www3.ccps
.virginia.edu/career_prospects/briefs/P-S/SummaryStage.html
(23 July 2004).

"Performing Arts Career Facts—Stage Technology." Lansing
Community College. http://www.lcc.edu/hums/
performing_arts/careerfacts/stage.htm (8 August 2004).

"Standards of Apprenticeship adopted by IATSE #15 Theatrical Stage
Technicians Apprenticeship Committee." Washington State
Apprenticeship and Training Council, January 16, 1998.

Thrall, Anne. "Glass Blowing History." Gaffer's Guild Homepage,
http://www.public.iastate.edu/~fed/gaffersguild/history/
history.html (2 September 2003).

"The Unbreakable Glass of Ancient Rome." Corning Museum
of Glass, http://www.cmog/org/index/asp?pageId=742
(28 July 2004).

CHAPTER 5: HEALTH CARE CAREERS

"Address Critical Nursing Shortage With Washington State Pilot
Program (Press Release)." Council for Adult and Experiental
Learning and U.S. Department of 29 December 2003. http://
www.cael.org/LatestNews/CAEL_Press_Release_12_29.pdf,
(15 June 2004).

Bellis, Mary. "The History of Prosthetics." About.com. http://www
.inventors.about.com/library/inventors/blprosthetic.htm
(18 June 2004).

"Clinical Laboratory Technicians and Technologists." Career
Prospects in Virginia, Virginia Department of Education,
http://www3.ccps.virginia.edu/career_prospects/briefs/
A-D/ClinicalLabTechs.html (17 June 2004).

"The Cultural Body: History of Prostheses." University of Iowa's
Healthcare Medical Museum, http://www.uihealthcare.com/
depts/medmuseum/wallexhibits/body/histofpros/histofpros.html
(18 June 2004).

"Dentistry—Dental Assistants: Apprenticeship." National Skills
Standards Board http://www.nssb.org/certapps/
DentalAssistantApprenticeshipProgram.htm (17 June 2004).

"Details for Pharmacy Technicians." Occupational Information
Network. U.S. Department of Labor, O*NET OnLine.
http://online.onetcener.org/reprot?r=1&id=319 (17 June 2004)

"Details Report for Medical Appliance Technicians." Occupational
Information Network. U.S. Department of Labor O*NET
Online. http://online.onetcenter.org/report?r=1&id=931,
(17 June 2004).

Hall, Carl T. "Prosthetics Keep Pace with Technical Advances
of War: Modern Armor Results in Fewer Deaths—More
Amputees." *San Francisco Chronicle*. SFGate.com,
5 January 2004. http://www.nssb.org/certapps/
DentalAssistantApprenticeshipProgram.htm (18 June 2004).

"Health Care Apprenticeship Initiative." Wisconsin Department
of Workforce Development. http://www.dwd.state.wi.us/
healthcare/doc/apprenticeship_summation_1.doc (15 June
2004).

"Healthcare Practitioner and Technical Occupations." 2003 National
Occupational Employment and Wage Estimate. U.S.
Department of Labor, Bureau of Labor Statistics, http://www
.bls.gov/oes/2003/may/oes_29He.htm (21 June 2004).

"Healthcare Support Occupations." 2003 National Occupational
Employment and Wage Estimates. Bureau
of Labor Statistics, U.S. Department of Labor, http://www
.bls.gov/oes/2003/may/oes_31He.htm (15 June 2004).

"Health Services." Career Guide to the Industries, 2004–05 Edition.
U.S. Department of Labor, Bureau of Labor Statistic.
http://www.bls.gov/oco/cg/cgs035.htm (15 June 2004).

References

Janofsky, Michael. "Redefining the Front Lines in Reversing War's Toll." *The New York Times*, 21 June 2004. http://www.nytimes.com/2004/06/21/health21limbs.html (21 June 2004).

"Nursing Shortages: Innovative Solutions and Opportunities."Council for Adult and Experiential Learning and U.S. Department of Labor. http://www.cael.org/Lattice_Web.pdf (15 June 2004).

"Soldiering: Patent for Artificial Limbs." Smithsonian Institution." http://www.civilwar.si.edu/soldiering_limb_patent.html (18 June 2004).

"What's New: Apprenticeship Nursing Career Lattice Program." U.S. Department of Labor Employment and Training Agency. http://www.doleta.gov/atels_bat.cael.cfm (16 June 2004).

CHAPTER 6: INSTALLATION, MAINTENANCE, AND REPAIR

"AAIA Releases Collision Repair Trends Report Indicating Size of the Collision Repair Industry Increased Nearly 20 Percent Since 1997." *Collision Repair Industry Insight,* 4 October 2002. http://www.collision-insight.com/news/20021004-aaia.htm (5 July 2004).

"Aircraft and Avionics Equipment Mechanics and Service Technicians." *Occupational Outlook Handbook, 2004–05 Edition*, February 27, 2004. U.S. Department of Labor, Bureau of Labor Statistics. http://bls.gov/oco/ocos179.htm (5 August 2004).

"Automotive Body and Related Repairers." *Occupational Outlook Handbook, 2004–05 Edition*, 27 February 2004. U.S. Department of Labor, Bureau of Labor Statistics. http://bls.gov/oco/ocos180.htm (4 July 2004).

"Automotive Service Technicians and Mechanics" *Occupational Outlook Handbook, 2004–05 Edition*, 27 February, 2004. U.S. Department of Labor, Bureau of Labor Statistics. http://wbls.gov/oco/ocos181.htm (4 July 2004).

"Avionics Technician." Ontario, Canada: Baxter Group. EduNET Connect. http://www.edunetconnect.com/cat/caeeers/avion.html (6 August 2004).

"Bus and Truck Mechanics." May 2003 National Occupational Employment and Wage Estimates, 7 May 2004. U.S.

Department of Labor, Bureau of Labor Statistics. http://www
.bls.gov/oes/2003/May/oes493031.htm (4 July 2004).

"Details Report for Avionics Technicians." Occupational Information
Network. U.S. Department of Labor, O*NET OnLine, http://
www.online.onetcenter.org/report?r=1&id=472 (5 August
2004).

"Diesel Service Technicians and Mechanics." *Occupational Outlook
Handbook, 2004–05 Edition,* 27 February 2004.
U.S. Department of Labor, Bureau of Labor Statistics.
http://bls.gov/oco/ocos182.htm (4 July 2004).

"Electric Meter Apprentice." City of Riverside Human Resources
Department, Classification Specification, July 1, 1995.

Ford, Royal. "A Career Accelerates Greasy Days Gone, Well-Trained
Auto Technicians Much in Demand." *Boston Globe,* December
4, 2003, A1.

"Home Appliance Repairers." *Occupational Outlook Handbook,
2004–05 Edition,* 27 February 2004. U.S. Department of Labor,
Bureau of Labor Statistics. http://bls.gov/oco/ocos193.htm
(30 June 2004).

"Industrial Machinery Installation, Repair, and Maintenance
Workers, Except Millwrights." *Occupational Outlook
Handbook, 2004–05 Edition,* 27 February 2004. U.S.
Department of Labor, Bureau of Labor Statistics. http://bls.gov/
oco/ocos191htm (30 June 2004).

"Installation, Maintenance, and Repair Occupations." May 2003
National Occupational Employment and Wage Estimates,
7 May 2004. U.S. Department of Labor, Bureau of Labor
Statistics. http://www.bls.gov/oes/2003/may/oes_49In.htm
(30 June 2004).

"Maintenance and Repair Workers, General." *Occupational Outlook
Handbook, 2004–05 Edition,* 27 February 2004.U.S.
Department of Labor, Bureau of Labor Statistics. http://www
.bls.oco/ocos194.htm (30 June 2004).

"Millwrights." *Occupational Outlook Handbook, 2004–05 Edition,*
27 February 2004. U.S. Department of Labor, Bureau of Labor
Statistics. http://bls.gov/oco/ocos190.htm (26 June 2004).

"Summary Report for Industrial Machinery Mechanics."
Occupational Information Networks. U.S. Department
of Labor, O*NET OnLine. http://onine.onetcenter.org/
report?r=0&id=694 (2 July 2004).

"Top Ten Tips for Auto Technology Students From ASE-Certified Master Technicians." National Automotive Technicians Education Foundation. http://www.natef.org/career/topten.cfm (4 July 2004).

"What Does a Professional Locksmith Do?" Associated Locksmiths of America, http://www.aloa.org/about1.cfm (3 July 2004).

CHAPTER 7: PERSONAL CARE AND SERVICE

"Apprenticeship: Cosmetology Apprenticeship Program Approved Related Instruction." Wytheville, VA: Wytheville Community College. http://www.wc.cc.va.us/apprenticeship/ cos.asp (22 July 2004).

"Apprenticeship Fundamentals." American Culinary Institute. http://www.acfchefs.org/apprwhat.html (29 April 2003).

"Bakers." May 2003 National Occupational Employment and Wage Estimates, 7 May 2004. United States Department of Labor, Bureau of Labor Statistics. http://www.bls.gov/oes/2003/ may /oes513011.htm (29 July 2004).

"Barbers, Cosmetologists, and Other Personal Appearance Workers." *Occupational Outlook Handbook, 2004–2005 Edition*, 2 June 2004. U.S. Department of Labor, Bureau of Labor Statistics. http://www.bls.gov/oco/oco169.htm (22 July 2004).

"Blood, Bandages and Barber Poles." BBC, 22 November 2002. http://www.bbc.co.uk/dna/h2g2/brunel/A885062 (22 July 2004).

"Career: Costume and Wardrobe Specialists." Iseek. Minnesota Department of Education, May, 2004. http://www.iseek .org/sv/13000.jsp?id=100287&testOnly=Y (23 July 2004)

"Chefs and Head Cooks." May 2003 National Occupational Employment and Wage Estimates, 7 May 2004. U.S. Department of Labor, Bureau of Labor Statistics. http://www .bls.gov/oes/2003/may/oes351011.htm (29 July 2004).

"Chefs, Cooks, and Food Preparation Workers." *Occupational Outlook Handbook, 2004–05 Edition*. U.S. Department of Labor, Bureau of Labor Statistics. http://www.bls.gov/oco/ ocos161.htm (29 July 2004).

"Chefs Profiles." National Restaurant Association. http://www .restaurantorg/careers/profiles (1 August 2003).

"Cooks, Restaurant." May 2003 National Occupational Employment and Wage Estimates, May 7, 2004, U.S. Department of Labor,

Bureau of Labor Statistics. http://www.bls.gov/oes/2003/may/oes352014.htm (29 July 2004).

"Details Report for Bakers." U.S. Department of Labor, Occupational Information Network, O*NET Online. http://www.online.onetcenter.org/report?r=1&id=905 (1 August 2004).

"Details Report for Bakers, Bread and Pastry" U.S. Department of Labor, Occupational Information Network, O*NET Online. http://www.online.onetcenter.org/report?r=1&id=573 (1 August 2004).

"Details Report for Costume Attendants." U.S. Department of Labor, Occupational Information Network, O*NET Online. 2003. http://online.onetcenter.org/report?r=1&id=615 (22 July 2004).

"Funeral Directors." *Occupational Outlook Handbook, 2004–2005 Edition*, 27 February, 2004. U.S. Department of Labor, Bureau of Labor Statistics. http://www.bls.gov/oco/pring/ocos022.htm (21 July 2004).

"Funeral Service." Mt. Ida College Catalog, 2003–2004. Newton, Massachusetts: Mt. Ida College. http://www.mountida.edu/sp.cfm?pageid=919&id=37 (21 July 2004).

"Guide Dog Origins." Guide Dog Foundation for the Blind. http://www.guidedog.org/Aboutgdf/gd1usa.htm (30 September 2003).

Guide Dogs of America. http://www.guidedogsofamerica.org (23 July 2004).

"Overview of Careers in Animal Training." Career Prospects in Virginia. Virginia Department of Education. 18 June 2004. http://www3.ccps.virginia.edu/career_prospects/briefs/P-S/SummaryAnimalTrain.html (6 July 2004).

"Personal Care and Service Occupations." 2003 National Occupation Employment and Wage Estimates, 7 May 2004. U.S. Department of Labor. http://stats.bls.gov/oes/2003/may/oes_39Pe.htm (22 July 2004).

"Scenic Artist Apprenticeship Program." United Scenic Artists, Local USA 829, 2003 Scenic Artist Exam Info East—Revised May 7, 2003.

"Thinking About a Career in Funeral Service." National Funeral Directors Association. http://www.nfda.org/careers.php (21 July 2004).

"Training, Sea World/Busch Gardens Animal Information Database, 2002." http://www.seaworld.org/career-resources/info-books/careers/training.htm (6 July 2004).

"WBA Offering New Educational Programs!" Upper Midwest Bakers Alliance. http://www.umwba.org/WBA/scholarship%20information_files/Scholarship.htm (29 July 2004).

CHAPTER 8: PRODUCTION

"Apprenticeship." National Institute for Metalworking Skills, Inc. http://www.nims-skills.org/appren/appren.htm (27 June 2004).

"Career Profiles: Pattern Maker." SchoolsIntheUSA.com. http://www.schoolsintheusa.com/careerprofiles_details.cfm?CarID=1698 (26 June 2004).

Leno, Jay. "Calling All Machinists." *Popular Mechanics.* http://popularmechanics.mondosearch.com/cgi-bin/MsmGo.exe?grab_id=41&EXTRA_ARG=&CFGNAME=MssFind%2Ecfg&host_id=42&page_id=7606016&query=Calling+all+machinists&hiword=Calling+all+MACHINIST+machinists+CALLIES+ (27 June 2004).

"Machine Setters, Operators, and Tenders—Metal and Plastics." *Occupational Outlook Handbook, 2004–05 Edition*, March 21, 2004. U.S. Department of Labor, Bureau of Labor Statistics. http://www.bls.gov/oco/print/ocos224.htm (28 July 2004).

"Machinists." Occupational Outlook Handbook, 2004–2005 edition, May 18, 2004. http://www.bls.gov/oco/print/ocos223.htm.

"Machinists Make Replacement Tusks for Calgary Elephant." CBC News, 13 April 2002. http://www.cbc.ca/story/science/national/2002/04/12/elephant020412.html (27 June 2004).

"Pattern Maker Apprenticeship Training." Thomson Education Direct. http://www.workforcedevelopment.com/machinery/pattern.html (26 June 2004).

"Production Occupations." May 2003 National Occupational Employment and Wage Estimates, 7 May 2004. United States Department of Labor, Bureau of Labor Statistics. http://www.bls.gov/oes/2003/may/oes_51Pr.htm (28 May 2004).

"Steel Manufacturing." *The 2004–05 Career Guide to Industries.* United States Department of Labor, Bureau of Labor Statistics. http://bls.gov/oco/cg/cgs014.htm (26 June 2004).

"Summary Report for Model Makers, Metal and Plastic." Occupational Information Network. U.S. Department of Labor, O*NET OnLine. http://www.online.onetcenter.org/report?r=0&id=852 (26 June 2004).

"Tool and Die Makers." Career Prospects in Virginia/ Virginia
    Department of Education. http://www3.ccps.virginia.edu/
    career_prospects/briefs/T-Z (26 June 2004).
"Welder Apprentice Training." Thomson Education Direct,
    http://www.workforcedevelopment.com/machinery/welder.html
    (26 June 2004)
"Welding, Soldering, and Brazing Workers" *Occupational Outlook
    Handbook, 2004–05 Edition*, February 17, 2004. Bureau of
    Labor Statistics. http://www.bls.gov/oco/ocos226.htm (26 June
    2004).

CHAPTER 9: PROTECTIVE AND INVESTIGATIVE SERVICES

"Correctional Officers." Bureau of Prisons, Job Information, U.S.
    Department of Justice. http://www.bop.gov (25 June 2004).
"Corrections Officers." Career Prospects in Virginia. Virginia
    Department of Education. http://www3.ccps.virginia.edu/
    career_prospects/briefs/A-D/Corrections.html (25 June 2004).
"Firefighting Occupations." *Occupational Outlook Handbook,
    2004–05 Edition*, 21 March 2004. U.S. Department of Labor,
    Bureau of Labor Statistics. http://wbls.gov/oco/ocos157.htm
    (23 June 2004).
Lajoie, John M. *How to Become a Private Investigator.*
    (prepublication manuscript).
"On the Line of Fire: The Men and Women Who Battle America's
    Wildland Blazes." Maryland Department of Natural Resources.
    http://www.dnr.state.md.us/forests/otheragencies/fire.html
    (24 June 2004).
Petkus, Janetta. "You Can't Hide From the Private Investigator of the
    Year." Holden, MA, *The Landmark*, September, 2003.
"Police and Detectives." *Occupational Outlook Handbook,
    2004–2005 Edition*, 18 May 2004. U.S. Department of Labor,
    Bureau of Labor Statistics. http://www.bls.gov/oco/ocos160.htm
    (24 June 2004).
"Police and Detectives, Protective Service Occupations." May 2003
    National Occupational Employment and Wage Estimates,
    7 May 2004. U.S. Department of Labor, Bureau of Labor
    Statistics. http://www.bls.gov/oes/2003/may/oes_33Pr.htm
    (22 June 2004).

"Private Detectives and Investigators." *Occupational Outlook Handbook, 2004–05 Edition,* 21 March 2003. U.S. Department of Labor, Bureau of Labor Statistics. http://wbls.gov/oco/ocos158.htm (23 June 2004).

"Standards of Apprenticeship." Olympia Firefighters Apprenticeship Committee, April, 1994. http://www.lni.wa.gov/TradesLicensing/Apprenticeship/files/standards/0539.pdf (24 June 2004).

"State and Local Government, Excluding Education and Hospitals." *2004–05 Career Guide to Industries.* U.S. Department of Labor, Bureau of Labor Statistics. http://www.bls.gov/oco/cg/pring/cgs042.htm (23 June 2004).

"Training Track Suggestions. Massachusetts Department of Fire Services. http://www.mass.gov/dfs/mfa/training/indes.htm (24 June 2004).

"Wildland Firefighter Apprenticeship Program." USDA Forest Service, Fire and Aviation Management, Pacific Southwest Region, Region 5, Recruitment Notice, April 2004. http://www.fs.fed.us/r5/sixrivers/documents/fire2004/2004-application.pdf (20 June 2004).

"Wildland Firefighter Apprenticeship Program." USDA Forest Service, USDI Bureau of Land Management, USDI National Park Service, June 2003. http://www.wfap.net/ (20 June 2004).

CHAPTER 10: SOCIAL SERVICE CAREERS

"Apprenticeship for Youth Workers Why? And How?" National Clearinghouse for YDPA Programs, The Sar Levitan Center, Johns Hopkins University.

"Child Care Workers." May 2003 National Occupational Employment and Wage Estimates, 7 May 2004. U.S. Department of Labor, U.S. Bureau of Labor Statistics. http://www.bls.gov/oes/2003/may/oes399011.htm (15 July 2004).

"Child Daycare Services" *The 2004–05 Career Guide to Industries.* U.S. Department of Labor Bureau of Labor Statistics, 27 February 2004. http://www.bls.gov/oco/cg/pring/cgs032.htm (14 July 2004).

"Child Development Specialist Apprenticeship Program." UAW, *Skill Magazine,* Fall/Winter, 2001. http://www.uaw.org/publications/skill/01/2/skill09.html (17 July 2004).

"Childcare Workers." *Occupational Outlook Handbook, 2004–2005 Edition*, 27 February 2004. U.S. Department of Labor Bureau of Labor Statistics. http://bls.gov/oco/ocos170.htm (14 July 2004).

"Creating Brighter Futures: Registered Apprenticeship for Careers in Child Development" (brochure). U.S. Department of Labor Employment and Training Administration, U.S. Department of Labor Office of Apprenticeship Training, Employer and Labor Services.

"Details Report for Child Care Workers." U.S. Department of Labor, Occupational Information Network, O*NET OnLine. http://online.onetcenter.org/report?r=1&id=617 (19 July 2003).

"Details Report for Employment Interviewers, Private or Public Employment Service." U.S. Department of Labor Occupational Information Network, O*NET OnLine. http://online.onetcenter .org/report?r=1&id=64 (20 July 2004).

"Employment, Recruitment, and Placement Specialists." May 2003 National Occupational Employment and Wage Estimates. U.S. Department of Labor Bureau of Labor Statistics, 7 May 2004. http://www.bls.gov/oes/2003/may/oes131071.htm (20 July 2004).

"Employment Services." *The 2004–05 Career Guide to Industries*, U.S. Department of Labor Bureau of Labor Statistics, February 27, 2004. http://www.bls.gov/oco/cg/pring/cgs039.htm (20 July 2004).

"Human Services Direct Support Professionals Apprenticeship Program, Standards of Apprenticeship, Appendix 1—Work Experience Outline." 28 November 2001. U.S. Department of Labor Employment and Training Administration Bulletin 2002–02.

"Preschool Care and Education—Child Care Development Specialists: Apprenticeship," Revised—April 13, 1999. National Skills Standards Board Institute. http://www.nssb.org/ certapp_details.cfm?certapp_id=90 (7 June 2003).

Salzman, Jeffrey, Micheline Magnotta, Peter Rumble. "Estimating Sustainability and Comprehensiveness in the Quality Child-Care Initiative, Final Report, April 30, 2003." Oakland, CA: Social Policy Research Associates.

Salzman, Jeffrey, Micheline Magnotta, Peter Rumble. "Evaluating the Quality Child-Care Initiative: Child-Care Worker Apprenticeships in the Western States, Final Report, April 30, 2003." Oakland, California: Social Policy Research Associates.

"Social and Human Service Assistants." May 2003 National Occupational Employment and Wage Estimates, 7 May 2004. U.S. Department of Labor Bureau of Labor Statistics. http://www.bls.gov/oes/2003/Mayoes211093.htm (20 July 2004).

"Social and Human Service Assistants." *Occupational Outlook Handbook, 2004–2005 Edition*, 27 February 2004. U.S. Department of Labor, Bureau of Labor Statistics. http://bls.gov/oco/ocos059.htm (19 July 2004).

Taylor, Marianne. "The Direct Support Workforce." Cambridge, Massachusetts: Human Services Research Institute, #101-61 February 1999 online at http://www.thearc.org/faqs/dsw.html (23 July 2004).

"YDPA: Professionalizing Youth Workers and Improving Youth Services Nationwide, YDPA Field Notes." National Clearinghouse for Youth Development Practitioner Apprenticeship Programs, Johns Hopkins University, Sar Levitan Center for Social Policy Studies.

"Youth Development Practitioner Apprenticeship Program Competency Descriptions." Somerville, MA: YouthBuild USA.

CHAPTER 11: MILITARY OPPORTUNITIES

"Helmets to Hardhats." http://www.helmetstohardhats.org (23 August 2004).

"Job Opportunities in the Armed Forces. U.S. Department of Labor, Bureau of Labor Statistics, *Occupational Outlook Handbook, 2003–04*. http://bls.gov/oco/ocos249.htm (5 August 2004).

"Military Careers." United States Department of Defense. http://www.careersinthemilitary.com (4 August 2004).

"Partners for Youth Success." United States Army. http://www.armypays.com (4 August 2004).

"Preparing for the Future." United States Services Military Apprenticeship Program. https://www.cnet.navy.mil/usmap/ (17 August 2002).

Shanker Thom. "Army Pushes a Sweeping Overhaul of Basic Training." *New York Times*, NYTimes.com. (4 August 2004). http://www.nytimes.com/2004/08/04/politics/04training.html?hp (4 August 2004).

United States Army. http://www.goarmy.com (4 August 2004).

CHAPTER 12: MAKING CHOICES—
FINDING OPPORTUNITIES

America's CareerInfoNet. http://www.acinet.org (4 August 2004).

Americorps. http://www.americorps.org/whoweare.html
(5 August 2004).

Bolles, Richard N. *What Color Is Your Parachute?* Berkeley: Ten
Speed, 2004.

Capacchione, Lucia, and Peggy Van Pelt. *Putting Your Talent to
Work.* Deerfield Beach, FL: Health Communications, 2003.

Gale, Linda. *Discover What You're Best At.* New York: Fireside,
1990.

Habitat for Humanity International. http://www.habitat.org
(5 August 2004).

"O*NET—Beyond Information—Intelligence." U.S. Department
of Labor Employment and Training Administration.
http://www.doleta.gov/programs/onet/ (13 August 2004).

"O*NET Interest Profiler." Occupational Information Network,
O*NET Consortium. http://www.onetcenter.org/IP.html
(5 August 2004).

"Occupational Outlook Handbook, 2004–2005 Edition."
U.S. Department of Labor, Bureau of Labor Statistics.
http://www.bls.gov/oco/home.htm (24 August 2004).

"The Official Job Corps Website." U.S. Department of Labor
Employment and Training Administration. http://jobcorps
.doleta.gov/ (24 August 2004).

"Registered School-to-Apprenticeship Program." U.S. Department
of Labor Employment and Training Administration.
http://www.dolega.gov/atels_bat/raprog.cfm (15 March 2004).

Index

Note: Italic entries indicate sidebars.

About the Author

Penny Hutchins Paquette is an educational writer and former school librarian. She has a wealth of experience helping teenagers find appropriate books to help them with their concerns. She is the author of *Asthma: The Ultimate Teen Guide* and the coauthor of *Learning Disabilities: The Ultimate Teen Guide, Parenting a Child with a Learning Disability, Parenting a Child with a Behavior Problem*, and *Thinking Games for Kids*.